TREES OF UTAH
and the
INTERMOUNTAIN WEST

TREES OF UTAH
and the
INTERMOUNTAIN WEST

A Guide to Identification and Use

Michael Kuhns

UTAH STATE UNIVERSITY PRESS
UTAH STATE UNIVERSITY EXTENSION
Logan, Utah
1998

Utah State University Press
Logan, Utah 84322-7800

Published in conjunction with Utah State University Extension

© 1998 Utah State University Press
All rights reserved

Printed in Canada

Typography by WolfPack
Cover design by Michelle Sellers

Library of Congress Cataloging-in-Publication Data
Kuhns, Michael Richard, 1955-
    Trees of Utah and the intermountain West : a guide to
identification and use / Michael Kuhns.
        p.   cm.
    Includes bibliographical references (p.   ) and index.
    ISBN 0-87421-244-8
    1. Trees—Utah—Identification. 2. Trees—Great Basin—
Identification. 3. Landscape plants—Utah—Identification.
4. Landscape plants—Great Basin—Identification. I. Title.
QK189.K84   1998
582. 16' 09792—dc21   98-17347
                                                       CIP

CONTENTS

ACKNOWLEDGMENTS

The production of this book was supported by Utah State University Cooperative Extension, USU's Department of Forest Resources and College of Natural Resources, the Utah Community Forest Council, Utah Division of Forestry, Fire & State Lands, and USDA Forest Service State and Private Forestry.

Thanks to Phil Allen, Tony Dietz, Dick Hildreth, Terry Sharik, and Marita Tewes for their detailed and valuable reviews of the manuscript. Larry Rupp, Extension Horticulture Specialist at Utah State University, provided much of the information included in the crabapple selection guide at the end of this book. Hardiness zone calculations were provided by the Utah Climate Center at Utah State University.

I thank my colleagues in the Department of Forest Resources, College of Natural Resources, and Extension at Utah State University for their support and encouragement. It is a pleasure to be associated with such an outstanding group of people.

Production of original drawings for the large number of species and topics covered in this book was not possible. I thank the following authors and publishers for permission to use some of their drawings. Sources for drawings are indicated by the author's name(s) in the drawing captions.

Apgar, Austin C. 1892. *Trees of the Northern United States.* NY: American Book Company. Copyright 1892, 1920 by American Book Company.

Barnes, Burton V. and Warren H. Wagner. 1981. *Michigan Trees.* Ann Arbor, MI: University of Michigan Press. Copyright 1981 by University of Michigan.

Behr, Eldon A. 1986. *Identifying Wood.* Extension Bulletin E-746. East Lansing, MI: Michigan State University.

Benson, Lyman and Robert A. Darrow. 1945. *Trees and Shrubs of the Southwestern Deserts.* Tucson, AZ: University of Arizona Press. Copyright 1945, 1954, 1981 by Arizona Board of Regents. Illustrations by Lucretia Breazeale Hamilton.

Britton, Nathaniel Lord and Addison Brown. 1896. *An Illustrated Flora of the Northern U.S., Canada, and the British Possessions, Vol. I.* NY: Charles Scribner's Sons. Copyright 1896 by Charles Scribner's Sons.

Britton, Nathaniel Lord and Addison Brown. 1897. *An Illustrated Flora of the Northern U.S., Canada, and the British Possessions, Vol. II.* NY: Charles Scribner's Sons. Copyright 1897 by Charles Scribner's Sons.

Cathey, Henry M. 1990. *USDA Plant Hardiness Zone Map.* USDA Ag. Research Service Miscellaneous Publication Number 1475.

Dirr, Michael A. 1975. *Manual of Woody Landscape Plants.* Champaign, IL: Stipes Publishing Company. Copyright 1975 by Michael A. Dirr.

Elmore, Francis H. 1976. *Shrubs and Trees of the Southwest Uplands.* Southwest Parks and Monuments Assn. Copyright 1976 by Southwest Parks and Monuments Association. Illustrations by Jeanne R. Janish.

Farrar, John Laird. 1995. *Trees of the Northern United States and Canada.* Reproduced with permission from *Trees in Canada*, 1995, by John Laird Farrar, copublished by the Canadian Forest Service, Natural Resources Canada, and Fitzhenry and Whiteside Limited; and with the permission of the Minister of Public Works and Government Services Canada.

Forest Products Laboratory. 1987. *Wood Handbook: Wood as an Engineering Material.* USDA Ag. Handbook 72.

Garcke, August. 1908. *Illustrierte Flora von Deutschland.* Berlin: Verlagsbuchhandlung Paul Parey. Copyright 1908 by Verlagsbuchhandlung Paul Parey.

Hayes, Doris W. and George A. Garrison. 1960. *Key to Important Woody Plants of Eastern Oregon and Washington.* USDA-Forest Service Ag. Handbook 148.

Otis, Charles Herbert. 1925. *Michigan Trees: A Handbook of the Native and Most Important Introduced Species.* University of Michigan Bulletin 27(4). Copyright 1925 by The University of Michigan.

Sargent, Charles S. 1905. *Manual of the Trees of North America*. Boston: Houghton-Mifflin. Copyright 1905 and 1922 by Charles Sprague Sargent.

Sudworth, George B. 1908. *Forest Trees of the Pacific Slope*. USDA-Forest Service.

Sudworth, George B. 1915. *The Cypress and Juniper Trees of the Rocky Mountain Region*. USDA-Forest Service Bulletin 207.

Sudworth, George B. 1917. *The Pine Trees of the Rocky Mountain Region*. USDA-Forest Service Bulletin 460.

USDA. 1949. *Trees: The Yearbook of Agriculture*. U.S. GPO.

Finally, I thank my family for their support and encouragement during the several years it has taken to write this book. I couldn't have done it without them.

Logan, Utah
1998

INTRODUCTION

Trees provide us with beauty, wildlife habitat, wind protection, shade, fruit, and wood. Individual types of trees, or species and cultivated varieties (cultivars), have different requirements for water, light, nutrients, and soil conditions. In order to know what trees to plant, and to properly manage existing trees, you need to know these requirements. And before you can select a tree that is well-suited to your site, you need to know how to tell one tree from another. This book covers tree identification, interesting facts about tree species and cultivars, and uses of trees in the landscape. Identification and cultural characteristics of 219 tree species are covered, including all native and common introduced trees from Utah and parts of the surrounding states.

NATIVE OR NON-NATIVE?

Native and introduced trees are referred to throughout this book. The term *native* refers to trees that naturally occurred in the area prior to European settlement. Most of these trees are found in the mountains, or near streams and other water sources at lower elevations. Few native trees are planted in our cultivated landscapes, though many would make good ornamental trees. Trees native to Utah and to portions of surrounding states are noted in this book with the symbol ❖. Most of the species that we see in our towns and cities are not native, but are planted for their ornamental or other characteristics and are called *introduced* species. A few are *naturalized*; they are not native but have escaped cultivation and are growing and reproducing in the wild.

   Growing native trees in cultivated landscapes generally is a good idea and should be encouraged. Many wonderful and interesting native tree species do well on a variety of sites in Utah and the Intermountain West, from high alpine areas to mountain stream-sides to desert canyons. Remember, however, that a tree is really only native to specific sites where it grows naturally. For example, while quaking aspen (*Populus tremuloides*) is native to moist mountain sites in much of the West, it should not be thought of as a native in lower elevation valleys, where heat and low humidity cause many problems. Knowing your site and the characteristics of the species or cultivar you are planting will help ensure that you end up with a tree well-suited to your location, whether it is a native or is introduced. The individual tree descriptions and tree selection guide found later in this book will help you match trees to your site.

Be aware that some introduced trees can become weeds. For example, Russian-olive (*Elaeagnus angustifolia*) was introduced from Asia and has spread aggressively in many parts of the West. Such species usually should be avoided, and are illegal to propagate and must be controlled if they have been declared noxious weeds. To date Russian-olive is the only tree species that has been declared a noxious weed in parts of Utah: in Carbon, Duchesne, and Uintah counties. It is illegal to sell Russian-olive seeds or plants in those counties, and landowners are required to attempt to control the spread of the species.

TREES OF UTAH'S "DIXIE"

This book includes all trees native to Utah and parts of the surrounding states, including most of the trees found in extreme southern Utah's canyons, some of which are usually shrubby but can reach tree size. It also includes many of the introduced trees commonly planted in extreme southwestern Utah ("Dixie"). However, Utah's "Dixie" area is so much warmer than the rest of the state, with USDA plant hardiness zones of 7 and 8 (see hardiness zone explanation on page 277) and with hard freezes relatively uncommon, that many more species can be planted than could be included here. For a more complete discussion of trees for these warmer climates, check the following references:

Almeria, Francis H. 1976. *Shrubs and Trees of the Southwest Uplands*. Tucson, AZ: Southwest Parks and Monuments Assn.

2

Benson, Lyman and Robert A. Darrow. 1981. *Trees and Shrubs of the Southwestern Deserts*. Tucson, AZ: University of Arizona Press.

Sunset Books. 1997. *Sunset Western Garden Book*. Menlo Park, CA: Sunset Publishing Corp.

Vines, Robert A. 1960. *Trees, Shrubs and Woody Vines of the Southwest*. Austin, TX: University of Texas Press.

COMMON NAMES AND LATIN NAMES— WHY YOU SHOULD KNOW THE DIFFERENCE

We know most trees by their *common names*, such as "white poplar" or "cottonwood". These names are useful, but the same species may have more than one common name. For example, white poplar is also called silver poplar and sometimes even silver maple. Bigtooth maple is also called canyon maple. This local variation in tree names led to the creation of standard names, also called *scientific names* or Latin names because they use Latin words. These Latin names are used world-wide to describe a particular species.

Latin names are always underlined or italicized to set them apart. The Latin name for Gambel oak is *Quercus gambelii*. The first word, in this case *Quercus*, is the *genus* or *generic name* (plural of genus is *genera*) of the tree. A genus is a broad group of species that are alike in some ways but not enough to be the same species. Members of different genera rarely interbreed, whereas hybrids or interbreeding between various species within a genus are quite common. The genus *Quercus* includes all the oaks, and *Ulmus* all the elms. The second word in the scientific name is the *specific name*, such as *gambelii* in *Quercus gambelii*. The genus and specific name together make-up the *species* name (species ends in an "s" whether it is singular or plural). Trees of the same species are very alike in fruit, flowers, and other parts. If the word 'species' or the abbreviation 'spp.' is placed after a genus the author is referring to more than one species in that particular genus or to the genus in general. *Quercus* spp., for example, could mean several oaks or all oaks in general.

Sometimes you will see a full or abbreviated name of a person right after the Latin name, for example *Quercus gambelii* Nutt. This name is called the "authority" and refers to the person who first described and named the tree. In this example, Thomas Nuttall is the person who first described the species we know as Gambel oak. Authorities will not be used in this book.

Another name you will see used in this book is the *family* name. A family is a group of genera that are closely related. The first part of the family name comes from the most common or typical genus in that family. Plant family names always end in "-*aceae*," pronounced "AY-cee-ee". An example of a family is the Ulmaceae, which includes the elms (*Ulmus* genus), hackberries (*Celtis* genus), and others.

Knowing Latin names and being ready to use them can help you avoid confusion. If you go to a nursery and ask for a red maple and also use the Latin name of *Acer rubrum* there is little chance to mistake what you want. On the other hand, if you ask for a red maple without using its Latin name, you may get a variety of Norway maple (*Acer platanoides*) with reddish-purple leaves that also is sometimes called red maple. Of course, such confusion can only be avoided if both parties understand and use Latin names. In this book Latin names are generally included, especially the first time a species is mentioned.

A few other naming practices need to be mentioned. An "×" between the genus and species name, as in *Aesculus × carnea*, is a short way to indicate a hybrid or cross between two species. In this example, the hybrid red horsechestnut is a cross between horsechestnut (*Aesculus hippocastanum*) and red buckeye (*Aesculus pavia*). A *variety* is a subset of a species grouping plants that differ considerably from others in the species, with these differences often staying true when plants are grown from seed. An example is the pink-flowering form of flowering dogwood (*Cornus florida* var. *rubra*). A cultivated variety or *cultivar* refers to plants chosen for specific traits and cultivated so that offspring retain those traits, either through asexual reproduction with rooted cuttings, grafting, or budding; or sexual reproduction with controlled crosses with known parents.

TREE PARTS

Ultimately trees are identified by the characteristics of their parts and how those parts go together. This section describes major tree parts and their variations.

Leaves

Shade Tolerance: Some tree species are more efficient at making food (through photosynthesis) under low-light conditions. These are called *shade tolerant*. Examples include firs, lindens, hackberries, and redbuds. *Shade intolerant* species include cottonwoods, willows, aspens, birches, and pines. Shade tolerant trees may do well in full sun, but shade intolerant species always need plenty of light to do well. Shade intolerant species generally appear early in the life of a forest and grow quickly in height, while tolerant species appear later under the shade of the intolerant species. Though slower growing, shade tolerant trees live longer and often are more desirable than shade intolerant species. Knowledge of shade tolerance is useful for understanding a tree's place in the natural landscape and can help you decide how to use a tree in a cultivated or "built" landscape.

Persistent or deciduous: A tree's leaves either remain attached (and green) through the winter (*persistent* or *evergreen*) or die and fall off in autumn (*deciduous*). Most broadleaves found in northern climates, like Utah's, are deciduous. However, many examples of evergreen broadleaves occur in the extreme southern portion of Utah, such as the native shrub live oak (*Quercus turbinella*). Most conifers have persistent or evergreen leaves. Sometimes a tree's leaves will die in autumn but will remain on the branch through most of the winter, as with many of the oaks. Moreover, a portion of the older leaves of some evergreen conifers turn color and are lost each fall, causing some people to erroneously think the trees are sick or dying.

Leaf type: There are several types of tree leaves, but they all fit into four general categories: *needle-like*, *scale-like*, *awl-like*, and *broadleaf*. Broadleaves are common on hardwoods (angiosperms), though one gymnosperm included here, ginkgo (*Ginkgo biloba*), has broad, flat-bladed leaves. Though the name broadleaf implies a wide leaf, these trees actually have leaves ranging from very wide (sycamore) to very narrow (willow).

Needle-like leaves are found on most conifers, other than the cypress family. Pine needles are nearly always held in bunches or *fascicles* of two to five. Singleleaf pinyon (*Pinus monophylla*) is an exception, having one needle per fascicle. *Hard pines*, such as ponderosa (*Pinus ponderosa*) or lodgepole (*Pinus contorta*) pine, have needles in fascicles of two to three with a scaly sheath around the base. *Soft* or *white pines*, such as limber pine (*Pinus flexilis*), typically have five needles per fascicle without a persistent scaly sheath.

Spruces (genus *Picea*), true firs (genus *Abies*), Douglas-fir (*Pseudotsuga menziesii*), cedars (genus *Cedrus*), and larches (genus *Larix*) have single needles that are flat (most true firs, Douglas-fir, cedars, and larches) or diamond-shaped (most spruces) in cross-section. Fir, Douglas-fir, and spruce needles and needles on current year twigs of cedars and larches are arranged individually along the twig. Cedar and larch needles on older growth are arranged in whorls or bundles of many on short spur shoots.

Scale- and awl-like leaves are both found on junipers or redcedars (genus *Juniperus*) and on giant sequoia (*Sequoiadendron Giganteum*). Younger twigs generally have the shorter scale-like leaves while older twigs and branches have the longer, pointed awl-like leaves. Both awl- and scale-like leaves cover the twig surface completely.

Leaf Type (drawings from Dirr)

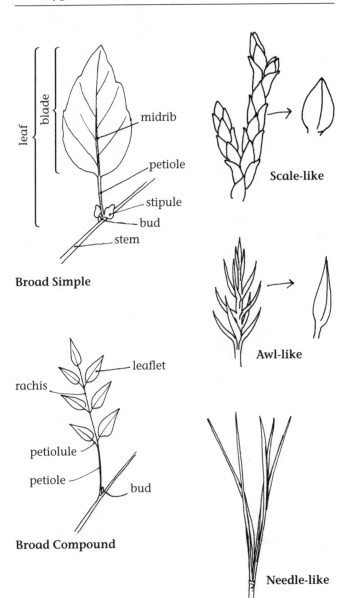

midrib

petiole

stipule

bud

stem

leaf

blade

Broad Simple

Scale-like

Awl-like

leaflet

rachis

petiolule

petiole

bud

Broad Compound

Needle-like

Leaf arrangement: Conifer leaves are arranged either *alternately* (generally scattered along the twig in a spiral fashion) or in pairs *opposite* each other on a twig. Broadleaves are arranged either *opposite* each other on a twig (two at each *node* or point of attachment), *subopposite* (nearly, but not quite opposite), *alternate* (one at each node), or *whorled* (more than two leaves at each node; usually three). Most broadleaved tree species have alternate leaves. One way to remember many of the species with opposite leaves is to remember "*MAD Buck*". This stands for *M*aple, *A*sh, *D*ogwood, and the *Buck*eye (horsechestnut) family, all of which have opposite leaves.

When the leaves are on the tree, you can determine leaf arrangement by following the leaf stalk or *petiole* back to where it is attached to the twig. There will be a bud at this point on all but new growth, though the bud may sometimes be hidden under the base of the petiole. If leaves have fallen off, look at the arrangement of leaf scars and buds on the stem.

Leaf Arrangement   (drawings from Dirr)

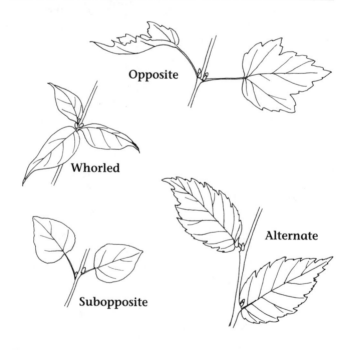

Opposite

Whorled

Suboppsite

Alternate

Leaf shape: Leaf shape or outline is sometimes a good indicator of a species. This feature can be variable though, depending on leaf development, shade, position in the crown, and genetic variation.

Leaf Shape (drawings from Dirr)

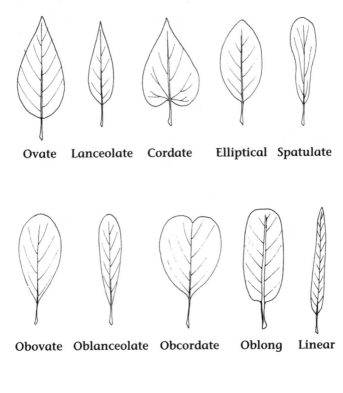

Ovate   Lanceolate   Cordate   Elliptical   Spatulate

Obovate   Oblanceolate   Obcordate   Oblong   Linear

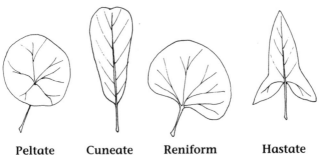

Peltate   Cuneate   Reniform   Hastate

Leaf composition: Broadleaves are classified as *simple* or *compound*. Simple leaves have one *blade* attached to a petiole or stalk, which is then connected to the twig. Compound leaves have a few to many leaflets or small leaf blades attached to a stalk or stalks. Leaflets in a compound leaf are attached to a stalk called a *rachis*, which is then attached to the twig by a petiole. Compound leaves are either *palmately compound*, *pinnately compound*, or may be more than once pinnately compound (example: *twice-pinnately compound*).

You often can tell leaflets of compound leaves from simple leaves by looking at the point where they attach to the stalk or stem. If a bud is found, you have a complete leaf; if there is no bud, you have a leaflet. You also can look at which part of the leaf falls off in autumn (look on the ground under the tree at other times of year). While entire leaves generally come off the tree in fall, the stalks of some compound leaves, like black walnut (*Juglans nigra*), may not fall until mid or late winter. In some cases, such as baldcypress (*Taxodium distichum*), the leaves are simple but are attached to a branchlet that falls off with the leaves.

Leaf margins: Margins or edges of leaves are either *entire* (smooth, with no teeth), lobed, or toothed. Toothed leaves, sometimes called *serrate*, can be coarsely or finely serrate, singly or doubly serrate (teeth on teeth), and can have sharp (pointed or angled) or blunt (rounded) teeth. Many other names are used to describe different types or shapes of teeth.

Leaf Composition   (drawings from Dirr)

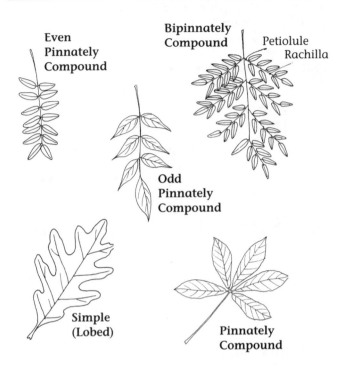

Even Pinnately Compound

Bipinnately Compound

Petiolule

Rachilla

Odd Pinnately Compound

Simple (Lobed)

Pinnately Compound

Leaf Margins   (drawings from Dirr)

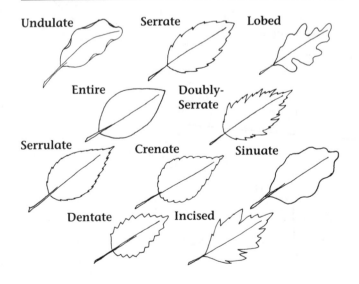

Undulate

Serrate

Lobed

Entire

Doubly-Serrate

Serrulate

Crenate

Sinuate

Dentate

Incised

Leaf tips and bases: The shapes of leaf tips and bases are very useful characteristics in tree identification. Several examples are shown below.

Leaf Tips   (drawings from Dirr)

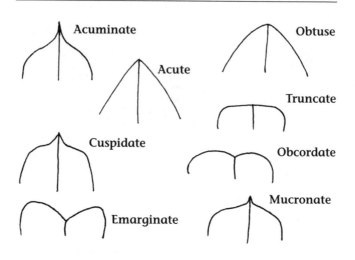

Leaf Bases   (drawings from Dirr)

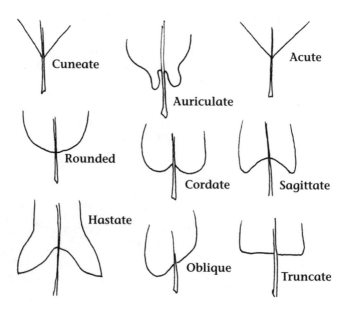

Leaf surfaces: Leaf surfaces can be lightly or densely hairy (*pubescent*), rough, glabrous (smooth, without hairs, scales, etc.), shiny, scaly, or waxy. Top surfaces often are very different from bottom surfaces.

Stipules: Stipules are small appendages attached in pairs at the base of a petiole that are leafy or scaly in appearance. Leaves without stipules are termed *estipulate*. Stipules vary widely in their persistence, shape, size, margins, and in the scars they leave on a twig and are useful in identifying some species. Stipules and stipule scars are mentioned in this book where important for identification.

Twigs

Twigs, the smallest branches of a tree, can be rough, glabrous, hairy, shiny, ridged, straight, zig-zag, or waxy. *Pith*, or the tissue in the middle of a twig, may be chambered or solid and variously colored, or it may not show at all. Sizes and shapes of leaf scars and stipule scars also vary between species and can be useful identification tools.

Pith Types   (drawings from Dirr)

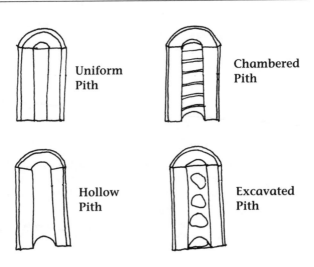

Uniform Pith

Chambered Pith

Hollow Pith

Excavated Pith

Buds

Buds hold the small leaves, flowers, and twigs that will grow the next year. Buds can be *terminal* (at the twig tip) or *lateral* (on the side of the twig). Some twigs do not have a terminal bud, but instead have one located at the tip but off to one side. Such buds are called *pseudo-terminal*. Oaks have several buds clustered around the twig tip. Some lateral buds may be hidden under the base of the petiole, as in sycamore (*Platanus occidentalis*).

Buds   (drawings from Dirr)

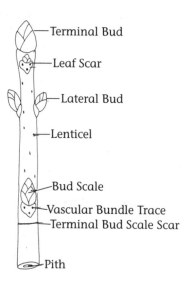

— Terminal Bud

— Leaf Scar

— Lateral Bud

— Lenticel

— Bud Scale
— Vascular Bundle Trace
— Terminal Bud Scale Scar

— Pith

Flowers

Flowers are the reproductive parts of a plant. In many woody plants flowers are small and inconspicuous and may not be present during much of the year. Some vegetatively propagated varieties and many young trees also may not bear flowers and fruit. The usefulness of flowers for tree identification is therefore sometimes quite limited. However, plants

14

are classified botanically by flower structure, so some knowledge of flowers is useful. In addition, many ornamental trees are prized for their conspicuous, colorful flowers.

Floral descriptions are included under the detailed descriptions for most species in this book. For a more complete description of flower parts and arrangement see the references listed on page 296.

Several rather complicated terms are used in this book to describe the types of flowers you will find on a particular tree species. Understanding these floral characteristics is useful for identifying and selecting trees. With this information, you will know whether a species has male-only trees and female-only trees and whether all trees will bear fruit (only trees with female or perfect flowers can bear fruit). A discussion of these terms follows.

Flowers that have actively functioning organs of both sexes (*stamens* and *pistils*) are *bisexual* and are called *perfect flowers*. Perfect flowers are typical of the elm, magnolia, rose, linden, and several other families. If a flower lacks either functioning stamens or pistils it is *imperfect* or *unisexual*. Unisexual flowers can be either *staminate* (male) or *pistillate* (female). When a species has only unisexual flowers, and both staminate and pistillate flowers are found on the same tree, that species is called *monoecious* (for the Greek "one house"). Monoecious families include pine, walnut, birch, oak, and others. *Dioecious* ("two houses") species have staminate flowers on one tree and pistillate flowers on a separate tree, as in the willow and mulberry families.

If both perfect and imperfect flowers are found on the same tree, the species is called *polygamous*. *Polygamo-dioecious* species have unisexual flowers, with staminate and pistillate flowers borne on different trees, but also have some perfect flowers on each tree. Examples are honeylocust (*Gleditsia triacanthos*) and Kentucky coffeetree (*Gymnocladus dioicus*). *Polygamo-monoecious* species have staminate and pistillate flowers borne on the same tree, along with some perfect flowers on each tree, as in hackberry (*Celtis occidentalis*). Typically trees are self-infertile and thus must receive pollen from another nearby tree to produce viable seeds. Polygamous species are indicated here as monoecious or dioecious with a note that perfect flowers also are present.

15

Fruits

Fruits develop from flowers with female parts and are the seed-bearing organs of a plant. They can be very helpful for tree identification. The term "fruit" is used here to describe the seeds and the parts that surround them, whether or not they are edible by people. An *aggregate* fruit is actually a cluster of many individual fruits formed from one flower with many pistils. A *multiple* fruit is a cluster of individual fruits formed from pistils from different flowers attached to a common receptacle. Never eat fruits or other parts of plants unless you are sure they are safe. Several fruit types and examples are:

1. *drupe*—fleshy with a single stone or pit containing a seed within (example—cherry).
2. *berry*—fleshy with several seeds (example—blue elder).
3. *pome*—leathery skin, fleshy middle layer, and plastic-like inner layer containing several seeds (example—apple, pear, serviceberry).
4. *legume*—dry, elongated pod that splits in two length-wise with several seeds along one edge (example—honeylocust, redbud).
5. *capsule*—dry fruit that splits to reveal many seeds inside (example—catalpa).
6. *achene*—small, dry, and hard one-seeded fruit (example—a sycamore "fruit" is actually hundreds of achenes).
7. *samara*—a dry fruit with one or two flat wings attached to a seed (example—maple, elm, ash).
8. *nut*—hard throughout and typically partly or fully enclosed in a leafy or leathery structure (example—black walnut). A nutlet is a small nut (example—hornbeam).
9. *acorn*—nut-like fruit of an oak, with a scaly or warty cap.
10. *follicle*—a dry fruit that splits open along one line and is the product of a simple ovary (example—a magnolia's fruit is an aggregate of follicles).
11. *cone*—seed bearing structure of a conifer (example—spruce, pine, fir).

Bark

Bark is the outer covering on the trunk, twigs, and roots of a tree. The outermost bark on all but the youngest stems has no live cells. New bark is constantly being made on the

Fruit Types   (drawings from Dirr and others)

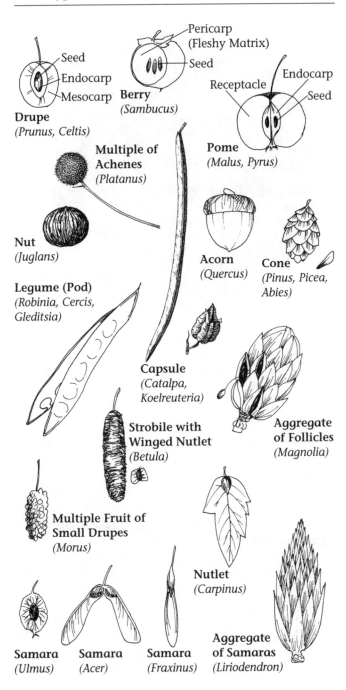

Drupe
(Prunus, Celtis)
Seed
Endocarp
Mesocarp

Berry
(Sambucus)
Pericarp
(Fleshy Matrix)
Seed

Pome
(Malus, Pyrus)
Receptacle
Endocarp
Seed

Multiple of Achenes
(Platanus)

Nut
(Juglans)

Legume (Pod)
(Robinia, Cercis, Gleditsia)

Acorn
(Quercus)

Cone
(Pinus, Picea, Abies)

Capsule
(Catalpa, Koelreuteria)

Aggregate of Follicles
(Magnolia)

Strobile with Winged Nutlet
(Betula)

Multiple Fruit of Small Drupes
(Morus)

Nutlet
(Carpinus)

Samara
(Ulmus)

Samara
(Acer)

Samara
(Fraxinus)

Aggregate of Samaras
(Liriodendron)

Tree Trunk Parts   (photo from Wood Handbook)

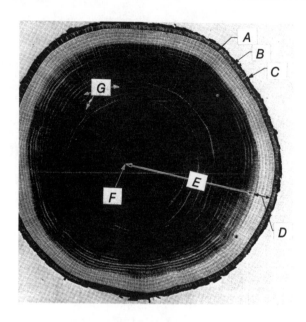

A—cambium, B—phloem, C—outer bark, D—sapwood with several growth rings, E—heartwood with many growth rings, F—Pith, G—rays

inside and pushed out. This is why older trunks usually have rough outer bark that peels or flakes away. Bark is highly variable, though young trees generally have fairly smooth bark. To see what a tree's bark looked like when it was young, look at the young bark on upper branches and twigs. Some tree species, like sycamore, white poplar, and Scotch pine, can be easily identified by bark characteristics.

The inner bark, or *phloem*, is a live spongy tissue that moves food throughout the tree. It eventually is pushed out and its cells die, becoming part of the outer bark, though new layers of living phloem are constantly being made to replace the old phloem. Just inside the inner bark, but outside the wood, is a layer of cells called the *cambium*. This layer divides and forms layers of cells to the inside that become wood and to the outside that become phloem and other bark tissues.

Cork cambium or *phellogen* also forms outside the phloem and produces corky bark tissues that help protect the stem.

Wood

The wood is everything inside the cambium on tree trunks, branches, twigs, and roots. Wood can also be called *xylem*. Wood is made up of *fibers* for strength, hollow tubes of different sizes and types, and parenchyma. These tubes, like straws, conduct water from the roots to the leaves. Most of the larger tubes are called *vessels* and look like pores in cut wood. Smaller tubes are called *tracheids* and are too small to be seen without a magnifier. *Parenchyma* are undifferentiated cells that make up much of the cells of many plant tissues and have various functions like food storage.

Softwoods and hardwoods: Trees can be divided into two general classes called *softwoods* and *hardwoods*. Softwood is another name for a *conifer* or cone-bearing tree like a pine, spruce, or fir. The wood of many of these trees is fairly soft and light. They sometimes are called *non-porous* because they have no large vessels, only very small tubes or tracheids that cannot be seen easily. Hardwoods also are called *broadleaves* and include trees such as elm, ash, oak, and cottonwood. They are often called *porous* woods because their wood is mostly made up of small to large vessels that appear as pores or holes in a cross-section. Some woods classified as hardwoods, such as cottonwood, actually have softer wood than is found in a true softwood, such as Douglas-fir. In other words, the terms softwood and hardwood do not clearly indicate the wood density or hardness.

Annual rings: As trees grow in temperate climates like Utah's, a new layer of wood is produced each year. This layer is called an *annual ring* or growth ring. The inner part of an annual ring (the side away from the bark) is formed early in the year and is called *spring-wood*. Spring-wood generally has larger vessels or pores with thinner walls and may be lighter in color. *Summer-wood*, on the outside of an annual ring, has smaller pores or vessels packed closer together with thicker walls and may be darker in color.

Sapwood and heartwood: Each year as a new annual ring is added by the cambium to the outside of a tree's stem, some of the wood in the middle of the tree is chemically

Softwood Cross-Section   (photo from Behr)

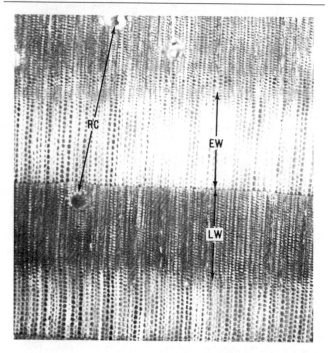

Cross-section of a pine stem with thin-walled early-wood or spring-wood (EW) from one growth ring, thicker walled latewood or summer-wood (LW) from an older growth ring, and resin canals or ducts (RC) (about 10×). The center of the stem is down in the photo.

altered and becomes *heartwood*. Heartwood often is filled with dark colored substances that help it resist decay, though wood may also be darkened by mineral stains and injury. The wood on the outside of the stem, one to many rings wide, is called the *sapwood*. It is usually lighter in color than the heartwood and is responsible for water and mineral movement through the stem and for defense against injury.

Rays: *Rays* are ribbon-like groups of tracheids and parenchyma that move water and other substances in the xylem from the outer rings in or from the inner rings out. They also connect with the phloem. Rays may be large and

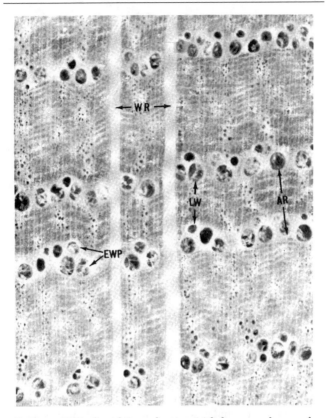

Cross-section of a white oak stem with large early-wood pores or vessels (EWP), small late-wood pores (LW), an annual growth ring consisting of early- and late-wood (AR), and large rays (WR) (about 10×). The center of the stem is down in the photo.

easily seen, as in the oaks, or small and hard to see, as in cottonwood. They show up best and largest in cross-sections and surfaces cut lengthwise through the middle of the trunk.

Ring-porous and diffuse porous: Wood of broadleaved trees can be classified as *ring-porous*, *diffuse-porous*, or *semi-ring-porous*. Ring-porous wood has vessels or pores in the

Diffuse-porous Cross-Section (photo from Behr)

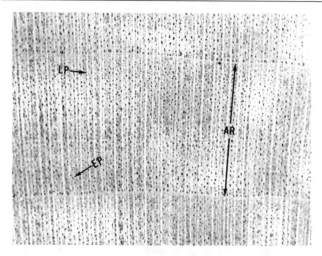

Cross-section of a maple stem with indistinct early-wood (EP) and late-wood pores (LP) and an annual growth ring (AR) (about 10×). The center of the stem is down in the photo.

spring-wood much larger than in the summer-wood. Examples are oak, ash, and elm. Trees with diffuse-porous wood produce similar-sized vessels throughout spring and summer, as in cottonwood and willow. Semi-ring-porous species have characteristics between ring-porous and diffuse-porous, as in black walnut and black cherry (*Prunus serotina*).

LIST OF INCLUDED TREES

The following is a list of the 219 tree species described in this book. As mentioned previously, this list does not include every tree found in Utah or the surrounding region, but does include all native and most introduced species. One or more common names and the scientific name for each species is given. The species are listed in order of their appearance in the species description section, with the page number of their description on the right. This order roughly relates to common botanical classifications which keep similar species close together. Species indented below another species usually are less common and have a shortened description that is included within the description for the major species. These species also usually are not included in the identification keys. Species listed under "Other...." all have individual descriptions, but with less detail.

24

SPECIES DESCRIPTIONS

The following pages contain descriptions and illustrations of the 219 species covered in this manual, including all native and most introduced species. One to several common names and the scientific name for each species is given. The species are listed in an order that relates to common botanical classifications which keep similar species close together. Species mentioned within another species' description generally are less common and have not been included in the identification keys above.

For most species there are descriptions of the leaves, twigs/buds, flowers/fruit, bark, wood, general comments about the species' native habitat, and a description of its uses in cultivated landscapes, including its USDA Plant Hardiness Zone designation (see page 277 for a description of hardiness zones). Some species have more abbreviated descriptions and may not be illustrated. A species' mode of bearing flowers (monoecious, dioecious, perfect flowers, etc.) is noted under the flower/fruit description (see page 15 for a discussion of these terms). Flowering dates, when noted, will be much later for trees grown on cooler than normal sites or at high elevations. Very distinctive characteristics are indicated by bold lettering. The species in this list are organized by family and genus. The families are organized under the broad groups gymnosperms and angiosperms. Trees native to Utah and portions of the surrounding states are denoted by a ❖symbol preceding the common name.

More detailed ornamental characteristics and names and characteristics of common cultivars can be found after this section in the tree selection guide. A crabapple selection guide also follows this section. Identification keys for most species also are included (see page 295).

GYMNOSPERMS

Gymnosperms include many of the world's most interesting and useful trees. They have an ancient ancestry, going back well before the angiosperms. The main characteristic that separates them from the angiosperms is their naked or uncovered seed, usually held on a scale in a cone. The Latin *"gymno/spermae"* actually means *"naked/seed"*. (*Angiosperms*, on the other hand, have their seeds covered with protective tissue called an ovary.) Technically, gymnosperms are not flowering plants, though they have pollen- and seed-bearing structures that resemble flowers and that will be referred to as flowers here. Leaves for gymnosperms are evergreen except where noted.

GINGKOACEAE

Ginkgo family. Only one species, gingko (*Ginkgo biloba*), occurs in this family. Native only to China and Japan.

Ginkgo ♦ Maidenhair Tree *(Ginkgo biloba)*

Leaves: Broad; deciduous; **fan-shaped**; with or without notched margin; **branching or dichotomous venation, gives appearance of long, flowing "maiden's hair"**; spiral or alternate arrangement on young twigs; on older branches only occur on short spur shoots; bright yellow-green; turn bright yellow in fall; petiole 2" to 4" long.

Twigs/Buds: Stout; light brown first year, becoming gray with stringy, peeling bark; short spur shoots on older twigs. Buds with overlapping scales, brown.

Flowers/Fruit: Green male flowers borne in 1" long catkins in spring; female flowers inconspicuous; dioecious. Fruit plum-like in shape and size; about 1" to 1-1/2" long; tan to orange; fleshy covering very messy and bad smelling.

Bark: Light gray-brown; tight ridges with darker furrows on older stems.

Wood: Unimportant.

General: A native of China and Japan, where it has long been cultivated in temple gardens. Thought of as a "living fossil", since it has likely been around in some form for 150 million years and once was native to North America. Ginkgo is one of the few broadleaved gymnosperms, and is the only one covered in this book. Tolerates a very broad range of soil and environmental conditions. Shade intolerant.

Landscape Use: Does very well in cultivated landscapes in Utah. Very strong, upright growth form. Tolerates urban environments including smoke, compacted soil, and salt. Does well in soils with high pH and tolerates heat. Only trees known to be male should be planted because of bad smelling, messy fruit born by females. Excellent golden fall color, though it doesn't last long. These are excellent landscape trees that should be planted more often. A number of cultivars are available that vary in crown shape, size, and fall color characteristics. Zones 3-9.

ginkgo (*Ginkgo biloba*)

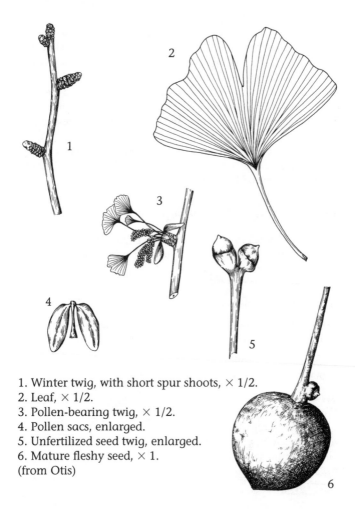

1. Winter twig, with short spur shoots, × 1/2.
2. Leaf, × 1/2.
3. Pollen-bearing twig, × 1/2.
4. Pollen sacs, enlarged.
5. Unfertilized seed twig, enlarged.
6. Mature fleshy seed, × 1.
(from Otis)

PINACEAE

Pine family. Cone-bearing trees with **needle-like** or **linear** leaves. Contains nine genera and about 210 species worldwide, mostly found in the Northern Hemisphere. Many species are very important timber trees. All species are monoecious. Pollen cones of most species are more abundant lower in the crown, while seed cones are found higher in the crown.

Pine   Genus *Pinus*

This genus contains about 95 species, with 36 native to the U.S. and Canada and 6 native to Utah. Needles are arranged in **bundles of 2 to 5** (arranged singly in one species); a sheath near the base of the needle bundle may or may not persist. Pines have orange, yellow, or red male catkin-like pollen cones grouped at the new shoot base, shedding pollen in spring and then falling off. Female flowers are small cones that are pollinated in the spring and grow and mature in two seasons into **woody seed-bearing cones with winged or unwinged seeds**. White or soft pines generally have 5 needles per bundle and hard or yellow pines have 2 to 3 needles per bundle. The pinyon or nut pines have 1 to 4 needles per bundle and large, edible seeds. In general pines are intolerant of shade and well-adapted to a wide variety of soils and environmental conditions. Monoecious.

❖Limber Pine   *(Pinus flexilis)*

Leaves: **Needles in groups of 5**; 1-1/2" to 3" long; rigid; dark green; covered with lengthwise rows of fine, white lines; evergreen; remain on tree 5-6 years.

Twigs/Buds: Twigs stout; **very flexible**; glabrous; silver-white to gray. Buds 1/3" to 1/2" long; pointed.

Flowers/Fruit: Fruit a woody cone; short stalked; 3" to 8" long; light brown; thick, non-pointed scales; large, wingless seeds.

Bark: Thin; smooth; white to gray.

Wood: Unimportant; light and soft.

General: Native to higher elevations in Utah and the interior West. Often very long-lived and slow growing, occurring on dry, harsh sites. Very shade intolerant. **Southwestern white pine** (*Pinus strobiformis*) is thought by some to be a variety of limber pine (*P. flexilis* var. *reflexa*); it has cone scale tips that curve back toward the base.

limber pine (*Pinus flexilis*)

Twig with
clusters of
leaves, × 1/3.

Open seed
cone, × 1/3.

Cone scale with
seeds, × 1/2.

(from Sudworth 1908)

southwestern white pine (*Pinus strobiformis*)

Twig with clusters
of leaves, ×1/6.

Open seed
cone, ×1/3.

(from Sudworth 1917)

35

Landscape Use: Seldom used but should be more often; nice dark green color and very tough; don't over-water. Zones 4-7. **Southwestern white pine** (*Pinus strobiformis*) could be used in Utah landscapes; it has a nice blue-green needle color and makes a good Christmas tree. Zones 5-9.

❖Bristlecone Pine   *(Pinus aristata)*

Leaves: Needles in groups of 5; 1" to 1-1/2" long; dark green; curved; stiff; evergreen, remain on tree 10-17 years; usually lightly covered with white specks of dried resin.

Twigs/Buds: Twigs orange-brown, becoming black when older. Buds 1/3" long; covered with brown scales.

Flowers/Fruit: Fruit a woody cone; short stalk; about 3" to 3-1/2" long; brown; scales thick and **tipped with a long bristle**; seeds smaller than limber pine and winged.

Bark: Thin, smooth, and gray-white on young stems; furrowed and red-brown on older stems.

Wood: Unimportant; fairly soft; heartwood light red-brown.

General: Native in scattered mountainous areas in the interior West, including Utah. Slow growing and very long-lived (over 4,000 years old) on dry, tough sites. Shade intolerant.

Landscape Use: Seldom used but should be more often; can be found at nurseries; very slow-growing; nice dark green color and interesting, sometimes contorted form; needs little or no supplemental water once established. Zones 5-7. Welsh *et al.* consider the bristlecone pine growing in Utah to be *Pinus longaeva*.

❖Pinyon ◆ Colorado Pinyon   *(Pinus edulis)*

Leaves: Needles in groups of 2; 1" to 2" long; fairly stiff; yellow-green; evergreen, remain on tree 3-9 years.

Twigs/Buds: Twigs fairly stout; orange to brown colored. Buds small, oval, brown.

Flowers/Fruit: Fruit a woody cone with very short or no stalk; 1" to 2-1/2" long; oval to round; reddish-brown; scales few and not tipped with a prickle; **seeds wingless and large**, about 1/2" long, thin-shelled, edible.

Bark: Fairly thin; ridged.

Wood: Unimportant except for firewood and occasionally fence posts; fairly hard.

General: Native throughout most of southern, central, and eastern Utah at mid-elevations; and throughout the southwestern U.S. The fruit (seed) is an important food for certain southwestern Indians. Grows on dry sites, often mixed with junipers. Shade intolerant.

bristlecone pine (*Pinus aristata*)

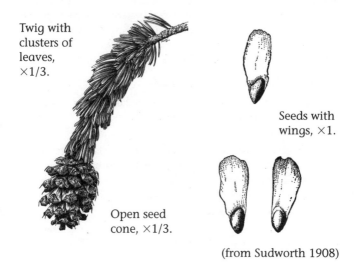

Twig with clusters of leaves, ×1/3.

Seeds with wings, ×1.

Open seed cone, ×1/3.

(from Sudworth 1908)

pinyon (*Pinus edulis*)

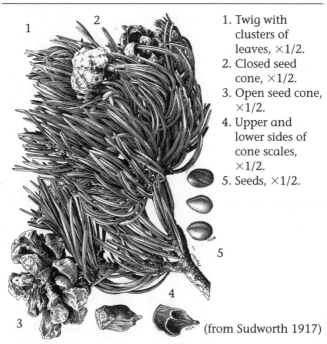

1. Twig with clusters of leaves, ×1/2.
2. Closed seed cone, ×1/2.
3. Open seed cone, ×1/2.
4. Upper and lower sides of cone scales, ×1/2.
5. Seeds, ×1/2.

(from Sudworth 1917)

Landscape Use: Seldom planted, though could do well on dry sites. Sometimes present as native trees in housing developments—trees in this situation often do poorly due to over-watering and root damage; pinyons in these situations also pose a fire hazard. Zones 4-8.

❖Singleleaf Pinyon   *(Pinus monophylla)*

Major differences from **Pinyon** include:

Leaves: Needles not in groups—borne singly (this is the only pine with needles borne individually on the twig); evergreen, remain on tree 4-12 years.

General: Native to mid-elevations in a few, isolated locations in northern Utah, throughout Nevada, and in parts of central and southern California and Baja California. The seeds are edible as with pinyon. Dry sites. Shade intolerant.

Landscape Use: Rarely used—similar to pinyon. Zones 5-9.

❖Ponderosa Pine   *(Pinus ponderosa)*

Leaves: Needles in groups of 2 and 3; 3" to 10" long; yellow-green; less sharp-pointed than those of Austrian pine; somewhat twisted; evergreen, remain on tree 3-6 years.

Twigs/Buds: Twigs stout; orange-brown; smell like turpentine when crushed. Buds about 1/2" long; usually covered with resin droplets; cinnamon-brown colored.

Flowers/Fruit: Fruit a woody cone; very short to no stalk; 3" to 6" long; reddish-brown; **each scale armed with a short, sharp spine**.

Bark: Dark brown to black on younger trees; older trees have large, thick plates, orange to cinnamon-red, separated by deep furrows; inner bark has vanilla smell.

Wood: Very important; sapwood white to yellow; heartwood yellow to light brown; growth rings distinct; used for lumber, millwork, and railroad ties.

General: Native to mountainous areas in southern two-thirds of Utah and throughout the West. Normal growth rate is relatively slow. Resists fires with thick bark. Drought resistant. Shade intolerant.

Landscape Use: Occasionally planted when a large, long-needled pine is desired in the landscape. Austrian pine is similar in appearance and more readily available in nurseries. Zones 3-7.

singleleaf pinyon (*Pinus monophylla*)

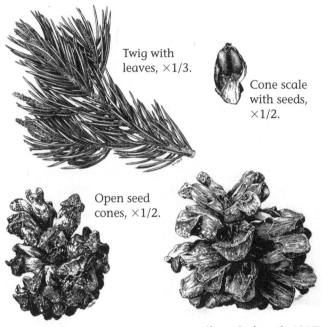

Twig with leaves, ×1/3.

Cone scale with seeds, ×1/2.

Open seed cones, ×1/2.

(from Sudworth 1917)

ponderosa pine (*Pinus ponderosa*)

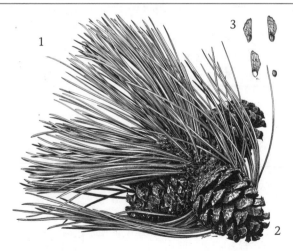

1. Twig with clusters of leaves ×1/3.
2. Open seed cones, ×1/3.
3. Seed with and without twigs, ×1/3.

(from Sudworth 1917)

39

❖**Lodgepole Pine** *(Pinus contorta* or
P. contorta var. *latifolia)*

Leaves: **Needles in groups of 2**; 1" to 3" long; yellow-green; stout; evergreen, remain on tree 4-6 years.

Twigs/Buds: Twigs stout; orange-brown to black when older. Buds about 1/4" long; covered with resin; dark brown.

Flowers/Fruit: Fruit a woody cone; very short to no stalk; **3/4" to 2" long**; oval; brown turning gray; each scale tipped with a prickle; cones often stay on trees and remain tightly closed for many years (such cones are called *serotinous*).

Bark: Orange-brown to gray; thin, even on older trees; scaly.

Wood: Moderately important; sapwood thick; heartwood light brown; used for lumber, posts, poles, and railroad ties.

General: Native to higher elevations in northern Utah and throughout the West and western Canada. Normal growth rate is relatively slow. Grows in dense, single-species stands formed when it seeds-in heavily after fires. Fairly drought resistant. Shade intolerant.

Landscape Use: Rarely planted in the landscape. Could be used occasionally where a natural, less manicured appearance is desired. Zones 2-6.

Austrian Pine   *(Pinus nigra)*

Leaves: **Needles in bundles of 2**; 3" to 6" long; slender; stiff; sharp-pointed; yellow-green to blue-green; evergreen, remain on tree 3-4 years.

Twigs/Buds: Twigs orange-brown; glabrous. Buds silvery and striped, 1/2" to 3/4" long.

Flowers/Fruit: Fruit a woody cone; about 2" to 3" long; reddish-brown; **non-pointed scales**.

Bark: Rough; platy; dark brown turning gray when older.

Wood: Sapwood nearly white; heartwood red-brown, somewhat oily and resinous; growth rings distinct.

General: A native of Europe, but grows well in Utah. Similar in size and habit to native ponderosa pine, but can be separated from ponderosa by the cone, needle, and bud characteristics described above. Shade intolerant.

Landscape Use: Widely planted in landscapes throughout Utah and the West. Nice, long-needled pine that is quite tough. Has been fairly disease- and insect-free in Utah, though Zimmerman pine moth, *Diplodia* tip blight, and *Dothistroma* needle blight have caused considerable problems elsewhere. Good individually or in a mass planting. Zones 4-7.

40

lodgepole pine (*Pinus contorta*)

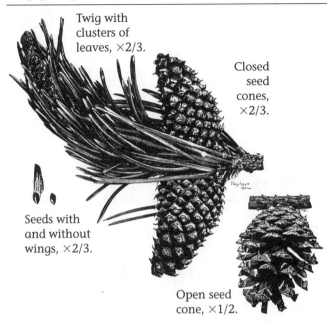

Twig with clusters of leaves, ×2/3.

Closed seed cones, ×2/3.

Seeds with and without wings, ×2/3.

Open seed cone, ×1/2.

(from Sudworth 1908)

Austrian pine (*Pinus nigra*)

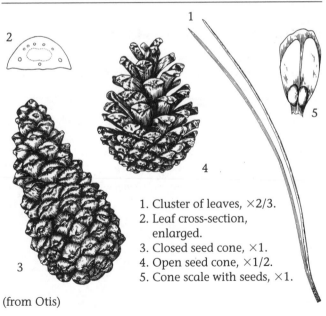

1. Cluster of leaves, ×2/3.
2. Leaf cross-section, enlarged.
3. Closed seed cone, ×1.
4. Open seed cone, ×1/2.
5. Cone scale with seeds, ×1.

(from Otis)

41

Scotch Pine ◆ Scots Pine *(Pinus sylvestris)*

Leaves: Needles in groups of 2; about 1-1/2" to 3" long; blue-green, may turn yellow-green in winter; **often twisted**; evergreen, remain on tree 3 years.

Twigs/Buds: Twigs medium-thick; dull gray-yellow; roughened by scales at base of leaf clusters. Buds 1/4" to 1/2" long; pointed; with fringed scales; red-brown; resinous.

Flowers/Fruit: Fruit a woody cone; 1-1/2" to 2" long; reddish-brown; scales with raised pyramid-shaped tips.

Bark: **Distinctively orange colored on upper limbs and trunk**.

Wood: Little used in the U.S. wood products industry; little information available.

General: Native throughout Europe, but widely planted in Utah. A very desirable species, preferred for Christmas tree production. Shade intolerant.

Landscape Use: Fairly widely planted in landscapes throughout Utah and the West. I have seen many old, stately trees in Logan. Needle and upper bark color are very nice. Fairly disease- and insect-free, though it shows some chlorosis (needle yellowing) when planted on our highest pH (most alkaline) soils and when overwatered. Zones 2-8.

Other Pines

Eastern White Pine *(Pinus strobus)*

Leaves: **Needles in groups of 5**; 3" to 5" long; dark blue-green, turning light green in winter in Utah; straight; slender; flexible; remain on tree 2-3 years.

Twigs/Buds: Twigs orange-brown; glabrous or with only a few, fine hairs. Buds covered with thin, red or orange-brown, non-pointed scales.

Flowers/Fruit: Fruit a woody cone; **about 4" to 8" (usually 5") long**; narrow; stalked; thin, non-pointed scales.

Bark: Thin, smooth, and gray on young stems; breaks into rectangular plates on older stems.

Wood: Important, especially historically; sapwood nearly white; heartwood darker; growth rings distinct; used for lumber, fine millwork, sailing-ship masts.

General: Native to eastern U.S. Shade tolerant when young, intolerant when older.

Scotch pine (*Pinus sylvestris*)

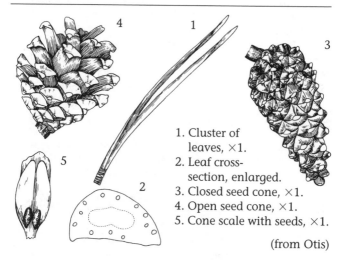

1. Cluster of leaves, ×1.
2. Leaf cross-section, enlarged.
3. Closed seed cone, ×1.
4. Open seed cone, ×1.
5. Cone scale with seeds, ×1.

(from Otis)

eastern white pine (*Pinus strobus*)

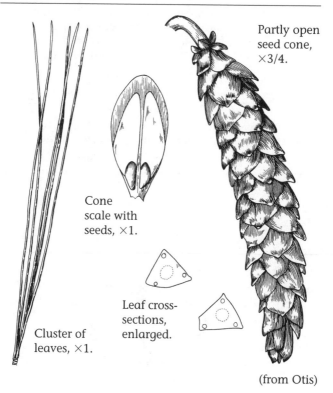

Partly open seed cone, ×3/4.

Cone scale with seeds, ×1.

Leaf cross-sections, enlarged.

Cluster of leaves, ×1.

(from Otis)

Landscape Use: A very nice tree with fast growth on good sites. Unfortunately, this tree is usually chlorotic in Utah due to high soil pH. Nevertheless, it seems fairly readily available in the nurseries. Zones 3-8. **Western white pine** (*Pinus monticola*) also is sometimes planted in Utah and I hear it does well, though I have not seen it. It differs from eastern white pine in having cones 5" to 15" long and needles that persist 3 to 4 years. Zones 5(4?)-8.

Himalayan Pine ◆ Bhutan Pine   (*Pinus wallichiana*)

Leaves: Needles in **bundles of 5; 5" to 8" long; slender, drooping, and feathery when older**; needle often bent sharply at base to hang down; grayish-green; evergreen, remain on tree 3 to 4 years.

Flowers/Fruit: Fruit a woody cone; 1" to 2" stalk; **cone 8" to 10" long** and 2" wide; light-brown when ripe.

General: Native to Afghanistan, Nepal, and China; occasionally planted in Utah. Potentially a large tree. Needs average moisture; shade intolerant.

Landscape Use: Very nice long-needled pine with interesting large cones. Fairly tough, but best planted in a location sheltered from dry summer winds and late-day winter sun. I have seen this doing well in a somewhat sheltered location in Logan, Utah (hardiness zone 4-5), but it may be marginally cold-hardy. Zones 5-7.

Mugo Pine ◆ Swiss Mountain Pine   (*Pinus mugo*)

Leaves: Needles in bundles of 2; 1-1/2" to 3" long; stiff; medium green; evergreen, remain on tree 5 or more years.

Flowers/Fruit: Fruit a woody cone; **1" to 2" long**; ovoid, with an uneven base; no spine on the tips of the scales; little or no stalk; gray-black when mature.

Bark: Scaly; gray-brown; not orange on upper trunk like *Pinus sylvestris*.

General: A **shrubby tree** native to mountains of central and southern Europe. Tough and tolerant of a variety of conditions, including cold, alkaline-soils, and some drought. Shade intolerant.

Landscape Use: A very common shrub planted throughout Utah, though some varieties can get quite large and almost tree-like. Usually used in mass plantings and rarely planted with enough room for its eventual size. If planting in a small area be sure to use true dwarf cultivars. Zones 2-8.

western white pine (*Pinus monticola*)

Open seed cone, ×1/4.

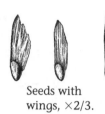

Seeds with wings, ×2/3.

Twig with clusters of leaves, ×1/4.

(from Sudworth 1917)

Mugo pine (*Pinus mugo*)

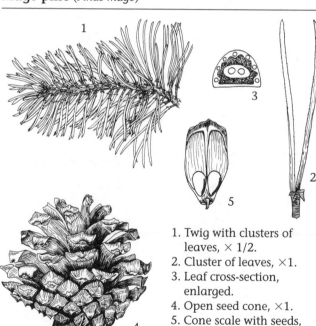

1. Twig with clusters of leaves, × 1/2.
2. Cluster of leaves, ×1.
3. Leaf cross-section, enlarged.
4. Open seed cone, ×1.
5. Cone scale with seeds, ×1-1/2

(from Barnes & Wagner)

Japanese White Pine *(Pinus parviflora)*

Leaves: Needles in **bundles of 5; 1-1/4" to 2-1/2" long**; stiff; twisted; tufted near branch ends; bluish-green; evergreen, remain on tree 3 to 4 years.

Flowers/Fruit: Fruit a woody cone; short or no stalk; 1-1/2" to 4" long; reddish-brown; **persists on tree 6 to 7 years**.

General: Native to Japan. Stays fairly short (25' to 50'). More cold hardy than Himalayan pine. Needs average moisture; tolerant of salt; shade intolerant.

Landscape Use: Good tree like all of the white (5-needled) pines because of its fine-textured foliage. Desirable and could be planted more in Utah. Zones 4-7.

Lacebark Pine *(Pinus bungeana)*

Leaves: **Needles in bundles of 3**; 2" to 4" long; stiff; dark green; evergreen, remain on tree 3 to 4 years.

Flowers/Fruit: Fruit a woody cone; 2" to 3" long; curved, triangular spine on the tips of the scales.

Bark: **Scaly bark that comes off in patches like a London planetree**; irregular patches of green, white, and brown; very distinctive.

General: Native to China. Tolerant of a variety of conditions, including pavement nearby. Fairly cold and alkaline-soil tolerant; shade intolerant.

Landscape Use: Very desirable tree. Use as a specimen tree where showy bark can be observed. Foliage and crown shape and size remind me of a Scotch pine. Should be planted more often. Zones 4-8.

Japanese Black Pine *(Pinus thunbergiana)*

Leaves: Needles in bundles of 2; 2" to 4" long; stiff; dark green; evergreen, remain on tree 3 to 5 years.

Flowers/Fruit: Fruit a woody cone; 1-1/2" to 2-1/2" long; brown; **scale tips rounded** or with a very small prickle.

General: Native to Japan. Large, tough tree, though not extremely cold hardy. Salt and drought tolerant; shade intolerant.

Landscape Use: Could be used more to vary our choices in pines. Does well in Utah. Nice dark green foliage. Somewhat irregular shape. Zones 5-9.

Japanese Red Pine   *(Pinus densiflora)*

Leaves: Needles in bundles of 2; 3" to 5" long; slender; twisted; bright to dark green; evergreen, remain on tree 3 years.

Flowers/Fruit: Fruit a woody cone; 1-1/2" to 2" long; dull yellow; remain on tree 2 to 3 years.

Bark: **Orange-red when young, peels off in scales**; turning grayish near the base when older.

General: Native to Japan, Korea, and China. Very cold hardy. Potentially large tree, though slow-growing. Needs average water and soil; shade intolerant.

Landscape Use: Nice large tree. Attractive bark. Irregular and interesting crown and trunk form. Zones 3-7.

Aleppo Pine   *(Pinus halepensis)*

Leaves: Needles in bundles of 2 or sometimes 3; 2-1/2" to 4-1/2" long; slender; curved; gray-green; evergreen.

Flowers/Fruit: Fruit a woody cone; very short stalk; oval to conical; 3" long; red to yellow-brown.

General: Native to southern Europe, northern Africa, and parts of Asia. Not cold hardy; adapted well to hot, dry desert climates. Needs little water. Shade intolerant.

Landscape Use: Use in warm desert climates where a pine is desired. Do not plant where it will encounter hard frosts on a regular basis. Zones 8-10.

Larch   Genus *Larix*

This genus of **deciduous** conifers (needles turn yellow and fall off in autumn) contains about 10 species with 3 native to North America and none native to Utah. Needles are arranged in whorls or clusters on short, spur-like branches or individually on new growth. Larches have round or elongated, yellow, catkin-like pollen cones at the ends of shoots that shed pollen in spring and then fall off. Seed cones are small and red, yellow, or green at pollination, growing into fairly small **upright, woody seed-bearing cones** with small winged seeds. Larches are intolerant of shade. Only one larch, European larch, is commonly planted in Utah, and another is planted occasionally. Monoecious.

European Larch   *(Larix decidua)*

Leaves: Needles borne singly; 3/4" to 1-1/4" long; **deciduous**; bright green, turning yellow in fall; triangular or 4-sided in cross-section; soft; alternately arranged on new growth, on older growth occurring in dense clusters of 30 to 40 on spur shoots.

Twigs/Buds: Twigs slender; glabrous; orange-brown; obvious spur shoots on older growth. Buds round; dark red-brown.

Flowers/Fruit: Fruit a cone; **3/4" to 1-1/2" long; upright; 40 to 50 thin scales**; green or purple turning brown at maturity.

Bark: Thin and smooth on young stems; gray-brown and scaly on older stems.

Wood: Not widely used; sapwood yellowish-white; heartwood yellowish-brown; strong; hard; durable; used for poles, railroad ties, lumber.

General: Native to the mountains of northern and central Europe. Does well in Utah with a moderate growth rate and is quite cold-tolerant; prefers moist soils. Shade intolerant.

Landscape Use: Beautiful tree with great, golden fall color. Deciduous character is interesting but not everyone likes its winter appearance. Trees I have seen are generally large with strongly pointed, cone-shaped crowns. Zones 2-6. **Japanese larch** (*Larix kaempferi*) also is sometimes planted in Utah. This larch has more blue-green needles and the tips of the cone scales are curved back, giving the cone a rosette appearance. It has similar requirements to European larch. Zones 4-7.

Cedar   Genus *Cedrus*

True cedars. This genus contains 4 species that are native to northern Africa and southern Asia and none that are native to North America. The leaves are evergreen, needle-like, flattened in cross-section, and **arranged on twigs like larch needles**. Pollen cones are similar in appearance to seed cones, shedding pollen in the fall. Seed cones resemble fir cones and are generally **upright**, contain large winged seeds, and mature in 2 to 3 years. Cedars are fairly intolerant of shade and prefer deep soils and moist, somewhat protected sites. Monoecious.

Atlas Cedar   *(Cedrus atlantica)*

Leaves: Needles borne singly; 3/4" to 1-1/2" long; stiff; evergreen; bluish or dark-green; four-sided but somewhat flattened in cross-section; pointed tip; spirally arranged on new growth, on older growth occurring in dense clusters of **30 to 40 on short spur shoots**.

eastern larch (*Larix laricina*)
                for
European larch (*Larix decidua*)

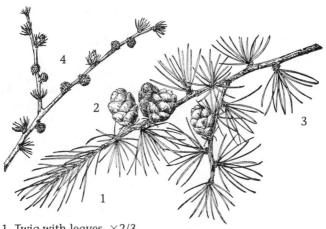

1. Twig with leaves, ×2/3.
2. Upright seed cones, ×2/3.
3. Leaves on spur shoots, ×2/3.
4. Twig with pollen cones, ×2/3.   (from Sargent)

Atlas cedar (*Cedrus atlantica*)

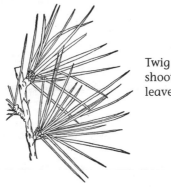

Twig with spur
shoots and
leaves, ×1.

(from Apgar)

Twigs/Buds: Twigs somewhat downy or glabrous; less densely-branched than *Cedrus libani*. Buds small and ovoid, with few scales.

Flowers/Fruit: Seed cones fir-like, upright; mature in two seasons; **about 2" to 3" long and 2" wide**; green when young, brown at maturity.

49

Bark: Smooth and gray on young stems; older stems with dark gray-brown furrowed bark.

Wood: Not important except locally where native.

General: Native to the Atlas Mountains in Morocco and Algeria. Slow to medium growth rate. Likes warm sites, with good moisture but deep, well-drained soils. Shade intolerant.

Landscape Use: Excellent specimen tree with beautiful crown and good color. Supposedly zones 6-9, but doing well in several Salt Lake City locations and in Utah County at BYU, and a young one is doing well on the northwest side of a building on the USU campus.

Other Cedars

Deodar Cedar   *(Cedrus deodara)*

Leaves: Similar to Atlas cedar but **needles 1-1/2" to 2" long** with clusters of 15 to 20 on spur shoots.

Flowers/Fruit: Seed cones held singly or in pairs and **about 3" to 4" long and 3" wide**.

General: Native to the Himalayas. Slow to medium growth rate. Not as cold hardy as Atlas cedar. Top often dies back due to diseases or cold. Shade intolerant.

Landscape Use: Very attractive tree with a sweeping, graceful habit; flat-topped when old. Zones 7-9, but doing well in several Salt Lake City locations.

Cedar of Lebanon   *(Cedrus libani)*

Leaves: Similar to Atlas cedar.

Flowers/Fruit: Seed cones held singly and **about 3" to 5" long and 2" to 2-1/2" wide**.

General: Native to the Taurus Mountains, Turkey, and Lebanon. Slow growth rate. More cold-hardy than Deodar cedar. Shade intolerant.

Landscape Use: Very good specimen tree with wide-spreading branches and dark green leaves; flat-topped when old. Zones 5-7.

Spruce   Genus *Picea*

There are about 30 species of spruces with 7 native to North America and 2 native to Utah. The needles are evergreen, **4-angled** or occasionally flattened in cross-section, arranged individually on the twigs, and persist for 7 to 10 years. Pollen cones are

Deodar cedar (*Cedrus deodara*)

Spur shoot
with leaves,
× 1/2.

(from USDA 1949)

cedar of Lebanon (*Cedrus libani*)

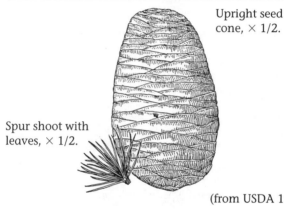

Upright seed
cone, × 1/2.

Spur shoot with
leaves, × 1/2.

(from USDA 1949)

catkin-like and borne on the previous year's shoot, shedding pollen
in the spring and then falling off. Spruce seed cones are erect and
purplish when very young, **hang down after pollination, have
papery scales** and small winged seeds, and mature in one season.
Spruces are fairly shade tolerant and prefer moist, cool sites, generally at higher elevations. Monoecious.

❖Engelmann Spruce *(Picea engelmannii)*

Leaves: Needles borne singly; about 1" long; evergreen; blue-
green to dark green; 4-angled; not as sharp pointed as blue spruce;
tend to be crowded on around upper side of twig; fragrant when
crushed.

Twigs/Buds: Leaves attached with a short stalk that remains part
of the twig, so twig rough; young twigs with minute hairs. **Buds
with scales that lie fairly flat.**

51

Flowers/Fruit: Fruit a papery cone that hangs down; **about 1" to 2-1/2" long**; light chestnut-brown; papery scales are slightly round-toothed at tip.

Bark: Red to purple-brown; made-up of thin scales; thinner than blue spruce.

Wood: Moderate importance; heartwood not distinct; nearly white to light brown; growth rings distinct; used for lumber, poles, ties, and fuel.

General: Native throughout the Rocky Mountains and parts of the Pacific Northwest and western Canada. Slow growing. Likes cool, moist sites and good soil. Wind-throw (trees being blown over) is a problem if the site is disturbed. Shade tolerant.

Landscape Use: Rarely used, though some mountain homes are built in Engelmann spruce stands. Probably would not do well at lower, warmer, drier locations. Blue spruce is more available and has good cultivars. Zones 2-5.

❖Blue Spruce ◆ Colorado Blue Spruce
(Picea pungens)

Leaves: Needles borne singly; about 1" long; evergreen; blue-white to dark green; 4-angled; sharp pointed; extend at right angles all around twig; very fragrant when crushed.

Twigs/Buds: Twigs glabrous; leaves on a short stalk that remains part of the twig, so twig rough. **Buds with scales that tend to turn out into a rosette**, especially in spring.

Flowers/Fruit: Fruit a papery cone that hangs down; **about 2-1/2" to 4" long**; light chestnut-brown; papery scales are slightly round-toothed at tip.

Bark: Light to dark gray; made-up of thin scales; wide, thick ridges on older trees.

Wood: Minor importance; similar to Engelmann spruce.

General: Utah's official state tree. Native to Utah, the Rocky Mountains and Intermountain states. Slow growing. Likes moisture and good soil; may not do well with extreme heat or hot, dry winds. Wind-throw can be a problem. Intermediate shade tolerance.

Landscape Use: Beautiful, slow-growing tree but allow enough room—can eventually get quite tall and wide. Best if it is allowed to keep branches and foliage right to the ground. Will as often be green as blue in nature, but blue-foliage cultivars are available. Good visual, sound, and wind screen. Cooley spruce gall adelgid can cause unsightly brown galls to form on twig tips on blue spruces in the landscape. This is a very good tree, but it is over-used in many areas. Zones 2-7.

Engelmann spruce (*Picea engelmannii*)

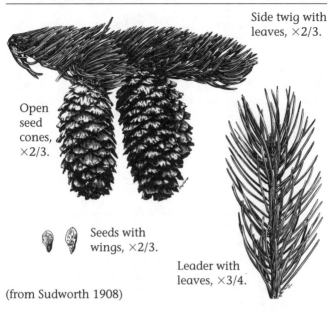

Side twig with leaves, ×2/3.

Open seed cones, ×2/3.

Seeds with wings, ×2/3.

Leader with leaves, ×3/4.

(from Sudworth 1908)

blue spruce (*Picea pungens*)

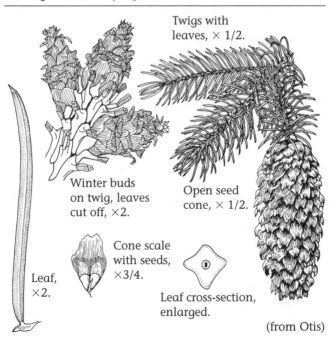

Twigs with leaves, × 1/2.

Winter buds on twig, leaves cut off, ×2.

Open seed cone, × 1/2.

Leaf, ×2.

Cone scale with seeds, ×3/4.

Leaf cross-section, enlarged.

(from Otis)

White Spruce ◆ Black Hills Spruce *(Picea glauca)*

Leaves: Needles borne singly; **1/3" to 3/4" long**; often crowded on upper side of branch by twisting of needles from the lower side; tips pointed but not sharp; evergreen; blue-green, sometimes with white tinge; 4-angled; pungent when crushed.

Twigs/Buds: Twigs glabrous; slender, orange-brown to gray; pungent odor when crushed. Buds 1/8" to 1/4" long; red-brown or light brown; not resinous; tips of scales often curve back.

Flowers/Fruit: Fruit a papery cone that hangs down; **1-1/2" to 2-1/2" long**; light brown colored; margins of cone scales rounded, entire.

Bark: Thin, gray-brown; flaky or scaly; newly exposed inner bark silvery.

Wood: Important in native range; light colored, with little difference between heartwood and sapwood; used for pulp, millwork, boxes, and piano sounding boards.

General: Native in Black Hills, northern Lake States, northeastern U.S., and throughout Canada and Alaska; but not in Utah. Slow growing. Prefers moist sites with good soil, but fairly adaptable. Shade tolerant.

Landscape Use: Seldom planted in Utah (except for dwarf Alberta spruce—see below), but a very desirable landscape tree. Narrow-crown and short needles make it interesting. As with other spruces, looks best when foliage and branches are maintained to the ground. **Dwarf Alberta spruce** *(Picea glauca* 'Conica') is a commonly available cultivar that is overused in many landscapes. Winter desiccation and spider mites are potential problems. Zones 2-6.

Norway Spruce   *(Picea abies)*

Leaves: Needles borne singly; about 1" long; sharp; evergreen; dark green; 4-angled, but **somewhat flattened in cross-section**.

Twigs/Buds: On older trees of larger cultivars **long twigs often hang down and sway in the wind**; glabrous; leaves on a short stalk that remains part of the twig. Buds 1/4" long; red-brown or light brown; not resinous; scales often with spreading tips; rosette shaped.

Flowers/Fruit: Fruit a large papery cone that hangs down; **4" to 7" long**; light tan colored.

Bark: Light to dark gray; made-up of thin scales; in wide ridges on older trees.

Wood: Important in Europe and somewhat in eastern U.S.; light colored; indistinct heartwood; slightly resinous; used for pulp and paper.

white spruce (*Picea glauca*)

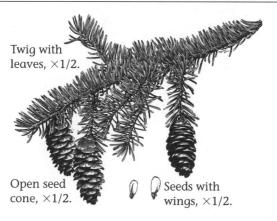

Twig with leaves, ×1/2.

Open seed cone, ×1/2.

Seeds with wings, ×1/2.

(from Sudworth 1908)

Norway spruce (*Picea abies*)

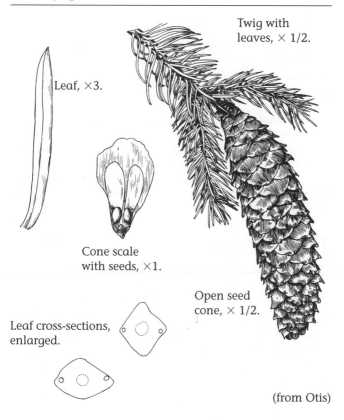

Twig with leaves, × 1/2.

Leaf, ×3.

Cone scale with seeds, ×1.

Open seed cone, × 1/2.

Leaf cross-sections, enlarged.

(from Otis)

General: Native to Europe. Widely planted ornamentally in U.S and fairly commonly planted in Utah. Gets taller and wider, grows faster than blue spruce. Intermediate shade tolerance.

Landscape Use: Beautiful and desirable, but highly variable depending on cultivar (see below). Medium growth rate and can get very tall and wide. Placing two or three together in a large-scale landscape can be very impressive. Long, weeping branchlets on some cultivars are very attractive. Zones 2-7.

Other Spruces

Serbian Spruce   *(Picea omorika)*

Leaves: Needles borne singly; about 1/2" to 1" long; sharp-pointed; evergreen; dark green above; **silver-green bands beneath**; somewhat flattened in cross-section but ridged.

Flowers/Fruit: Fruit a papery cone that hangs down; **1-1/4" to 2" long**; reddish brown when mature; scale edges rounded, entire.

General: Native to southeastern Europe. Potentially a large tree. Fairly tough tree adapted to a wide variety of soils and sites. Likes some shelter; fairly cold hardy; shade tolerant.

Landscape Use: Very desirable spruce with nice foliage. Rarely planted in Utah, but deserves more use. Zones 4-7.

Douglas-fir   Genus *Pseudotsuga*

Not true firs (genus *Abies*). This genus of evergreen conifers contains 6 species with 2 native to North America and one native to Utah. The needles are evergreen, fairly-flat in cross-section, arranged individually on the twigs, and attached by a short stalk. Douglas-fir pollen cones are yellow to orange and catkin-like, releasing their pollen in spring, then dying and falling off. **Seed cones hang down**, have flexible rounded scales with a **distinctive bract**, and mature in one season. Douglas-fir is intermediate in shade tolerance and prefers moist, cool sites, at medium to high elevations. The Douglas-fir native to Utah is the Rocky Mountain form, *Pseudotsuga menziesii* var. *glauca*. Monoecious.

❖Douglas-fir   *(Pseudotsuga menziesii)*

Leaves: Needles borne singly; about 1" long; **flat**; blunt; yellow-green to blue-green; evergreen; remain on tree 5-8 years.

Twigs/Buds: Twigs slender; flexible; covered with fine hairs; glabrous when leaves are detached; small bumps on young twigs where needles were attached. Buds cigar-shaped; sharp-pointed; about 1/2" long; brown.

Flowers/Fruit: Fruit a thin-scaled cone; about 3" long; **hangs down; each scale has a 3-pointed woody bract attached to it**.

Bark: Smooth; gray-brown; with resin blisters on young trees; rough and thick on older trees.

Wood: Very important; sapwood white to yellow; heartwood yellow to red; growth rings very distinct; used for high-quality lumber and plywood.

General: Native to the Pacific coastal states and Rocky Mountain states, including Utah. Not a true fir. Very valuable western timber tree. Narrower crown than many conifers. Intermediate shade tolerance.

Landscape Use: Does well in Utah but seldom seen away from native mountain sites. Does well in Utah's valleys with adequate moisture. Zones 4-6.

Douglas-fir (*Pseudotsuga menziesii*)

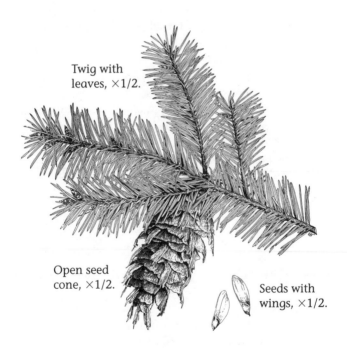

Twig with leaves, ×1/2.

Open seed cone, ×1/2.

Seeds with wings, ×1/2.

(from Sudworth 1908)

Fir Genus *Abies*

True firs. About 40 fir species exist world-wide with 9 native to North America and 2 native to Utah. The needles are evergreen, **flattened in cross-section**, without sharp-pointed tips (firs are "friendly"), arranged individually on the twigs, and persist for 7 to 10 years. Needles leave a conspicuous round scar where attached to the twig. Fir pollen cones are catkin-like and are borne amongst the previous year's needles, releasing their pollen in late spring. Seed cones are held **upright on upper branches and have deciduous scales** that fall from a persistent stalk, shedding seed in the process. Like spruces, firs are shade tolerant and prefer moist, cool sites, generally at higher elevations. Monoecious.

❖White Fir ◆ Concolor Fir *(Abies concolor)*

Leaves: Needles borne singly; **2" to 3" long**; flattened in cross-section; evergreen; silver-blue to silver-green.

Twigs/Buds: Twigs moderately stout; glabrous; yellow-green to brown-green; round leaf scar. Buds 1/4" long or less; tend to be sticky; yellow-brown.

Flowers/Fruit: Fruit a cone; 3" to 5" long; oblong; green to purple; **borne upright on upper branches; scales deciduous**.

Bark: Thin; smooth; gray; with resinous blisters; becoming furrowed and ridged on very old trunks.

Wood: Moderate importance; soft and brittle; white to yellow-brown; even grained; growth rings distinct.

General: Native to central and southern Rocky Mountains, including Utah, and to California. Prefers moist, cool, protected sites. Shade tolerant.

Landscape Use: Very desirable tree that needs some protection to do well on windy, exposed sites in Utah's valleys. Does not seem to like high soil pH. Still, very attractive with its nice conical form and blue-green foliage—sometimes confused with blue spruce. Zones 3-7.

❖Subalpine Fir ◆ Alpine Fir *(Abies lasiocarpa)*

Leaves: Needles borne singly; **1" to 1-1/2" long**; flattened in cross-section; evergreen; bluish-green.

Twigs/Buds: Twigs similar to white fir. Buds orange-brown.

Flowers/Fruit: Fruit a cone; 2" to 4" long; oblong; green to purple; **borne upright on upper branches; scales deciduous**.

Bark: Thin; smooth; gray; with resinous blisters; becoming shallowly furrowed on older trunks.

white fir (*Abies concolor*)

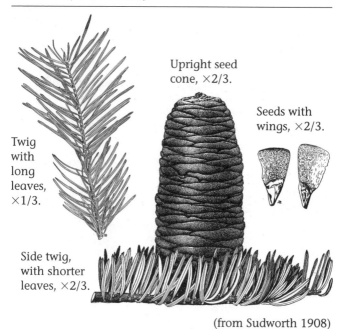

Upright seed cone, ×2/3.

Seeds with wings, ×2/3.

Twig with long leaves, ×1/3.

Side twig, with shorter leaves, ×2/3.

(from Sudworth 1908)

subalpine fir (*Abies lasiocarpa*)

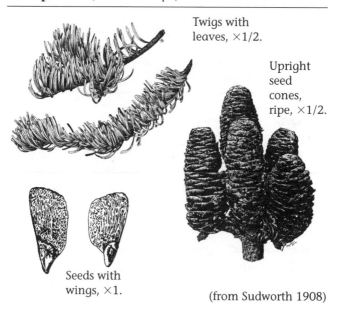

Twigs with leaves, ×1/2.

Upright seed cones, ripe, ×1/2.

Seeds with wings, ×1.

(from Sudworth 1908)

Wood: Moderate importance; similar to white fir.

General: Native to fairly high elevation, cool, moist sites from the southern Rockies to northwestern Canada, including Utah. Many native trees in Utah are dying due to insects, disease, drought, and old-age. Shade tolerant.

Landscape Use: Very narrow, spire-like crown, often with many leaders. Seldom, if ever, planted in Utah's valleys and may not do well with heat or dry conditions. Native trees are sensitive to construction damage when present on building sites. Zones 1-5.

TAXODIACEAE

Redwood family. Trees with small, woody cones; linear or awl-shaped leaves. Contains nine genera and 13-15 species, including redwood and sequoia. Located mostly in the Northern Hemisphere. Very important timber trees, though limited in number. All species are monoecious.

Baldcypress   Genus *Taxodium*

Not true cypresses (genus *Cupressus*). This genus contains 2 species that are native to the southeastern U.S. and Central America. The leaves are evergreen or deciduous, scaly or needle-like and flattened in cross-section. Pollen cones are small and borne on a drooping stalk, releasing pollen in spring. Seed cones are **round and woody with several fused scales** that fall apart at maturity to release the seeds. Native baldcypresses are swamp species, with large, buttressed bases and special "knees" that emerge from the water and may help in oxygen uptake for the roots. Only one species, the common baldcypress (*Taxodium distichum*), is planted in Utah. Monoecious.

Baldcypress   *(Taxodium distichum)*

Leaves: Linear or needle-like; 1/2" to 3/4" long; spirally or alternately arranged; **deciduous**; smallest twigs fall off in autumn with needles attached; small twigs and attached needles appear two-ranked and feather-like; yellow-green in summer turning rust colored in fall.

Twigs/Buds: Branch-end or terminal twigs have buds and are not deciduous; lateral or side twigs deciduous with needles still attached. Buds small; round; several overlapping scales.

Flowers/Fruit: Fruit a **woody cone; round**; 3/4" to 1-1/3" diameter; brown; 9 to 15 wrinkled, 4-sided, woody scales that break away when mature; mature in one year; seeds small, 3-winged.

baldcypress (*Taxodium distichum*)

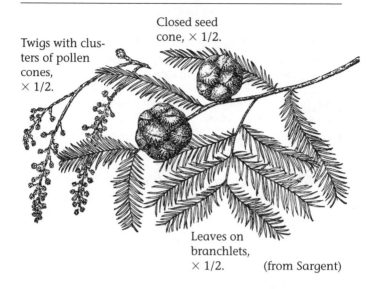

Closed seed cone, × 1/2.

Twigs with clusters of pollen cones, × 1/2.

Leaves on branchlets, × 1/2. (from Sargent)

Bark: Thin and scaly to fibrous; red-brown to gray.

Wood: Important; light to dark brown; very durable and rot resistant; used for construction, siding, shingles, etc.

General: Native throughout the southeast U.S. and as far north as southeast Missouri and southern Illinois; not native to Utah. Typically grows in swamps in the South. Can get 1,000 to 2,000 years old in native areas. Shade intolerant.

Landscape Use: This is a very interesting, large, deciduous conifer that has attractive, feathery foliage in summer, nice fall color, and an interesting shape and texture year-round. The fruit also is interesting. Not common in Utah, but will do well in a wide variety of soil conditions. Specimens are doing well on the BYU campus, in Salt Lake City, and on the USU campus in Logan. Zones 4-9.

Other *Taxodiaceae*

Giant Sequoia *(Sequoiadendron giganteum)*

Leaves: **Awl-shaped leaves**, 1/8" to 1/2" long, sometimes look scale-like, alternately or spirally arranged along twig; evergreen; blue-green; somewhat similar to junipers.

Twigs/Buds: Twigs slender; covered by leaves. Buds small; naked (no scales).

61

Flowers/Fruit: Fruit a **woody cone; oval**; 1-3/4" to 3-1/2" long; red-brown; hangs down after first year; 25 to 40 wrinkled scales with diamond shaped ends; mature in two years but cones may persist on tree with live seed for up to 20 years.

General: Native to a few groves in the western slopes of the Sierra Nevada in California; not native to Utah. Native trees grow rapidly, get very large (nearly 300' tall), and can be 4,000 to 5,000 years old. Extremely resistant to insects, diseases, and fire. Intermediate shade tolerance.

Landscape Use: This tree does surprisingly well in Utah where temperatures don't get too cold, but avoid very hot locations. Several good examples can be found in the Salt Lake area. It has a nice, dense, upright, conical crown. Likes a fair amount of moisture, but tolerates some drying. Zones 6-8.

giant sequoia (*Sequoiadendron giganteum*)

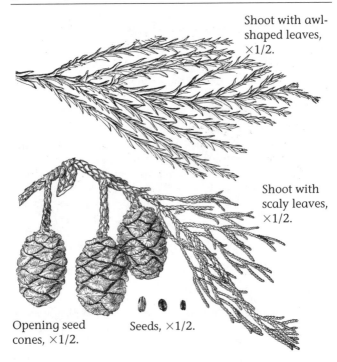

Shoot with awl-shaped leaves, ×1/2.

Shoot with scaly leaves, ×1/2.

Opening seed cones, ×1/2.

Seeds, ×1/2.

(from Sudworth 1908)

Dawn Redwood *(Metasequoia glyptostroboides)*

Key characteristics:

Leaves: Similar to baldcypress; **opposite arrangement on twig**; **deciduous**.

Flowers/Fruit: Fruit a round cone up to 1" in diameter; **with 20 to 30 triangular scales**.

General: Native to China. Prefers moist, well-drained soils that are slightly acid. Intermediate shade tolerance.

Landscape Use: Planted occasionally in Utah. Intolerance of high pH soils is a problem. Prefers full sun. Strong pyramid-shaped crown. Likely not as tolerant of high soil pH and poor soil drainage as baldcypress. Zones 4-8.

dawn redwood *(Metasequoia glyptostroboides)*

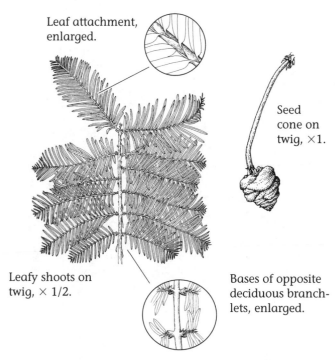

Leaf attachment, enlarged.

Seed cone on twig, ×1.

Leafy shoots on twig, × 1/2.

Bases of opposite deciduous branch-lets, enlarged.

(from Farrar)

CUPRESSACEAE

Cypress family. Trees with **fleshy, woody, or leathery cones**; **scale-like or awl-shaped leaves**. Contains 15 genera and about 140 species, located throughout the world. Includes many commercially important trees. Species are monoecious or dioecious.

Cypress Genus *Cupressus*

True cypresses. This genus includes about 15 species of trees and shrubs that are native to western North America, Mexico, the Mediterranean, and Asia. Five of these species are native to the west coast and one to the southwestern U.S., with none native to Utah. All species are monoecious.

Italian Cypress *(Cupressus sempervirens)*

Leaves: Scale-like or awl shaped on juvenile or fast-growing twigs; overlap in four rows to cover twig similar to junipers; evergreen; green to dark-green.

Twigs/Buds: Twigs covered by foliage so not noticed. Buds small; inconspicuous.

Flowers/Fruit: Pollen cones small, yellow, releasing pollen in spring; female cones nearly round, maturing in two growing seasons into a **round, woody cone**; 1" diameter; brown; with 6 to 8 **shield-shaped scales**, somewhat similar to baldcypress.

Bark: Scaly; red-brown.

Wood: Unimportant.

General: Native to southern Europe and western Asia. Naturally found in warm, fairly dry areas. Many of the native trees have the narrow, columnar crown commonly found in all of the cultivars. Shade intolerant.

Landscape Use: Only for use in warm, dry climates—not cold-hardy. Cultivars all have very narrow, tight, columnar crowns with upright branches. Foliage color of cultivars varies from yellow-green to dark blue-green. Only planted in Utah in low elevation, warm sites. Very formal appearance. Zones 7-9. **Arizona cypress** (*Cupressus arizonica*) is native to the southwestern U.S. and Mexico (not Utah) and has potential for planting in warm sites (Zones 7-9) in Utah.

Italian cypress (*Cupressus sempervirens*)

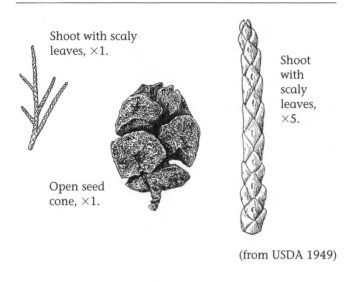

Shoot with scaly leaves, ×1.

Open seed cone, ×1.

Shoot with scaly leaves, ×5.

(from USDA 1949)

Arizona cypress (*Cupressus arizonica*)

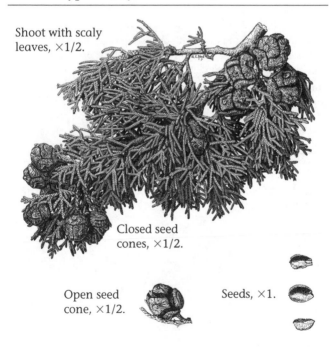

Shoot with scaly leaves, ×1/2.

Closed seed cones, ×1/2.

Open seed cone, ×1/2.

Seeds, ×1.

(from Sudworth 1915)

65

Falsecypress   Genus *Chamaecyparis*

This evergreen genus has six species, with two native to western coastal North America and one to the eastern United States. The scaly foliage resembles that of other genera in this family. The **round cones with 4 to 10 shield-shaped scales** are fairly distinctive.

Hinoki Falsecypress ◆ Hinoki Cypress
(Chamaecyparis obtusa)

Leaves: Small; scale-like; very similar to *Cupressus* and *Thuja*; attached in alternating pairs flattened along and clasping twig; 1/12" long or less; dark green above with white markings underneath; evergreen; persist 2 to 3 years; aromatic when crushed.

Twigs/Buds: Twigs slender; covered by foliage; arranged in flattened, somewhat drooping sprays. Buds very small; indistinct; not useful for identification purposes.

Flowers/Fruit: Fruit a **leathery cone; 1/3" to 1/2" diameter; round**; orange-brown; 8 to 10 shield-shaped scales with a bump on each one; matures in one year.

Bark: Fibrous; red-brown; coming off in long, narrow strips; distinctive.

Wood: Unimportant.

General: Native to Japan and Formosa. Not a true cypress. Small to medium-sized tree, depending on cultivar; medium to slow growth. Intermediate shade tolerance.

Landscape Use: This is a nice small evergreen that is little planted in Utah but should do well. It is easily confused with some of the arborvitaes with its scaly foliage in flattened sprays. I have two small ones growing in my yard in Logan in their second season, so the jury's still out. The foliage and crown texture are very attractive and several forms are available. Zones 4-8.

Hinoki falsecypress *(Chamaecyparis obtusa)*

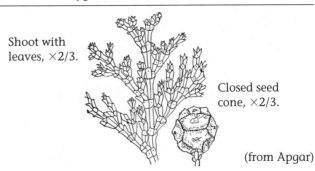

Shoot with leaves, ×2/3.

Closed seed cone, ×2/3.

(from Apgar)

Incense-cedar   Genus *Calocedrus*

A genus of evergreens with eight species in the Americas, Asia, and New Zealand, and one species native to North America. Also called *Libocedrus*. Scaly foliage is much like that of other genera in this family, but the **2-valved female cones** are distinctive.

Incense-cedar   *(Calocedrus decurrens* or *Libocedrus decurrens)*

Leaves: Small; scale-like; attached in whorls of four; flattened along and clasping twig; 1/8" to 1/2" long; dark green; evergreen; persist 3 to 5 years; aromatic when crushed.

Twigs/Buds: Twigs slender; covered by foliage; often flattened and arranged in vertical sprays. Buds very small; indistinct; not useful for identification purposes.

Flowers/Fruit: Fruit a **cone; 3/4" to 1-1/2" long; elongated**; red-brown; hangs-down; 6 scales, though only five are apparent, with 2 scales becoming very long at maturity, with the appearance

incense-cedar *(Calocedrus decurrens)*

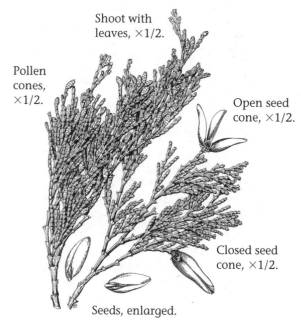

Shoot with leaves, ×1/2.

Pollen cones, ×1/2.

Open seed cone, ×1/2.

Closed seed cone, ×1/2.

Seeds, enlarged.

(from Sudworth 1908)

of a duck's bill as they open; matures by fall, but stays on tree through winter.

Bark: Scaly to fibrous; light brown to rusty-red; eventually becoming deeply furrowed; distinctive.

Wood: Important; sapwood nearly white and thin; heartwood reddish; light weight; soft; extensively used for pencils.

General: Native to mountainous areas in California, Oregon, and Washington. Not a true cedar. Medium to fairly large tree; medium to slow growth. Shade tolerant.

Landscape Use: A nice, large tree planted in Utah more in the past than presently. I have seen several in Salt Lake City growing in yards of 40 to 50 year-old houses and doing quite well. The bark is very attractive as it ages. The tree has an arborvitae-like look, but somehow different. Fairly heat tolerant and can stand a range of soil conditions. Zones 5-8(9).

Arborvitae ◆ White-cedar   Genus *Thuja*

Not true cedars (genus *Cedrus*). Five or six species of evergreen trees or large shrubs are included in this genus. Native habitat ranges from North America to east Asia. Only two species are native to North America and none to Utah, though both of the North American natives can be planted in cultivated landscapes in parts of Utah. Arborvitae translates to "Tree-of-Life". At first glance these trees look somewhat like junipers, but the **cones are woody, not fleshy**. Pollen cones are small, reddish, and are borne on the tips of branchlets, releasing pollen in early spring. Monoecious.

Northern White-cedar ◆ Eastern Arborvitae
(Thuja occidentalis)

Leaves: Small; scale-like; flattened along twig in pairs; yellow-green to green; evergreen.

Twigs/Buds: Twigs slender; covered by foliage; **arranged mostly in horizontally flattened or drooping sprays**. Buds very small; indistinct; not useful for identification purposes.

Flowers/Fruit: Fruit a cone; **1/3" to 1/2" long**; upright; 4 fertile scales plus several infertile scales; matures in one season.

Bark: Thin; narrow, interlacing ridges; red-brown to gray-brown; fibrous.

Wood: Moderately important; sapwood nearly white and thin; heartwood light brown; light weight; very resistant to decay; used for poles, railroad ties, fence posts, fencing, lumber.

General: Native to northeast U.S., Lake States, Appalachian Mountains, and southern Canada. Not a true cedar. Medium to fairly large tree, medium to slow growth. Often found in swampy areas. Intermediate shade tolerance.

Landscape Use: More commonly planted in Utah in the past than now, though these are very desirable trees. Many different crown forms are available, from shrubby, to large pyramidal, to weeping. Good as hedge, visual screen, windbreak, or as specimen trees. Cold hardy but may need protection on harsh, dry, windy sites. Does not like extreme heat and dry conditions. Few insect or disease problems. Zones 2-8. **Western redcedar** (*Thuja plicata*), also not a true cedar, is native to the rain-forests of the Pacific Northwest and to northern Idaho and western Montana. It is very rarely planted in Utah, but several of the cultivars may do well in zones 5-7.

northern white-cedar (*Thuja occidentalis*)

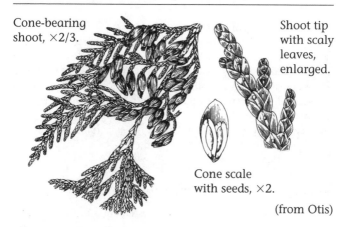

Cone-bearing shoot, ×2/3.

Shoot tip with scaly leaves, enlarged.

Cone scale with seeds, ×2.

(from Otis)

western redcedar (*Thuja plicata*)

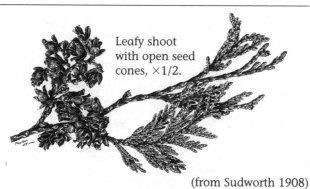

Leafy shoot with open seed cones, ×1/2.

(from Sudworth 1908)

Oriental Arborvitae *(Thuja orientalis*
or *Platycladus orientalis)*
*See **Northern White-Cedar** description and illustrations*

Major differences:

Twigs/Buds: **Twigs arranged in vertically flattened sprays**.

Flowers/Fruit: Fruit a cone; 1/3" to 1" long; upright; **6 to 8 scales**, thicker than above.

General: Native to Korea, Manchuria, and northern China. Medium to slow growth.

Landscape Use: Planted in Utah, but generally not very cold hardy and will winter burn. Not as desirable as *Thuja occidentalis*. Zones 6-9.

Juniper   Genus *Juniperus*

A common genus of evergreen coniferous trees and shrubs with **scaly or awl-shaped foliage** that clasps and covers the young twigs. There are about 50 to 70 juniper species with 13 native to the U.S. and two tree-sized species native to Utah. The **fruit is a fleshy, berry-like cone**; dioecious (rarely monoecious). Junipers are generally intolerant to moderately tolerant of shade and do well on dry sites that are warm or cool. All junipers are fairly trouble-free if not overwatered and given full sun. Junipers often are called cedars, but true cedars are in the Pinaceae family and the *Cedrus* genus.

❖Rocky Mountain Juniper   *(Juniperus scopulorum)*

Leaves: Awl-shaped or scale-like; pressed close to the twig; not arranged in overlapping pairs; variable in color; **retains blue-green color in winter**; evergreen.

Twigs/Buds: Twigs slender, older twigs red-brown and nearly glabrous; bark peeling off; finest twigs covered by foliage. Buds very small; indistinct; not useful for identification purposes.

Flowers/Fruit: Dioecious. Berry-like fruit **takes two years to mature**; nearly round; 1/4" to 1/3" in diameter; bright blue; often covered with a white coating; usually contains 2 seeds.

Bark: Brown to gray; fibrous; peels in narrow strips.

Wood: Soft; lightweight; light red heartwood with narrow white sapwood; see eastern redcedar for uses.

General: Occurs naturally from the western Great Plains throughout the Rocky Mountains and southwestern Canada, including Utah. Very drought resistant. Shade intolerant.

Oriental arborvitae (*Thuja orientalis*)

Seed cone, ×1.

Leafy shoot, ×1.

(from Apgar)

Rocky Mountain juniper (*Juniperus scopulorum*)

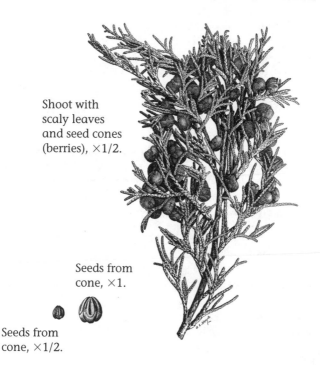

Shoot with scaly leaves and seed cones (berries), ×1/2.

Seeds from cone, ×1.

Seeds from cone, ×1/2.

(from Sudworth 1915)

Landscape Use: Often used in windbreaks due to its toughness and retention of lower branches; also good for visual screens and foundation plantings. Many cultivars in the landscape trade with a wide variety of foliage colors; needs (and wants) very little water once established. Zones 3-7.

Eastern Redcedar *(Juniperus virginiana)*
*See **Rocky Mountain Juniper** illustrations*

Major differences:

Leaves: Awl-shaped or scale-like, both kinds often on the same tree; similar to Rocky Mountain juniper but blue-green **turning a red-brown to purple color in winter**; arranged in overlapping pairs.

Flowers/Fruit: Dioecious. Fruit berry-like; round; about 1/4" in diameter; blue or purple; often with white, waxy coating; contains 2 or 3 hard seeds; **ripens in one season**.

Wood: Similar to Rocky Mountain juniper; moderate importance; sapwood nearly white; heartwood purple or rose-red to red-brown; characteristic odor; growth rings distinct; used for fence posts, closet and chest lining, novelties, ornamental purposes; oils and other materials are extracted from juniper wood and foliage for use in perfumes, medicines, and for other purposes. Juniper heartwood is very decay resistant, making all of these species good for fence posts.

General: Native from the eastern Great Plains east through the rest of the eastern U.S; not native to Utah. Often called cedar, but not a true cedar. Hardy and long-lived. Medium to slow growth. Intermediate shade tolerance.

Landscape Use: Very good windbreak or hedge tree, but winter color of species generally is not as nice as Rocky Mountain juniper. Some good cultivars available though. Zones 2-9.

❖Utah Juniper *(Juniperus osteosperma)*

Leaves: Small scale-shaped leaves that clasp and cover young twigs similar to other junipers; yellow-green; evergreen.

Twigs/Buds: Young, foliage covered twigs **coarser and stiffer than with Rocky Mountain juniper**; twigs are densely clumped at branch ends.

Flowers/Fruit: Usually monoecious. Berry-like fruit takes two years to mature; nearly round; 1/4" to 3/4" in diameter; **red-brown**; often covered with a white, waxy coating; usually contains 1 seed.

Bark: Gray; fibrous and scaly.

eastern redcedar (*Juniperus virginiana*)

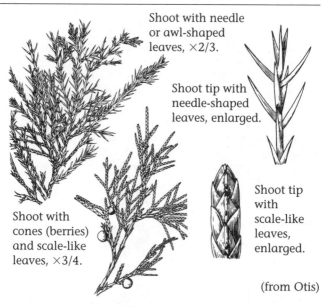

Shoot with needle or awl-shaped leaves, ×2/3.

Shoot tip with needle-shaped leaves, enlarged.

Shoot tip with scale-like leaves, enlarged.

Shoot with cones (berries) and scale-like leaves, ×3/4.

(from Otis)

Utah juniper (*Juniperus osteosperma*)

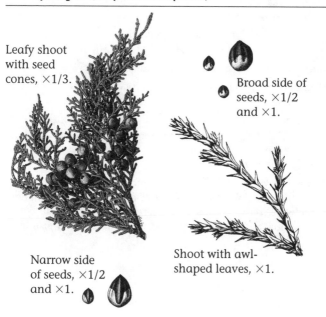

Leafy shoot with seed cones, ×1/3.

Broad side of seeds, ×1/2 and ×1.

Narrow side of seeds, ×1/2 and ×1.

Shoot with awl-shaped leaves, ×1.

(from Sudworth 1915)

Wood: Little used except for fence posts and firewood; properties and potential uses likely similar to Rocky Mountain juniper. Heartwood yellow-brown, very durable; sapwood white.

General: Native to the west-central Rockies and Great Basin at middle elevations, including most of Utah. Very drought, cold, and heat resistant and tolerant of a wide variety of soil conditions; does well on dry, rocky sites. Often shrubby but sometimes more upright; generally smaller (15' tall) than the biggest Rocky Mountain junipers. Shade intolerant.

Landscape Use: Little used in landscapes except where people build homes among existing trees. Could be used more in xeriscapes, but not easy to obtain from nurseries. Interesting texture. Zones 3-7.

Other Junipers

Chinese Juniper   *(Juniperus chinensis)*
See other juniper illustrations

Leaves: Small scale- and awl-shaped leaves on same plant very similar to Rocky Mountain juniper; colors vary widely depending on cultivar, from yellow to green to blue; evergreen.

Twigs/Buds: Young, foliage covered twigs are thin and flexible; buds are inconspicuous.

Flowers/Fruit: Dioecious. Berry-like fruit nearly round; 1/3" in diameter; bluish and white-waxy at first but **brown when mature**.

Bark: Gray-brown; fibrous and furrowed in thin strips.

Wood: Unimportant and little-used, but presumably similar to other junipers.

General: Native to China and Japan, but widely planted all over the world. Drought, cold, and heat resistant and tolerant of high pH soils; as with all junipers easy to over-water. Shrubby or upright. Shade intolerant.

Landscape Use: One of the most commonly planted ornamental junipers, with dozens of cultivars available from the common, shrubby Pfitzer ('Pfitzeriana'), to larger tree forms in all colors from yellow to blue. Good for hedges and foundation plantings. Zones 3-7.

ANGIOSPERMS

Angiosperms are the most common, complex, and widely distributed plants on Earth. Also known as flowering plants, they are found from the tropics to the tundra and from deserts to mountain tops. Some are small, primitive discs that float on water, while others are large trees like the bur oak. Most of our broad-leaved trees are angiosperms. As mentioned earlier, they are separated from the gymnosperms by the ovary covering their seeds. Most angiosperm trees introduced or native to Utah have deciduous leaves, though a number of evergreen angiosperms are grown—and a few are native—where winter temperatures don't get too cold.

SALICACEAE

Willow family. Contains two genera and 335 species. Widely distributed around the world, but more common in cooler areas of the Northern Hemisphere. Usually found in moist areas.

Willow   Genus *Salix*

About 300 species of willows, mostly shrubs with some trees, occur over most of the Northern Hemisphere, as well as in Indonesia, southern South America, and South Africa. Willows are pioneer species, coming in quickly after a flood or other disturbance. They nearly always are found where water is readily available, and occur at the northernmost reaches of tree growth north of the Arctic Circle, where they form mat-like shrubs. About 70 species of willow are native to North America, with about 38 occasionally reaching tree size and only about 12 of those commonly growing as trees. Willows can be very difficult to identify beyond the genus level. Small male and female flowers are borne on separate catkins, with seed and pollen catkins found on separate trees (dioecious).

❖Peachleaf Willow (*Salix amygdaloides*)

Leaves: Simple, **pale or bluish beneath**; finely serrate margin; lanceolate to ovate-lanceolate; 2" to 5" long, 3/4" to 1" wide; deciduous; more abruptly pointed than black willow; petiole short.

Twigs/Buds: Twigs slender to stout; often brittle; yellow or brownish. No terminal bud; lateral buds red-brown, small, covered by a single cap-like scale.

Flowers/Fruit: Fruit a **capsule; about 1/4" long**; short-stalked; many capsules attached to a stalk several inches long; seeds very small, hairy.

Bark: Brown-red; fairly thick; intertwining ridges.

Wood: Unimportant; see black willow for general characteristics.

General: Native throughout much of the northern U.S. and southern Canada, including northern Utah. Generally shrubby or a small tree. Like all willows, likes wet areas very near streams or lakes. Very shade intolerant.

Landscape Use: Rarely if ever planted in landscapes and no cultivars are available. Only recommended for sites well-suited for willows and where native plants are a high priority. Zones 2-8.

Other Willows
(All have alternate, simple, deciduous leaves; only tree-sized willows are discussed below)
*See also **Peachleaf Willow** description and illustrations*

Black Willow (*Salix nigra*)

Leaves: Leaves similar to peachleaf willow, but can be a little longer; bright green above and **pale green beneath**.

Bark: Brown to nearly black; thick on older trees; intertwining ridges.

Wood: Moderately important; sapwood white; heartwood light brown to red-brown; growth rings unclear; diffuse-porous; rays barely visible with a hand lens; used for pulp, charcoal, and lumber.

General: Native to most of the eastern U.S.; not Utah. Usually found on moist soils along the banks of streams and lakes. Usually tree-like; rarely shrubby. Grows rapidly and matures in 50 to 70 years. Can get very large—much larger than most North American willows. Very shade intolerant. Some sources claim that black willow is native here and there throughout the West, but this seems unlikely and may have been due to mis-identification.

Landscape Use: Probably planted a lot in pioneer landscapes in Utah and may have escaped cultivation. Little planted otherwise.

peachleaf willow (*Salix amygdaloides*)

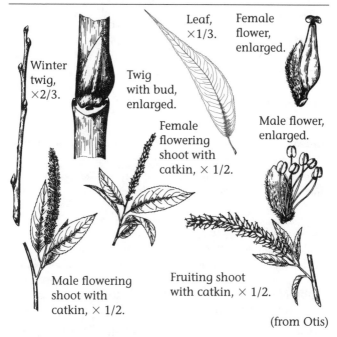

Winter twig, ×2/3.

Twig with bud, enlarged.

Leaf, ×1/3.

Female flower, enlarged.

Female flowering shoot with catkin, × 1/2.

Male flower, enlarged.

Male flowering shoot with catkin, × 1/2.

Fruiting shoot with catkin, × 1/2.

(from Otis)

black willow (*Salix nigra*)

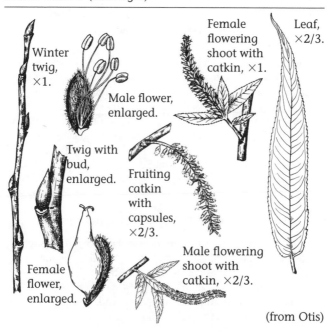

Winter twig, ×1.

Male flower, enlarged.

Twig with bud, enlarged.

Female flower, enlarged.

Female flowering shoot with catkin, ×1.

Leaf, ×2/3.

Fruiting catkin with capsules, ×2/3.

Male flowering shoot with catkin, ×2/3.

(from Otis)

Zones 4-9. **Crack willow** (*Salix fragilis*) is another large willow with a longer petiole (1/4" to 1" long) and brittle twigs that tend to break off at their base. Such twigs may actually float down streams and take root in stream banks. Several campgrounds in Logan Canyon and possibly elsewhere were planted with this willow decades ago. Zones 4-9.

Weeping Willow   *(Salix babylonica)*

Leaves: **Pale beneath**; narrow-lanceolate.

General: Native to China. Popular shade tree with a **weeping or drooping form**. Grows fast, short-lived.

Landscape Use: Many people like this tree. Like most willows, however, it has a lot going against it. It needs quite a bit of water, has weak wood from the trunk to the twigs, and grows too fast for most locations. Graceful, weeping habit is a plus, but this often can be achieved with better species. The form usually found is a female. **Golden weeping willow** (*Salix alba* 'Tristis') is another willow with a weeping form that also is called weeping willow. Zones 5-8.

Globe Navajo Willow ◆ Globe Willow
(Salix matsudana var. 'Navajo')

Leaves: Bright green above, **paler beneath**; narrow-lanceolate; 2" to 4" long, 1/4" to 1/2" wide.

General: Native to China. Very popular large tree because of its **broad, evenly rounded crown**. Like many other willows, grows fast but is short-lived.

Landscape Use: Tougher and hardier than many willows, and thus overused in Utah and the West. Rounded form and bright green leaves are nice from far away, but weak wood and susceptibility to slime flux and other disease and insect problems mean it should be planted less. Zones 4-9. Many other cultivars and hybrids of **Hankow willow** (*Salix matsudana*) also exist and some are planted in Utah. An example is 'Golden Curls', a hybrid between *Salix alba* var. 'Tristis' and *Salix matsudana* var. 'Tortuosa' that has strongly curled and slightly weeping stems.

Cottonwood, Poplar, Aspen   Genus *Populus*

A genus of about 35 species and many hybrids found throughout the Northern Hemisphere, including some north of the Arctic Circle. About 10 species are native to North America, but several non-natives are planted and may have escaped cultivation. These are shade intolerant pioneer species that tend to seed-in or root sprout after a disturbance. They tend to grow on moist sites near

crack willow (*Salix fragilis*)

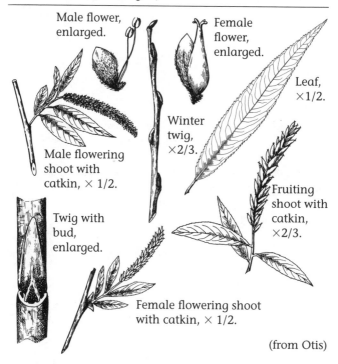

Male flower, enlarged.

Female flower, enlarged.

Leaf, ×1/2.

Winter twig, ×2/3.

Male flowering shoot with catkin, × 1/2.

Fruiting shoot with catkin, ×2/3.

Twig with bud, enlarged.

Female flowering shoot with catkin, × 1/2.

(from Otis)

weeping willow (*Salix babylonica*)

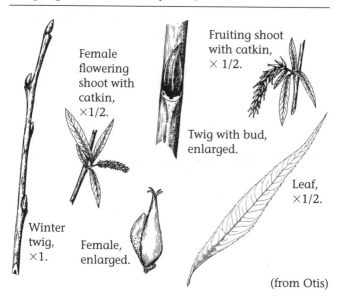

Female flowering shoot with catkin, ×1/2.

Fruiting shoot with catkin, × 1/2.

Twig with bud, enlarged.

Leaf, ×1/2.

Winter twig, ×1.

Female, enlarged.

(from Otis)

79

streams, especially in the West, though aspens often are found on more upland sites at higher elevations. Dioecious, with small male or female flowers found on separate catkins.

❖Quaking Aspen ◆ Trembling Aspen
(Populus tremuloides)

Leaves: Simple; alternate; **round to broadly ovate**; 1-1/2" to 3" diameter; deciduous; finely serrate margin; acute apex; glabrous; yellow-green to green, turning bright yellow to orange in fall; petiole 1-1/2" to 3" long, **flattened laterally**, causing leaf to flutter in the wind.

Twigs/Buds: Twigs slender; glabrous; red-brown. Terminal bud 1/4" to 1/2" long, sharp-pointed, sometimes resinous, covered by red-brown overlapping scales; lateral buds smaller, curve inward.

Flowers/Fruit: Fruit a capsule; narrow conical; 1/4" long; gray and hairy; seeds small, tufted, light brown.

Bark: Smooth; green-white to cream colored; becomes furrowed on older trunks.

Wood: Important; heartwood gray-white to light gray-brown; sapwood lighter and merges gradually into heartwood; straight grained; fine textured; growth rings unclear; diffuse-porous; used for lumber, pallets, crates, pulp, and matches.

General: Native in most of the northern and western U.S. and Canada, including higher elevations in Utah. Generally forms single aged stands through root sprouts after a fire or other disturbance; grows in clumps or "clones" that are genetically identical since stems are all attached to the same root system. Does not reproduce from seed in most of the West. Relatively short-lived. Grows in cool, moist areas. Very shade intolerant.

Landscape Use: Over-planted in Utah; also found where homes are built into native aspen areas. Native trees do well, but aspen does not like the heat and dry conditions in our lower valleys. Stressed aspens suffer from leaf scorch, leaf spot, borers, cankers, galls, occasionally iron chlorosis, and many other problems. Best grown in cooler high-mountain climates that it is used to. If grown at low elevations, avoid problems with older, larger trees by managing selected aspen sprouts in a large, mulched bed; remove stems before they get very large. Zones 3-7.

❖Narrowleaf Cottonwood *(Populus angustifolia)*

Leaves: **Lanceolate to ovate-lanceolate**; 2" to 4" long, 1/2" to 1-1/2" wide; narrowest leaf of the cottonwoods found in Utah; long, tapered apex; deciduous; finely to coarsely serrate; petiole short (less than 1/3 length of blade) and **not flattened laterally**.

quaking aspen (*Populus tremuloides*)

Fruiting catkin with capsules, × 1/2.

Leaves, ×1/2.

Male flowering catkin, × 1/2.

Male flower, enlarged.

Female flowering catkin, × 1/2.

Female flower, enlarged.

Winter twig, ×2.

(from Otis)

narrowleaf cottonwood (*Populus angustifolia*)

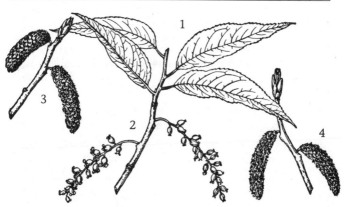

1. Twig with leaves, × 1/2.
2. Fruiting catkins with capsules, × 1/2.
3. Male flowering catkin, × 1/2.
4. Female flowering catkin, × 1/2.

(from Sargent)

81

Twigs/Buds: Twigs slender; round; glabrous; yellow-green when young and light gray when older. Terminal bud 1/4" to 3/4" long, sharp-pointed, resinous and aromatic, covered by brown overlapping scales.

Flowers/Fruit: Fruit an oval capsule, 1/4" long, several together on a slender stalk like a string of beads; seeds tufted, small, light brown.

Bark: Smooth and light yellow-green when young, becoming shallowly furrowed on older trunks.

Wood: Unimportant and seldom used. See eastern cottonwood for description.

General: Native from western Great Plains through the Intermountain West and from Mexico to Canada, including most of Utah. Grows along streams at moderate to low elevations; prefers moist soils and is shade intolerant. Utah's most common native cottonwood. Crowns tend to be somewhat narrow. Easily identified by its narrow leaves, but can hybridize with some cottonwoods. One common hybrid is **lanceleaf cottonwood** (*Populus* × *acuminata*), a wider-leaved cross between *P. angustifolia* and either *P. deltoides, P. fremontii,* or *P. balsamifera.*

Landscape Use: Rarely used and no cultivars are available. Would be alright where a cottonwood is appropriate (needs plenty of water). Cottonwoods and willows can easily be propagated by taking 10" or longer cuttings off of young branches in the winter and planting them in the spring with about an inch showing above ground. The resulting tree is genetically identical to the original. Zones 3-9.

❖Fremont Cottonwood   *(Populus fremontii)*

Leaves: **Deltoid to kidney-shaped**; 3" to 6" long, 4" to 5" wide; deciduous; rounded teeth on margin; pointed, short apex; glabrous; turn bright gold in fall; petiole 1-1/2" to 3" long, **flattened laterally**, causing leaf to flutter in the wind.

Twigs/Buds: Twigs yellow-brown and angular. Terminal buds 3/4" long, pointed, shiny-brown, resinous, fragrant when crushed.

Bark: Light green, smooth on young trunks; on older trunks thick, gray, deeply furrowed with flat-topped ridges.

Wood: Fairly unimportant. See eastern cottonwood for description.

General: Native from about the Wasatch Front south including lower-elevation river drainages (Green and Colorado) in southern Utah and throughout the Southwest. Usually found naturally along streams.

lanceleaf cottonwood (*Populus* × *acuminata*)

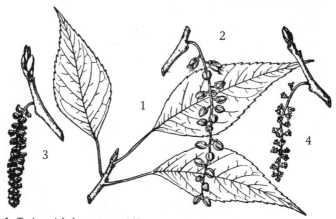

1. Twig with leaves, × 1/2.
2. Fruiting catkins with capsules, × 1/2.
3. Male flowering catkin, × 1/2.
4. Female flowering catkin, × 1/2.

(from Sargent)

Fremont cottonwood (*Populus fremontii*)

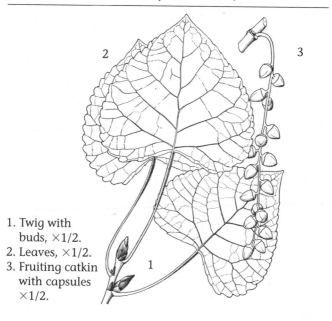

1. Twig with
   buds, ×1/2.
2. Leaves, ×1/2.
3. Fruiting catkin
   with capsules
   ×1/2.

(from Sudworth 1908)

Landscape Use: Rarely used and cultivars are not available, but it is a good, large cottonwood that would be worth having in the right setting. Zones 5-9.

Other Poplars, Cottonwoods

(All have alternate, deciduous leaves, are shade intolerant, and have capsule fruit filled with tufted seeds)

❖Black Cottonwood   *(Populus trichocarpa)*

Leaves: Ovate to ovate-lanceolate; rounded base and angled tip; 3" to 6" long, 3" to 4" wide; acute to acuminate apex; rounded base; finely serrate margin; **dark green above, paler beneath; petiole round**, slender, long.

General: Some sources show this as native to extreme northern Utah; at any rate uncommon.

Landscape Use: Not planted and no cultivars available. Zones 3-8.

black cottonwood (*Populus trichocarpa*)

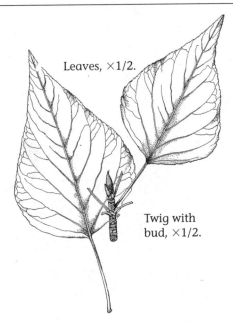

Leaves, ×1/2.

Twig with bud, ×1/2.

(from Sudworth 1908)

84

❖Balsam Poplar   *(Populus balsamifera)*

Leaves: Ovate to lanceolate; 3" to 6" long, 2" to 4" wide; pointed tip; rounded base; finely serrate margin; **dark green above, paler beneath; petiole round**, slender, long.

General: Some sources show this as native to extreme northeast Utah (confused with black cottonwood?); at any rate uncommon.

Landscape Use: Not planted and no cultivars available. Zones 2-5. **Balm-of-Gilead** *(Populus candicans)* is a somewhat similar poplar of confusing origin that has been planted quite a bit in Utah, especially in the south. It often is referred to as *Populus × gileadensis*, a hybrid of *P. deltoides* and *P. balsamifera*, though Rehder calls it a separate species. It grows fast, has many problems, and generally should be avoided. Zones 4-9.

balsam poplar *(Populus balsamifera)*

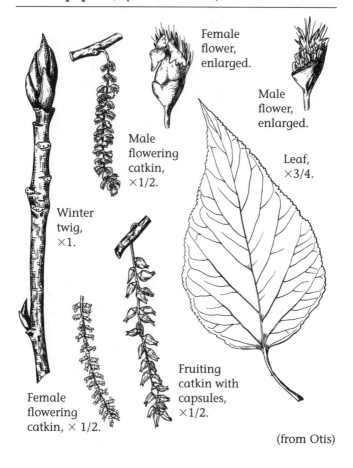

Female flower, enlarged.

Male flower, enlarged.

Male flowering catkin, ×1/2.

Leaf, ×3/4.

Winter twig, ×1.

Female flowering catkin, × 1/2.

Fruiting catkin with capsules, ×1/2.

(from Otis)

balm-of-Gilead (*Populus candicans*)

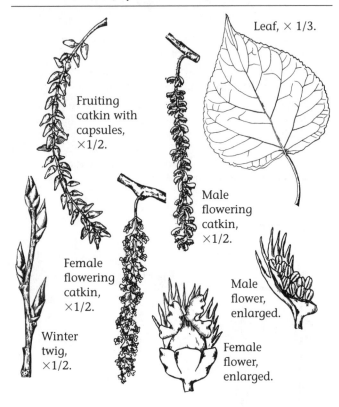

Leaf, × 1/3.

Fruiting catkin with capsules, ×1/2.

Male flowering catkin, ×1/2.

Female flowering catkin, ×1/2.

Male flower, enlarged.

Winter twig, ×1/2.

Female flower, enlarged.

(from Otis)

Eastern Cottonwood   *(Populus deltoides)*

Leaves: **Deltoid to ovate-deltoid**; glands or bumps where petiole and leaf blade meet; otherwise similar to Fremont cottonwood; turn bright gold in fall.

Twigs and Bark: Similar to Fremont cottonwood.

Wood: Important where native; sapwood white; heartwood gray; unclear change from sapwood to heartwood; growth rings unclear; diffuse-porous; rays not visible without magnification; used in lumber, pallets, veneer.

General: Native from the Great Plains east but planted occasionally in the West. Usually found naturally along streams and lakes.

Landscape Use: The species was originally planted quite a bit by Utah's settlers and some probably escaped cultivation. Those planted now are mostly hybrids with other species chosen for their fast growth rate, disease resistance, and cottonless characteristics (usually male trees). Zones 2-9.

eastern cottonwood (*Populus deltoides*)

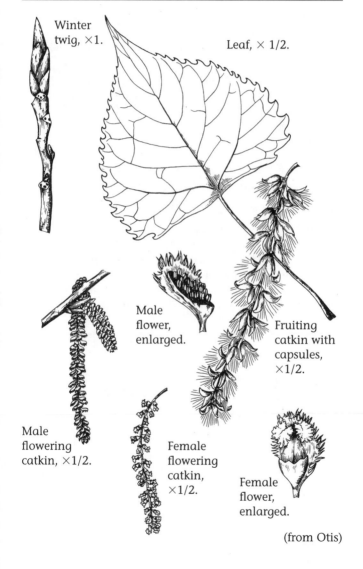

Winter twig, ×1.

Leaf, × 1/2.

Male flower, enlarged.

Fruiting catkin with capsules, ×1/2.

Male flowering catkin, ×1/2.

Female flowering catkin, ×1/2.

Female flower, enlarged.

(from Otis)

White Poplar   *(Populus alba)*

Leaves: Often resembles a maple leaf in shape with very coarse teeth or lobes on margin; base rounded; 1" to 4" long; dark green and glabrous above; **white and woolly beneath**; petioles hairy, 1/2" to 1-1/2" long, **not flattened laterally**.

Twigs/Buds: Twigs slender; green-gray; covered with fine white hairs. Terminal bud more or less woolly.

Bark: **Green-white to bright white**; with dark cracks and ridges when older; very characteristic.

General: Native to Europe. Sometimes wrongly called silver maple. A large, rapidly growing tree; thrives under less favorable conditions. Many root suckers (sprouts) occur around the tree.

Landscape Use: Planted in the past around farms and ranches and still sometimes seen in those locations, even if abandoned. Beautiful large tree, but root suckers are aggressive and wood is weak, similar to aspen. Some cultivars are available, but plant only in large, open areas where a troublesome tree will be less trouble. Golden fall color occasionally is nice. Zones 3-9.

Lombardy Poplar   *(Populus nigra* var. *italica)*
*See also **Eastern Cottonwood** description and illustrations*

Leaves: Similar to eastern cottonwood.

General: Native to western Asia and eastern Europe, but heavily planted in Utah, especially in the past. A sterile clone of *Populus nigra*.

Landscape Use: Once popular in Utah for its **narrow crown and upright form**. However, stressed trees weaken and die quickly (5 to 15 years) from stem cankers. Twigs break off in wind storms. Fall color occasionally nice in Utah. Grows fast, short-lived. Should be planted less, if at all. Zones 3-9.

white poplar (*Populus alba*)

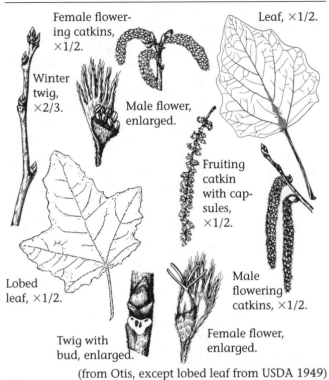

Female flower-ing catkins, ×1/2.

Leaf, ×1/2.

Winter twig, ×2/3.

Male flower, enlarged.

Fruiting catkin with cap-sules, ×1/2.

Lobed leaf, ×1/2.

Male flowering catkins, ×1/2.

Twig with bud, enlarged.

Female flower, enlarged.

(from Otis, except lobed leaf from USDA 1949)

Lombardy poplar (*Populus nigra* var. *italica*)

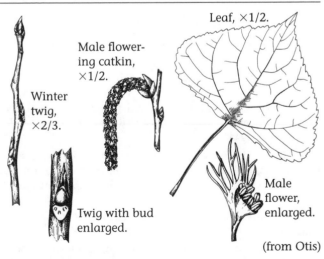

Leaf, ×1/2.

Male flower-ing catkin, ×1/2.

Winter twig, ×2/3.

Twig with bud enlarged.

Male flower, enlarged.

(from Otis)

89

Carolina Poplar and Hybrid Poplars
(Populus canadensis and others)*
***See also Eastern Cottonwood** description and illustrations**

General: Carolina poplar is a group of hybrids of *Populus deltoides* and *P. nigra*, and one particular hybrid seems to have been planted quite a bit in Utah in the past. Many other poplar hybrids also can be found in Utah. Most are noted for their fast growth, pest problems, and short lives. Shade intolerant.

Landscape Use: Carolina poplar has a narrower crown than many cottonwoods, but similar problems including weak wood, disease and insect problems, and growth that is too fast. With all hybrid poplars make sure that you select a seedless and canker-resistant clone and that you have plenty of room. Zones 3-9.

JUGLANDACEAE

Walnut family. Contains 6-7 genera and 60 species. Widely distributed through the temperate forests of the Northern Hemisphere. There are many valuable timber trees in this family. They also can be important food sources (nuts). Two species of *Juglans* and one *Carya* will be covered here, but several other *Carya* species (hickories) are worth trying in Utah.

Walnut   Genus *Juglans*

Containing about 20 species, this genus is scattered around the world with 6 species native to the U.S. None are native to Utah, but a few are planted. Monoecious.

Black Walnut   *(Juglans nigra)*

Leaves: Alternate; once pinnately compound; 1' to 2' long; with 15 to 23 leaflets; terminal leaflet often missing; deciduous; leaflets 3" to 4" long, ovate-lanceolate, serrate margins, glabrous above, hairy beneath; light yellow-green; characteristic odor when crushed; rachis stout, usually hairy; leaflets often deciduous before the rachis/petiole, which can persist well into the winter and is a good identifying characteristic.

Twigs/Buds: Twigs stout; light brown; **with yellow-brown to brown, chambered or divided pith**. Terminal bud short and blunt, hairy; laterals much smaller, often more than one at each leaf scar.

Flowers/Fruit: Flowers small; male flowers on long catkins; female borne in groups of one to four. Fruit a 1-1/2" to 2" diameter nut; round; covered by a thick, glabrous, yellow-green, fleshy

Carolina poplar (*Populus* × *canadensis*)

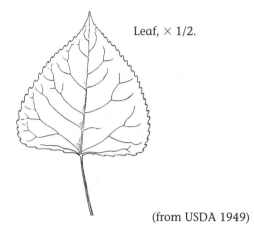

Leaf, × 1/2.

(from USDA 1949)

black walnut (*Juglans nigra*)

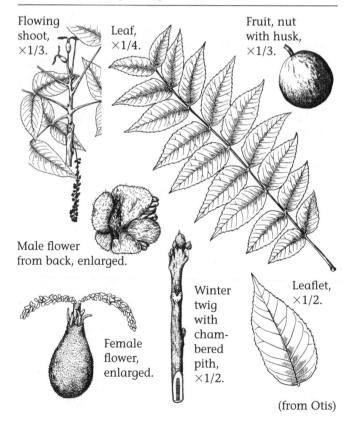

Flowing shoot, ×1/3.

Leaf, ×1/4.

Fruit, nut with husk, ×1/3.

Male flower from back, enlarged.

Female flower, enlarged.

Winter twig with chambered pith, ×1/2.

Leaflet, ×1/2.

(from Otis)

husk which becomes black and wrinkled; **nut inside with rough, dark, very hard shell**; sweet, oily, strong flavored nut meat within.

Bark: Dark brown to gray-black; broken pieces showing chocolate-brown; intertwining ridges forming a diamond pattern.

Wood: Important; sapwood white to light brown; heartwood chestnut-brown; growth rings distinct; semi-ring-porous; rays indistinct; hard; strong; used for lumber, fine furniture, veneer. This is our highest-valued hardwood, but it is not worth near as much in Utah as where it is native because of a lack of markets and the poorer quality of our trees for lumber and veneer.

General: Native to the eastern half of the U.S. but planted in Utah. It prefers rich, deep, well-drained bottom-land soil and under favorable conditions attains a large size. Very shade intolerant and adaptable to high soil pH.

Landscape Use: Planted more in Utah in the past than now, so most trees you see will be large. Nice golden-yellow fall color if leaves are not diseased or drought stressed. Black walnut can be a nice, large shade tree, but be prepared for some mess from the nuts. Few cultivars exist. Quite a few large black walnut trees in northern Utah recently have experienced branch dieback or have even been killed by borers or an unknown disease. Zones 4-9. Four native southwestern walnut species exist and at least one, **Arizona walnut** (*Juglans major*), might do well if planted in the warmest parts of Utah (Zones 7-8). **Butternut** (*Juglans cinerea*) is another similar species that also might do well in parts of Utah (Zones 3-7).

Other *Juglans*

English Walnut ◆ Persian Walnut   *(Juglans regia)*
See **Black Walnut** description and illustrations

Major differences:

Leaves: With **5 to 9 leaflets with entire margins** (rarely 13); leaflets elliptic to obovate.

Flowers/Fruit: Fruit a nut with **thinner, smoother shell** than black walnut; this is the most common commercially available walnut in the U.S.

General: Native to southeastern Europe to Himalayas and China, and widely planted throughout the world. Shade intolerant; prefers rich, deep soils.

Landscape Use: Can be planted in Utah in warmer, protected areas; generally not quite as cold hardy as black walnut. Two of the more cold-hardy cultivars are 'Carpathian' and 'Hansen'. Zones 4-8.

Arizona walnut (*Juglans major*)

Nut without husk, ×1/2.

Leaf, ×1/3.

Nut with husk, × 1/2.

(from Sargent)

butternut (*Juglans cinerea*)

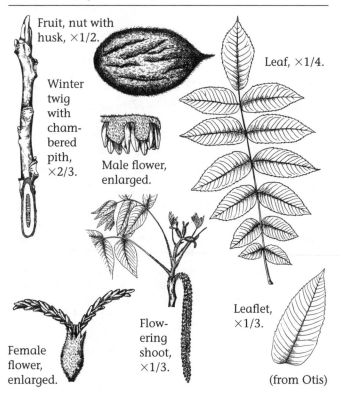

Fruit, nut with husk, ×1/2.

Leaf, ×1/4.

Winter twig with chambered pith, ×2/3.

Male flower, enlarged.

Female flower, enlarged.

Flowering shoot, ×1/3.

Leaflet, ×1/3.

(from Otis)

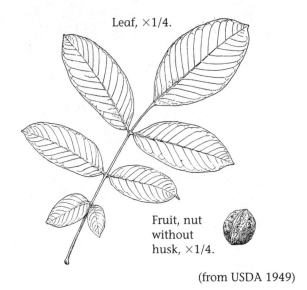

Leaf, ×1/4.

Fruit, nut without husk, ×1/4.

(from USDA 1949)

Hickory   Genus *Carya*

This genus contains about 17 species of trees native mostly to the eastern and southern U.S., though 2 are native to China and several to Mexico. Most are known for their **edible nuts**. Monoecious.

Pecan   *(Carya illinoensis)*

Leaves: Alternate; once pinnately compound; 12" to 20" long; 9-17 leaflets, 4" to 7" long, lanceolate to oblong-lanceolate, serrate margins, **terminal leaflet present**; rachis slender, glabrous.

Twigs/Buds: Twigs moderately stout; reddish-brown; pith solid. Terminal bud present, 1/4" to 1/2" long, yellow-brown.

Flowers/Fruit: Flowers inconspicuous; appear after the leaves expand. Fruit a nut; 1" to 2-1/2" long; **twice as long as wide**; with a thin, green turning dark brown, 4 part husk; husk splits readily to release oblong nut; nut smooth or slightly 4-ridged, with thin to medium-thick shell and sweet seed.

Bark: Light brown to brownish-gray; smooth when young breaking into scaly ridges.

Wood: Similar to bitternut hickory.

pecan (*Carya illinoensis*)

1. Flowering shoot with young leaves, ×1/4.
2. Leaf, ×1/3.
3. Twig with buds, × 1/2.
4. Nuts with husk, × 1/2.
5. Fruits, nut without husk, × 1/2.

(from Sargent)

General: Native throughout the Mississippi River valley from eastern Iowa to Louisiana, west to eastern Kansas and central Texas. Occurs naturally as scattered trees on moist but well drained soils. Intermediate shade tolerance.

Landscape Use: Planted throughout the southern U.S. for its fruit, this tree also has been grown successfully in plantations in Washington County. Warm sites are best, but this will likely vary widely with a tree's geographic origins. Zones 5-9.

BETULACEAE

Birch family. Contains 6 genera and 100 species. Generally found only in cooler regions in the Northern Hemisphere. All have deciduous leaves.

Birch   Genus *Betula*

About 40 species of birch exist and are found mostly in the Northern Hemisphere, with 15 species native mostly to the cooler regions of North America and one native to Utah. Small flowers are arranged on long male or female catkins; **male catkins form**

95

in late summer and over-winter on the tree, then lengthen, mature, and release pollen in spring. Monoecious.

❖Water Birch ◆ River Birch *(Betula occidentalis)*

Leaves: Alternate; simple; 1" to 2" long; 3/4" to 1-1/2" wide; deciduous; ovate or somewhat rounded; singly or doubly serrate margin; acute or acuminate apex; somewhat rounded base; glabrous; thin; dark green above; light yellow-green beneath; dull yellow in fall; petiole stout, 1/3" to 1/2" long.

Twigs/Buds: Twigs light green when young, becoming dark red-brown; glandular when young, covered with horizontal lenticels when older. No terminal bud; lateral buds 1/4" long, pointed, resinous, brown.

Flowers/Fruit: Fruit small winged nutlet arranged in a cone-like catkin; cylindrical; **hangs down**; 1" to 1-1/4" long; scaly; matures in fall.

Bark: Thin; smooth but broken by distinct, long, **horizontal lenticels; dark, shiny reddish-brown to almost purple**; very characteristic.

Wood: Unimportant; seldom used. Light colored sapwood; heartwood light brown; diffuse-porous; strong; used for firewood, fenceposts.

General: Native to much of the western U.S. and southern Canada. Utah's only native birch. Occurs naturally in moist areas along streams and lakes. Usually a small tree with many stems coming from the base, occasionally up to 30-40' tall. Intermediate shade tolerance.

Landscape Use: This is a nice, multi-stemmed tree that does well when planted in Utah's valleys if very hot, dry sites are avoided. Probably more borer resistant that other birches, and able to withstand moderately high soil pH. Zones 3-7.

European White Birch *(Betula pendula)*

Leaves: Alternate; simple; 1" to 3" long; 3/4" to 1-1/2" wide; deciduous; ovate to diamond-shaped; doubly serrate margin or finely-lobed on some cultivars; acute apex; rounded base; glabrous; dark green; petiole 1/2" to 3/4" long.

Twigs/Buds: Twigs slender; brown; glabrous to somewhat glandular (bumpy); usually hang down giving the tree its "weeping" appearance. No terminal bud; lateral buds curved, pointed, brownish-black.

Flowers/Fruit: Fruit small winged nutlets arranged in a cone-like catkin; cylindrical; hangs down; 3/4" to 1-1/4" long; scaly.

water birch (*Betula occidentalis*)

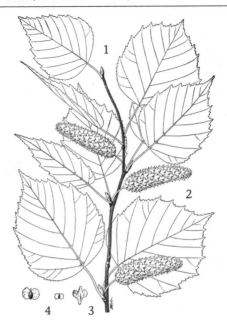

1. Fruiting shoot with leaves, ×1/2.
2. Fruiting catkin, ×1/2.
3. Female (fruit) bract, ×1/2.
4. Seeds, ×1 and ×1/2.

(from Sudworth 1908)

European white birch (*Betula pendula*)

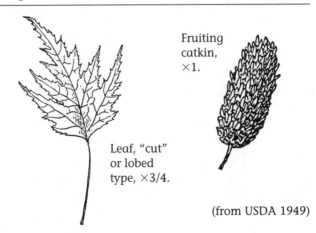

Fruiting catkin, ×1.

Leaf, "cut" or lobed type, ×3/4.

(from USDA 1949)

97

Bark: First brown; **later becoming chalky-white with horizontal lenticels**, occasionally splitting horizontally into thin papery strips, but not like paper birch; bark on older stems develops rough, black, vertical furrows.

Wood: Moderately important where native, but not in U.S. See water birch for general description.

General: Native to Europe and northern Asia. Often planted in Utah. Likes moist, well-drained soils but tolerates dryer soils and high soil pH. Shade intolerant.

Landscape Use: Beautiful tree with graceful, weeping habit and dramatic bark color; many cultivars. Severely affected by borers in much of Utah. However, I have seen many older, healthy, apparently borer-free trees in northern Utah (Box Elder and Cache Counties), so cooler, moister conditions may help ward-off infestations. Zones 2-7. **Paper birch** (*Betula papyrifera*), a native of northern North America, is very similar in appearance but with very papery, peeling bark and without the weeping habit. Though rarely planted in Utah, it would probably do well in cool, moist areas. Zones 2-7.

Other Birches

River Birch   (*Betula nigra*)

Leaves: Alternate; simple; 1-1/2" to 3-1/2" long; 3/4" to 2-1/2" wide; deciduous; rhombic-ovate; doubly serrate margin; wedge-shaped base; tapering sides; petiole short, hairy.

Twigs/Buds: Twigs slender; red-brown; more or less hairy below. No terminal bud; lateral buds pointed.

Flowers/Fruit: Fruit small winged nutlets arranged in a cone-like catkin; cylindrical; erect; hairy; with deciduous scales; matures in late spring.

Bark: Thin; **salmon-pink to red-brown; papery**.

Wood: Unimportant; see water birch for general description.

General: Native to eastern and southeastern U.S., not Utah. As with other birches, normally found along streams on cool, moist sites. Shade intolerant.

Landscape Use: Possible alternative to European white birch, since it seems to have less problems with borers. However, suffers from iron chlorosis on high pH soils. I have seen several of these planted in marginal conditions at the Ogden City Mall that were doing fairly well. Bark color and texture is beautiful. Trees often grown with two or three stems coming from the base. Zones 4-9.

paper birch *(Betula papyrifera)*

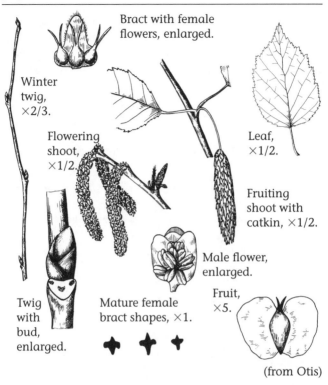

Bract with female flowers, enlarged.

Winter twig, ×2/3.

Flowering shoot, ×1/2.

Leaf, ×1/2.

Fruiting shoot with catkin, ×1/2.

Male flower, enlarged.

Twig with bud, enlarged.

Mature female bract shapes, ×1.

Fruit, ×5.

(from Otis)

river birch *(Betula nigra)*

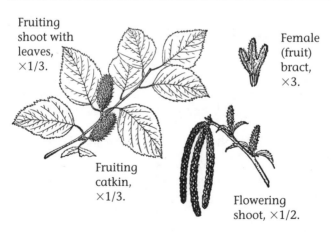

Fruiting shoot with leaves, ×1/3.

Female (fruit) bract, ×3.

Fruiting catkin, ×1/3.

Flowering shoot, ×1/2.

(from Sargent)

Other Betulaceae

Alder (*genus Alnus*: about 10 North American species),
Hophornbeam (genus *Ostrya*: 3 North American species),
Hornbeam (genus *Carpinus*: one North American species),
Filbert/Hazel (genus *Corylus*: 2 North American species).

All have simple, alternate, deciduous leaves with serrate margins;
tend to be small trees; have male catkins that are present in winter and release pollen in spring; and all are monoecious.

❖Thinleaf Alder ◆ Mountain Alder *(Alnus tenuifolia)*

Leaves: Alternate; simple; ovate-oblong; 2" to 4" long; deciduous; sometimes slightly lobed; doubly serrate; thin; pointed at the tip; glabrous; dark green above, pale yellow-green beneath; petiole short.

Twigs/Buds: Twigs slender; with orange lenticels or bumps; **buds stalked, bright red**, 1/4" to 1/3" long.

Flowers/Fruit: Fruit a small nutlet borne in small, **1/3" to 1/2" long, oval "cones"** (catkins or strobili).

Bark: Thin; smooth; brownish-red.

Wood: Unimportant. Alder wood in general is light and soft with conspicuous rays, white to pinkish color, and indistinct heartwood; used in furniture, veneer, and carvings; diffuse porous.

General: Shrubby tree native to much of the western U.S. and Canada, including moist canyon sites in Utah. Nitrogen fixer. Likes moist, cool sites along streams. Somewhat shade tolerant when young, but becomes intolerant when older. Welsh *et al.* consider this species to be *Alnus incana* or speckled alder.

Landscape Use: Seldom planted and no cultivars are available, but could be planted on appropriate, moist sites where native plants are desired. Zones 1-7. I have seen some very large, narrow crowned alders growing in Logan that were probably **European** or **common alder** (*Alnus glutinosa*). These were a little unkempt, but otherwise nice and several cultivars are available. Zones 3-7.

❖Knowlton Hophornbeam *(Ostrya knowltonii)*

Leaves: Alternate; simple; oblong-ovate; 1" to 2" long; deciduous; 5-8 pairs of veins; sharply, doubly serrate margin; acuminate apex; thin; tough; dark green above; paler and somewhat hairy beneath; yellow fall color; petiole short, hairy.

Twigs/Buds: Twigs slender; red-brown to dark brown. No terminal bud; lateral buds pointed, scales with green bases and brown tips.

thinleaf alder (*Alnus tenuifolia*)

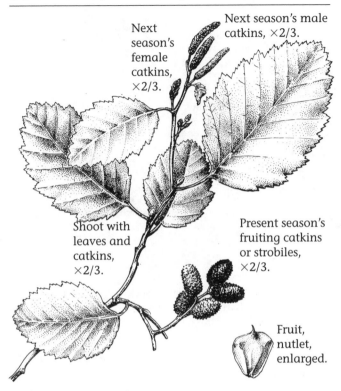

Next season's female catkins, ×2/3.

Next season's male catkins, ×2/3.

Shoot with leaves and catkins, ×2/3.

Present season's fruiting catkins or strobiles, ×2/3.

Fruit, nutlet, enlarged.

(from Hayes & Garrison)

European alder (*Alnus glutinosa*)

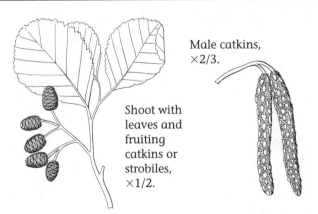

Male catkins, ×2/3.

Shoot with leaves and fruiting catkins or strobiles, ×1/2.

(from Britton & Brown Vol. I)

Knowlton hophornbeam *(Ostrya knowltonii)*

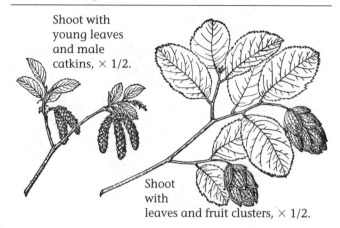

Shoot with young leaves and male catkins, × 1/2.

Shoot with leaves and fruit clusters, × 1/2.

(from Sargent)

Flowers/Fruit: Fruit a small nutlet; enclosed in an oval, flattened, papery sac; **sacs arranged in cone-like clusters, with the appearance of hops**.

Bark: Thin; gray-brown; with small, shreddy plates.

Wood: Extremely hard, so often called "ironwood"; resembles hickory; diffuse-porous; little used.

General: Native to southeastern Utah, northern Arizona, southeastern New Mexico, and west Texas. Slow growing, small tree. Uncommon and found in canyons. Shade tolerant.

Landscape Use: Essentially unknown in cultivated landscapes. No cultivars available and may be impossible to find in any nursery, but could be grown from seed or dug from public land with a permit. Might be a possibility for "native" landscapes. Zones 6(5?)-9. Another choice that is easier to obtain and makes a nice, medium-sized shade tree is **eastern hophornbeam** or **ironwood** (*Ostrya virginiana*), a native to most of the eastern U.S. It differs from Knowlton hophornbeam in having leaves that are 3" to 5" long with 11-15 pairs of veins. Zones 3-9.

European Hornbeam *(Carpinus betulus)*

Leaves: Alternate; simple; ovate to oblong-ovate; 2-1/2" to 5" long; 1" to 2" wide; deciduous; sharply, doubly serrate margin; rounded base; acuminate apex; dark green; hairy on veins beneath with tufts of hair where veins meet; yellow in fall; petiole 1/4" to 1/2" long, hairy.

Eastern hophornbeam (*Ostrya virginiana*)

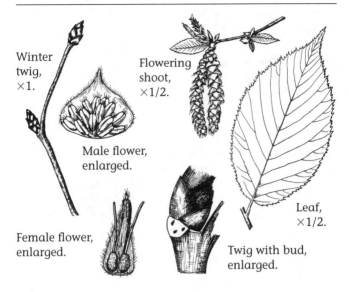

Winter twig, ×1.

Flowering shoot, ×1/2.

Male flower, enlarged.

Female flower, enlarged.

Twig with bud, enlarged.

Leaf, ×1/2.

(from Otis)

European hornbeam (*Carpinus betulus*)

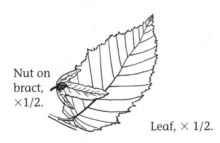

Nut on bract, ×1/2.

Leaf, × 1/2.

(from Apgar)

Twigs/Buds: Twigs glabrous; greenish-brown; with lenticels. No terminal bud; lateral buds 1/4" to 1/3" long, angled at tip, scaly with soft hair on scales, buds pressed against stem.

Flowers/Fruit: Fruit a small nutlet attached to a large, **3-lobed bract, 1" to 1-1/2" long; bracts arranged in loose clusters**.

Bark: Thin; gray; very smooth, with **stem having a sinewy feel**, sometimes called "musclewood".

103

Wood: Very hard and heavy, but not commonly used. Like hophornbeam, also called "ironwood". Sapwood white; heartwood light yellow or tan; diffuse-porous.

General: Native to Europe and Asia minor. Slow growing, small to medium-sized tree. Likes well-drained conditions, but otherwise tolerates a wide range of soils, including high pH. Shade tolerant.

Landscape Use: Very good tree that is not planted much in Utah, but is gaining popularity. Cultivars are available with a wide variety of forms, leaf colors, and leaf shapes. Zones 4-8. Another good, closely related tree is **American hornbeam** or **musclewood** (also called blue beech, *Carpinus caroliniana*), a native to most of the eastern U.S. Its leaves are thinner than European hornbeam's, with buds smaller and not pressed to the stem, and a more effective, orange-yellow fall color. One cultivar is available. Zones 3-9.

American hornbeam (*Carpinus caroliniana*)

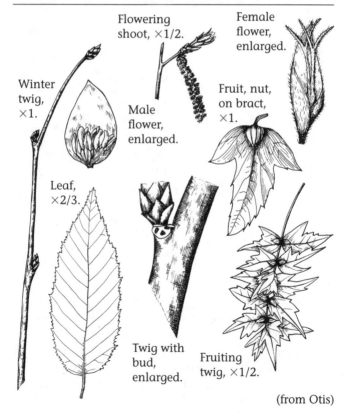

Flowering shoot, ×1/2.

Female flower, enlarged.

Winter twig, ×1.

Male flower, enlarged.

Fruit, nut, on bract, ×1.

Leaf, ×2/3.

Twig with bud, enlarged.

Fruiting twig, ×1/2.

(from Otis)

Turkish Filbert ♦ Turkish Hazel   *(Corylus colurna)*

Leaves: Alternate; simple; wide and ovate to obovate; 2-1/2" to 6" long; deciduous; sharply, doubly serrate margin; rounded to **heart-shaped base**; acuminate apex; dark green and glabrous above; hairy on veins beneath; yellow to purple in fall but not effective; petiole 1/2" to 1" long.

Twigs/Buds: Twigs pubescent and bumpy; grayish-brown; with small cracks developing with age down the length of the stem. No terminal bud; lateral buds 1/3" long, rounded, downy scales, green-brown.

Flowers/Fruit: Fruit an edible nut, 1/2" to 5/8" diameter, attached to a large, leafy bract

Bark: Light brown; flaky; **orange-brown inner bark exposed as scales fall off.**

Wood: Unimportant; little used. Diffuse-porous.

General: Native to southeast Europe and western Asia. Medium growth rate, medium-sized tree. Tolerates a wide variety of conditions including high soil pH, and moderate drought, and fairly cold temperatures. Shade intolerant.

Turkish filbert *(Corylus colurna)*

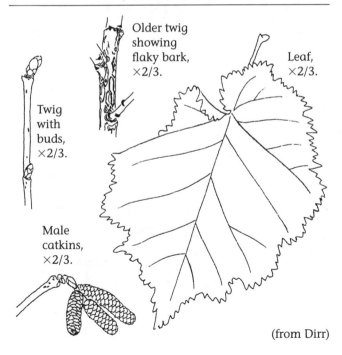

Older twig showing flaky bark, ×2/3.

Leaf, ×2/3.

Twig with buds, ×2/3.

Male catkins, ×2/3.

(from Dirr)

105

Landscape Use: Another very good tree that is not planted enough and will be difficult to find. Zones 4-8. Other, shrubby hazels with edible nuts worth trying in Utah are **American hazelnut** (*Corylus americana*) and **beaked hazelnut** (*Corylus cornuta* and *C. cornuta* var. *californica*).

American hazelnut (*Corylus americana*)

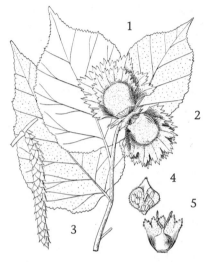

1. Leaves, ×1/2.
2. Nuts with leafy enclosures, ×1/2.
3. Male catkin, ×1/2.
4. Male flower, enlarged.
5. Female flower, enlarged.

(from Britton & Brown Vol. I)

beaked hazelnut (*Corylus cornuta*)

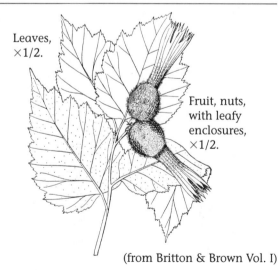

Leaves, ×1/2.

Fruit, nuts, with leafy enclosures, ×1/2.

(from Britton & Brown Vol. I)

106

FAGACEAE

Beech and oak family. Contains 6 genera and about 600 species. Widely distributed in both hemispheres, but most common in northern temperate forests. Many very important lumber producing trees. All have alternate, simple leaves, most with short petioles.

Beech   Genus *Fagus*

This genus contains about 10 species, all found in the Northern Hemisphere, with one found in North America. Monoecious.

European Beech   *(Fagus sylvatica)*

Leaves: Alternate; simple; ovate; 2" to 4" long, 1-1/2" to 2-1/2" wide; deciduous; entire or with few, small teeth; acuminate apex; shiny dark-green above, lighter green beneath; **5 to 9 pairs of veins**; glabrous when mature; petiole 1/4" to 1/2" long; fall color very attractive golden-yellow to reddish-orange.

Twigs/Buds: Twigs thin; zig-zag from bud to bud; glabrous; light gray and somewhat shiny when mature. Terminal and lateral buds 3/4" to 1" long; brown; sharply pointed; with many overlapping scales.

Flowers/Fruit: Flowers inconspicuous, in small groups appearing as leaves open. **Fruit a triangular, 5/8" long, edible nut, 2 to 3 enclosed in a woody, 4-part bur**; matures in one year.

Bark: Thin; smooth; beautiful dark gray color; roughens some with old age.

Wood: Very important timber tree in Europe; light colored; growth rings distinct; wider rays easily visible; diffuse-porous; strong; heavy; used for flooring, tool handles, furniture.

European beech (*Fagus sylvatica*)

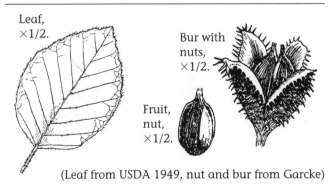

Leaf, ×1/2.

Bur with nuts, ×1/2.

Fruit, nut, ×1/2.

(Leaf from USDA 1949, nut and bur from Garcke)

American beech (*Fagus grandifolia*)

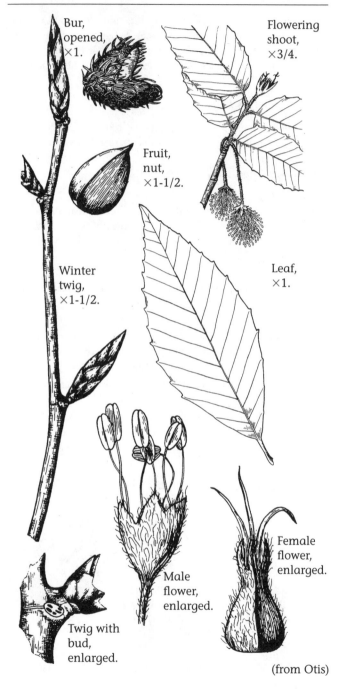

Bur, opened, ×1.

Flowering shoot, ×3/4.

Fruit, nut, ×1-1/2.

Winter twig, ×1-1/2.

Leaf, ×1.

Male flower, enlarged.

Female flower, enlarged.

Twig with bud, enlarged.

(from Otis)

General: Native to Europe, but widely planted in cooler climates around the world. Likes cool, moist, but not wet sites. Prefers acid soils but tolerates moderately high soil pH. Very shade tolerant.

Landscape Use: Beeches are beautiful large trees that should be planted more often. They stand shady spots or full sun equally well, as long as they get enough water. Many cultivars are available that vary greatly in crown form, leaf color and shape, and branch character. Cultivars with purple and variegated leaves suffer severe leaf scorch in hot locations with full sun. Zones 4-7. **American beech** (*Fagus grandifolia*) is a similar species native to the eastern U.S. that could be planted in Utah, but it is not readily available from nurseries. It has bigger leaves than European beech (11 to 15 pairs of veins) and lighter colored bark. Zones 3-9.

Chestnut   Genus *Castanea*

This genus contains about 10 species of trees native to eastern and southwestern Asia, southern Europe, northern Africa, and the eastern U.S. Several have edible nuts, with the Chinese chestnut (*Castanea mollissima*) and Japanese chestnut (*Castanea crenata*) being most popular. American chestnut (*Castanea dentata*) is native to parts of the eastern U.S. and was famous for its wood and nuts until it was nearly wiped out by the imported chestnut blight disease starting in 1906. The chinkapins are also members of this genus, but are not found in Utah. Horsechestnuts (genus *Aesculus*) are not true chestnuts, nor are they closely related. Monoecious.

Chinese Chestnut   *(Castanea mollissima)*

Leaves: Alternate; simple; elliptic-oblong to oblong-lanceolate; 4" to 8" long, 2" to 3" wide; deciduous; coarsely and sharply serrate margin with bristle or hair tipped teeth; acuminate apex; thin; yellow-green; with **whitish to greenish soft hair beneath**; petiole 1/4" to 1/2" long, hairy.

Twigs/Buds: Twigs stout; green-brown; hairy. No terminal bud; lateral buds 1/8" to 1/4" long, brown, with 2 or 3 scales, pubescent.

Flowers/Fruit: Flowers small; male on semi-upright catkins; female individual or in small groups, appearing when leaves are near fully grown. **Fruit a 2" to 2-1/2" diameter bur, splits at maturity into 2 to 4 sections, covered with sharp, branched spines**; bur encloses **2 to 3 edible nuts**, 1/2" to 1" wide.

Bark: Thick; dark brown to gray-brown; furrowed into broad, flat ridges.

American Chestnut (*Castanea dentata*)
for
Chinese chestnut (*Castanea mollissima*)

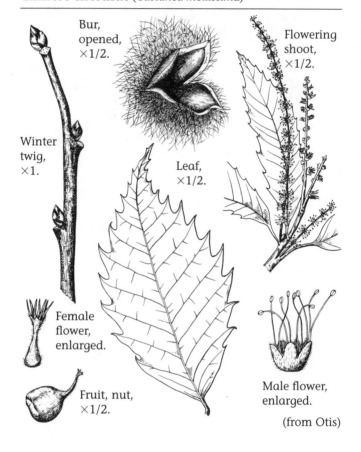

Bur, opened, ×1/2.

Flowering shoot, ×1/2.

Winter twig, ×1.

Leaf, ×1/2.

Female flower, enlarged.

Fruit, nut, ×1/2.

Male flower, enlarged.

(from Otis)

Wood: Not important in U.S. **American chestnut** (*Castanea dentata*) wood was very important before the species was nearly wiped out by chestnut blight; sapwood narrow and almost white; heartwood gray-brown to brown and darker with age; growth rings very distinct; ring-porous; soft; durable; rot resistant; used for furniture, poles, posts, ties.

General: Native to northern China and Korea. Resistant but not immune to chestnut blight. Intermediate shade tolerance, but likes full sun and heat.

Landscape Use: This medium to large tree can be planted in Utah, but there may be some cold-hardiness problems in the coldest valley sites. It can be used as a landscape tree but the burs and nuts produced can be messy. No cultivars are available. Zones 4-9.

Norway maple (*Acer platanoides*) fall color.

Bristlecone pine (*Pinus aristata*) shoot in cultivated landscape.

Canyon maple (*Acer grandidentatum*) fall color.

White fir (*Abies concolor*).

English hawthorn (*Crataegus laevigata*) in flower.

European Larch (*Larix decidua*) fall color.

Lacebark elm (*Ulmus parvifolia*) bark.

Blue elder (*Sambucus cerulea*) fruit.

Japanese zelkova (*Zelkova serrata*) fall color and fruit.

Joshua-tree (*Yucca brevifolia*) in flower.

Eastern redbud (*Cercis canadensis*) in flower.

Bark of native netleaf hackberry (*Celtis reticulata*).

Oak · Genus *Quercus*

This large, well-known, and very important genus includes 200 to 300 species found mostly throughout the Northern Hemisphere. About 60 to 70 oaks are native to the U.S. with about 58 reaching tree size; three oaks are native to Utah. Oaks all have acorns for fruit (monoecious) and ring-porous wood, but are highly variable. The red oak group or subgenus has leaves with entire margins, bristled teeth, or sharp lobes; bitter acorns with woolly inner shells that mature in two years; and large wood vessels that are mostly open and angled (see shrub live, northern red, pin, Shumard, sawtooth, and shingle oaks below). The white oak group has rounded lobes or teeth without bristle-tips; sweeter acorns maturing in one season with a glabrous inner shell surface; and large wood vessels that are round and often blocked with bubble-like structures (see Gambel, white, bur, chinkapin, and swamp white oaks below). Most oak leaves are deciduous, except for the live oaks that have evergreen leaves. Oaks are monoecious, with small male flowers on drooping catkins that release pollen in spring; female flowers small, arranged singly or in small groups in leaf axils. Oaks are some of the best ornamental trees in the world; more should be planted in Utah.

❖Gambel Oak ◆ Scrub Oak ◆ Rocky Mountain White Oak   *(Quercus gambelii)*

Leaves: Alternate; simple; oblong to obovate; 2-1/2" to 7" long; deciduous; margin with 7 to 9 **rounded lobes**; dark green and glabrous above; pale and hairy beneath; orange-yellow to brown in fall; thick; petiole 1/2" long.

Gambel oak *(Quercus gambelii)*

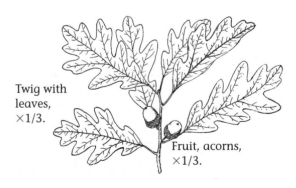

Twig with leaves, ×1/3.

Fruit, acorns, ×1/3.

(from Sargent)

111

Twigs/Buds: Twigs stout; orange- to red-brown; hairy. Terminal buds clustered at end of twig, blunt; lateral buds smaller; buds brown.

Flowers/Fruit: Fruit an acorn; short-stalked or no stalk; 1/2" to 3/4" long; brown; 1/4 to 1/2 enclosed by warty, hairy cap; matures in one season.

Bark: Gray-brown; somewhat platy-scaly but can be ridged.

Wood: Unimportant; similar to bur oak (below); mainly used for firewood. Ring-porous.

General: Native to most of the foothills of Utah and throughout the Intermountain West and the southern and central Rockies. Grows on fairly dry lower mountain slopes; this is the common "scrub" oak along the foothills of the Wasatch. It grows in clumps and is usually fairly shrubby, forming fairly dense, pure stands with a lot of open spaces. Can reach 60 feet tall. Reproduces vigorously from root sprouts after a fire or other disturbance. Very drought tolerant. Shade intolerant.

Landscape Use: This is a desirable landscape tree in many ways, with its attractive, clumpy growth form, its interesting leaves and fruit, and its good to fair fall color. Unfortunately, it also is fire-prone on native sites and should be thinned around buildings to reduce fuel. Occasionally planted and good for tough, dry sites, but availability is somewhat limited. No cultivars are available, though some nurseries have hybrids of Gambel and bur oaks. Zones 4-8.

❖Shrub Live Oak   *(Quercus turbinella)*

Leaves: Alternate; simple; ovate; 1/2" to 1-1/4" long; **evergreen**; wavy margin with **sharp, spiny teeth**, can look like a small holly leaf; blue-green and whitish-waxy.

Twigs/Buds: Twigs slender; brown. Terminal buds small; clustered at end of twig, brown.

Flowers/Fruit: Fruit an acorn; short-stalked or no stalk; 1/2" long; light-brown; shell glabrous inside; 1/2 enclosed by warty cap; matures in one season.

Bark: Gray-brown and scaly or flaky.

Wood: Unimportant and little known or used; ring porous.

General: Native to low canyon sites in southwestern Utah. Likely needs a fairly warm climate and can withstand some drought. Clumpy and shrubby, only getting up to about 8 feet tall. Shade intolerant.

Landscape Use: Rarely (if ever) planted; might occasionally find native plants in developed areas. Likely would need little water or care. Zones 7-9, though one is growing on the east side of a building in Provo. ❖**Wavyleaf oak** (*Quercus undulata*—called *Quercus*

shrub live oak (*Quercus turbinella*)

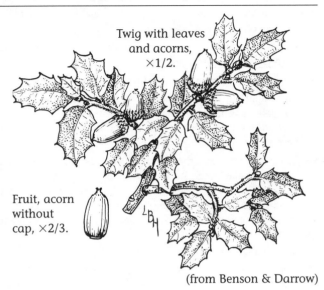

Twig with leaves
and acorns,
×1/2.

Fruit, acorn
without
cap, ×2/3.

(from Benson & Darrow)

wavyleaf oak (*Quercus undulata*)

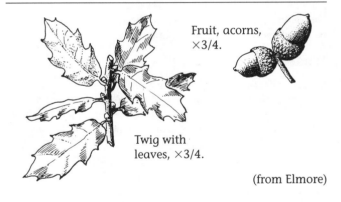

Fruit, acorns,
×3/4.

Twig with
leaves, ×3/4.

(from Elmore)

havardii or shinnery oak by Welsh *et al.*) is another small, shrubby, evergreen oak native to southern Utah that has slightly crinkled or wavy leaves. Zones 7-9.

Bur Oak ◆ Mossycup Oak   (*Quercus macrocarpa*)

Leaves: Alternate; simple; oblong to obovate; 6" to 10" long, 3" to 5" wide; deciduous; margin with 5 to 9 **rounded lobes**; variable shape; dark green and glabrous above; pale and hairy beneath; yellow to brown fall color; petiole 1" long, hairy.

113

Twigs/Buds: Twigs stout; yellow-brown; becoming ashen or brown; hairy; often with corky ridges. Terminal buds clustered at end of twig, blunt; lateral buds smaller.

Flowers/Fruit: Fruit an acorn; short-stalked; about 1" long; **1/2 or more enclosed by fringed cap**; matures in one season.

Bark: Thick; gray-brown; deeply furrowed and ridged.

Wood: Important; sapwood white to light brown; heartwood light to dark brown; growth rings very distinct; ring-porous; rays visible to naked eye; pores normally filled by hardened bubbles; used for lumber, furniture, barrels, etc.

General: Native from the Great Plains east throughout the Midwest and Lake States. An important tree species where native that grows on fairly dry upland sites as well as lower wetter sites. It can also be found in fairly dense forests or as scattered trees on the edges of the prairie. It is long lived and drought tolerant. Intermediate shade tolerance.

Landscape Use: This is one of the best introduced trees for planting in most parts of Utah. Many of these oaks that grow into the edges of the Great Plains do well in Utah because of their adaptations to high soil pH, moderate to severe drought, heat, cold, and winds that are common on the Plains. Bur oak grows at a medium rate and gets fairly large; has an excellent broad crown and beautiful dark-green leaves; is affected by few pests; and is becoming more available in nurseries. Zones 2-8.

White Oak   *(Quercus alba)*

Leaves: Alternate; simple; oblong to obovate; 5" to 9" long, 2" to 4" wide; deciduous; margin with 7 to 9 **rounded lobes**; deep to shallow areas between lobes; bright green and glabrous above; paler beneath; turns brown to deep red in fall; petiole 1" long.

Twigs/Buds: Twigs moderately stout; purple-gray to green-red; without corky ridges. Terminal buds 1/8" to 3/16" long, round to oval, clustered at end of twig; red-brown, glabrous; lateral buds similar but smaller.

Flowers/Fruit: Fruit an acorn; no stalk or short-stalked; 1/2" to 3/4" long; **cap with warty scales covers 1/4 of the acorn**; matures in one season.

Bark: Light ash-gray; variable; young to medium-sized trees with chunky, vertical blocks, older trees with scaly plates attached at one side.

Wood: Very important; sapwood white to light brown; heartwood gray-brown; growth rings very distinct; ring-porous; rays visible to naked eye; pores normally filled by hardened bubbles; used for lumber, furniture, floors, barrels, etc.

bur oak (*Quercus macrocarpa*)

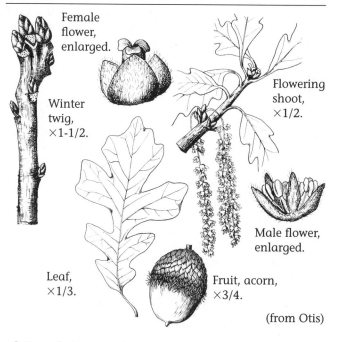

Female flower, enlarged.

Winter twig, ×1-1/2.

Flowering shoot, ×1/2.

Male flower, enlarged.

Leaf, ×1/3.

Fruit, acorn, ×3/4.

(from Otis)

white oak (*Quercus alba*)

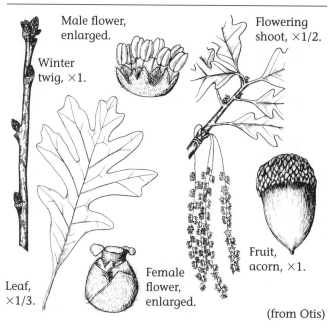

Male flower, enlarged.

Winter twig, ×1.

Flowering shoot, ×1/2.

Leaf, ×1/3.

Female flower, enlarged.

Fruit, acorn, ×1.

(from Otis)

General: Native throughout the eastern half of the U.S. as far west as the eastern edge of the Great Plains. It is long lived and fairly drought tolerant and is found on fairly dry, upland sites. White oak leaves sometimes resemble bur oak leaves, but acorns are very different. Intermediate shade tolerance.

Landscape Use: Good introduced oak for planting in most of Utah, though not yet very common. Tolerates moderately high soil pH, heat, and cold. It grows at a medium rate and can get fairly large. It has a nice, wide crown and casts dense shade and is fairly free of problems. Not common in Utah landscapes but should be planted more often. Zones 3-9.

Northern Red Oak *(Quercus rubra)*

Leaves: Alternate; simple; oblong to obovate; 5" to 8" long, 4" to 5" wide; deciduous; 7 to 11, **coarse-serrate, pointed lobes on margin**; dark green, glabrous, **and lustrous to dull above**; paler beneath but with occasional small tufts of hair where veins meet; deep red to red-orange fall color; petiole 1" to 2" long, yellowish, glabrous.

northern red oak *(Quercus rubra)*

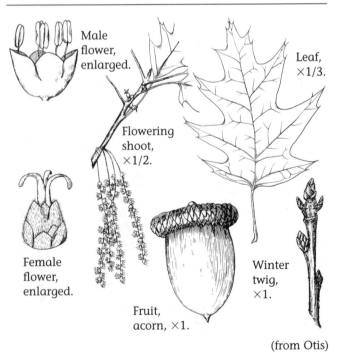

Male flower, enlarged.

Leaf, ×1/3.

Flowering shoot, ×1/2.

Female flower, enlarged.

Fruit, acorn, ×1.

Winter twig, ×1.

(from Otis)

116

Twigs/Buds: Twigs moderately stout; red-brown to green-brown. Terminal buds 1/4" long, clustered, pointed, with many red-brown scales; lateral buds smaller.

Flowers/Fruit: Fruit an acorn; 1" long, red-brown, inner surface of nut shell woolly; cap shallow, saucer-shaped, usually covering only the base of the nut; matures in two seasons.

Bark: Smooth on young stems; eventually brown to nearly black with shallow furrows and wide, flat-topped ridges.

Wood: Very important; sapwood white to pale, red-brown; heartwood pink to light red-brown; growth rings very distinct; ring-porous; rays conspicuous to naked eye; valuable wood used for flooring, cabinets, and furniture.

General: Native throughout most of the eastern U.S. Usually found naturally on fairly good sites. Intermediate shade tolerance.

Landscape Use: This is a good oak for planting in Utah where soil pH is not too high. It is a good alternative to pin oak because it is more tolerant of high soil pH and less likely to exhibit iron chlorosis. It is fairly tough and free of problems but needs more water than bur oak. Has a large, broad crown and very nice branch structure; grows at a medium rate and gets large. Very good red fall color. Zones 4-8.

English Oak   *(Quercus robur)*
*See also **White Oak** description and illustrations*

Leaves: Like white oak's but **smaller, 2-1/2" to 5" long; leaf base usually ear-lobe-like**; short petiole.

Flowers/Fruit: Fruit an acorn; **1" to 3" long stalk**; nut 1" to 2" long; cap covering 1/3 of acorn.

English oak *(Quercus robur)*

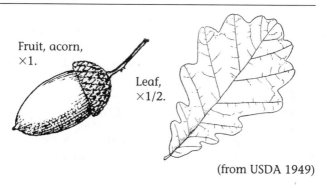

Fruit, acorn, ×1.

Leaf, ×1/2.

(from USDA 1949)

117

General: Native to Europe, northern Africa, and western Asia. Prefers well-drained soil. Shade intolerant.

Landscape Use: Commonly planted in European landscapes and does well in Utah. Leaf is very interesting and narrow or wide crown forms are available. Zones 4-8.

Other Oaks

(All have alternate, simple deciduous leaves and clustered terminal buds)

Chinkapin Oak   *(Quercus muehlenbergii)*

Leaves: 4" to 7" long; **coarsely serrate margin with sharp teeth**; thick; petiole 1" to 1-1/4" long.

Flowers/Fruit: Fruit an acorn; short-stalked; 1/2" to 3/4" long, chestnut-brown to dark brown; **shallow cap with hairy scales encloses 1/2 of the acorn**; matures in one season.

General: Native to most of the eastern half of the U.S. east of the Great Plains. Typically found on dry, wooded sites. Intermediate shade tolerance.

Landscape Use: This is another good, introduced oak worth planting more in Utah. It makes an attractive specimen or can be planted in groups of a few to many in yards, parks, or along streets. Fairly nice yellow to orange-brown fall color. It is seldom planted here and will not be easy to find, but is worth the effort. Zones 4-7.

Swamp White Oak   *(Quercus bicolor)*

Leaves: 5" to 7" long, 2" to 4" wide; shallowly lobed to coarsely serrate margin, teeth rounded; dark green and glossy above; paler and hairy to woolly beneath.

Twigs/Buds: **Bark peeling into curly, papery scales on older twigs**.

Flowers/Fruit: Fruit an acorn; **1" to 4" long stalk**; 3/4" to 1-1/4" long, cap hairy, fringed, covers 1/3 of the acorn; matures in one season.

General: Native to northern half of the eastern U.S. Naturally found on moist or low lying sites, though fairly drought resistant. Intermediate shade tolerance.

Landscape Use: Though native to fairly moist sites, needs only moderate water. Definitely worth planting more in Utah because of its pleasing form and good cultural characteristics. Dead, brown leaves stay on the twigs into the winter. Again, seldom planted in Utah and may be hard to find. Yellow fall color. Zones 3-8.

chinkapin oak (*Quercus muehlenbergii*)

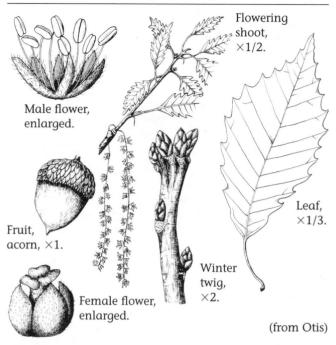

Male flower, enlarged.

Flowering shoot, ×1/2.

Fruit, acorn, ×1.

Female flower, enlarged.

Winter twig, ×2.

Leaf, ×1/3.

(from Otis)

swamp white oak (*Quercus bicolor*)

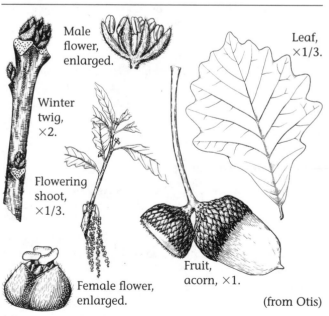

Male flower, enlarged.

Leaf, ×1/3.

Winter twig, ×2.

Flowering shoot, ×1/3.

Female flower, enlarged.

Fruit, acorn, ×1.

(from Otis)

Pin Oak   *(Quercus palustris)*

Leaves: 3" to 5" long, 2" to 5" wide; margin with 5 to 9 lobes; **openings between lobes extending 2/3 or more to the midrib**; lobes bristle-tipped; petiole up to 2" long, slender.

Flowers/Fruit: Fruit an acorn; 1/2" long, **often striped**, nearly hemispherical; thin, saucer-like cap encloses acorn only at the base; matures in two seasons.

Bark: Thick; gray-brown; smooth for many years; eventually with low, tight, scaly ridges.

General: Native to east-central U.S. where it is found mostly on moist, low-lying sites. Shade intolerant.

Landscape Use: Widely planted in the east as an ornamental because of its attractive, upright crown and nice fall color. Occasionally planted in Utah and can be found in nurseries, but suffers severely from iron chlorosis on our high pH soils and rarely should be planted. Zones 4-8.

Shumard Oak   *(Quercus shumardii)*

Leaves: 6" to 8" long; margin with 5 to 9 lobes; **openings between lobes extending more than halfway to the midrib**; lobes bristle-tipped with many coarse teeth; good deep red fall color; petiole slender.

Flowers/Fruit: Fruit an acorn; 3/4" to 1-1/4" long, red-brown, ovoid, short or no stalk; base covered with **thick, saucer-like cap** covered with small, shingle-like scales; matures in two seasons.

General: Native to eastern and southeastern U.S. on moist sites. Tolerates high soil pH and some drought. Intermediate shade tolerance.

Landscape Use: Used similarly to pin oak, but less prone to iron chlorosis. Good fall color. Rarely planted in Utah but could be more; hard to find. Zones 5-9.

Turkey Oak   *(Quercus cerris)*

Leaves: 3" to 5" long, 1" to 3" wide; **coarsely toothed to pinnately lobed**; dark green and shiny above, paler beneath; petiole 1/8" to 3/4" long.

Flowers/Fruit: Fruit an acorn; 1" long, brown, ovoid, no stalk; half covered with a cap with **long, curled-back scales**; matures in two seasons.

General: Native to western Asia and southern Europe. Intermediate shade tolerance.

pin oak (*Quercus palustris*)

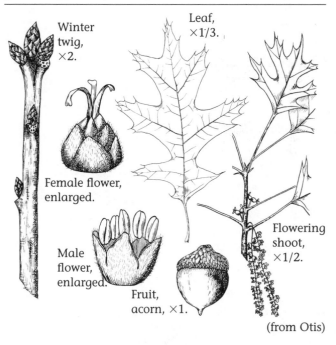

Winter twig, ×2.

Leaf, ×1/3.

Female flower, enlarged.

Male flower, enlarged.

Fruit, acorn, ×1.

Flowering shoot, ×1/2.

(from Otis)

Shumard oak (*Quercus shumardii*)

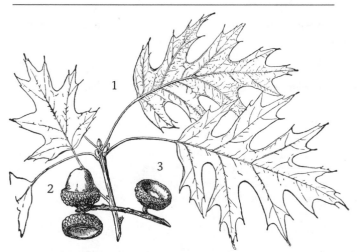

1. Leaves on twig, ×1/2.
2. Fruit, acorn, ×1/2.
3. Acorn cap, ×1/2.

(from Sargent)

121

turkey oak *(Quercus cerris)*

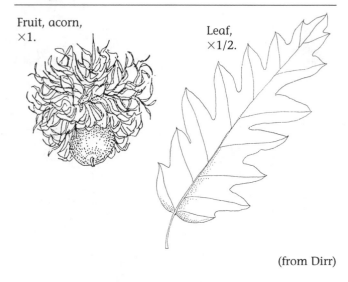

Fruit, acorn,
×1.

Leaf,
×1/2.

(from Dirr)

Landscape Use: Very desirable tree that is rarely planted in Utah or elsewhere in the U.S. Tolerates drought, high soil pH, and clay soils. Interesting acorn and leaf. Zones 5-7.

Sawtooth Oak   *(Quercus acutissima)*

Leaves: 3" to 7" long, 1" to 2" wide; **serrate margin with long bristles at the ends of teeth**; fall color yellow to golden-brown; looks similar to chestnut leaf.

Flowers/Fruit: Fruit an acorn; 1" long, brown, round, no stalk; 2/3 of nut covered with **thick cap covered with long, curved scales**.

General: Native to eastern Asia and Japan. Prefers acid, well-drained soils. Intermediate shade tolerance.

Landscape Use: Great tree with wide adaptability, but be careful on very high pH soils. However, I have seen this tree grow nearly an inch a year in trunk diameter over a several year period in the Midwest on moderately high pH soils (pH about 7.2). Zones 5(4?)-9.

Shingle Oak ◆ Laurel Oak   *(Quercus imbricaria)*

Leaves: 3" to 6" long, 1" to 3" wide; **entire margin, no lobes or teeth but somewhat wavy**; acute apex; shiny dark green above and paler and finely pubescent beneath; fall color red-brown to yellow-brown; petiole short.

sawtooth oak (*Quercus acutissima*)

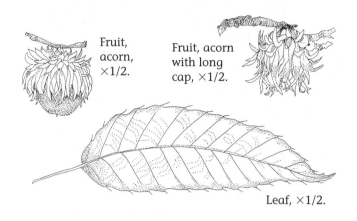

Fruit, acorn, ×1/2.

Fruit, acorn with long cap, ×1/2.

Leaf, ×1/2.

(from Dirr)

shingle oak (*Quercus imbricaria*)

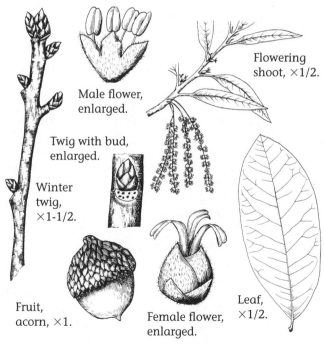

Male flower, enlarged.

Twig with bud, enlarged.

Winter twig, ×1-1/2.

Flowering shoot, ×1/2.

Fruit, acorn, ×1.

Female flower, enlarged.

Leaf, ×1/2.

(from Otis)

Flowers/Fruit: Fruit an acorn; 1/2" to 3/4" long, brown, ovoid, **short stalk**; 1/3 to 1/2 of acorn covered with a cap covered by shingle-like scales; matures in two seasons.

General: Native to east central U.S. on moist sites. Intermediate shade tolerance.

Landscape Use: Good tree for landscapes and more tolerant of high soil pH than pin oak, but less so than many of the other oaks listed above. Also rarely planted in Utah and would be hard to find. Zones 4-8.

ULMACEAE

Elm family. Contains 15 genera and more than 150 species mostly found throughout the world's temperate regions. Five of these genera are native to the U.S., but only two are very common.

Elm   Genus *Ulmus*

This genus contains about 18 species of trees native to Europe, Asia, and eastern North America. None are native to the western U.S., though several are planted and at least one, Siberian elm (*Ulmus pumila*), is common in Utah and has escaped cultivation. All have alternate, simple deciduous leaves with **serrate margins**. Perfect flowers are small and inconspicuous with no petals.

American Elm ◆ White Elm   *(Ulmus americana)*

Leaves: Alternate; simple; oblong-obovate to elliptic; 4" to 6" long, 1" to 3" wide; deciduous; coarsely doubly serrate margin; acuminate apex; dark green and **glabrous or slightly rough above**; pale and glabrous or somewhat hairy beneath; unequal base; petiole very short.

Twigs/Buds: Twigs slender; zigzag; generally glabrous; brown. No terminal bud; lateral buds about 1/4" long, oval, not sharp-pointed, chestnut-brown.

Flowers/Fruit: Fruit a samara; about 1/2" long; oval; a flat thin wing around the seed, wing hairy-fringed and **notched at tip; seed cavity distinct**; ripens in spring.

Bark: Ash-gray; divided into flat-topped ridges with diamond-shaped furrows in between; on older trees can become rough and without a definite pattern; **a broken piece of outer bark will have alternating light and dark layers**.

Wood: Important; sapwood gray to light brown; heartwood light brown to brown; growth rings distinct; ring-porous; rays not distinct to naked eye; used for boxes, crates, furniture, and veneer.

General: Native to most of the eastern half of the U.S. Intermediate shade tolerance.

Landscape Use: Formerly widely planted as a street tree throughout the U.S. and prized for its graceful, vase-like crown shape and dense shade. Unfortunately, over the last several decades it has been largely wiped out by Dutch elm disease. Surviving trees can be found in Utah, but they probably have escaped the disease by chance rather than true resistance. Risky to plant. Resistant cultivars are occasionally released, but many of these have not been proven resistant long-term, and some are crosses that have no American elm in them. Try lacebark elm instead (see below). Zones 2-9. Various elm hybrids, such as **English elm** (*Ulmus procera*), are likely to be encountered occasionally in Utah and are difficult to identify.

American elm (*Ulmus americana*)

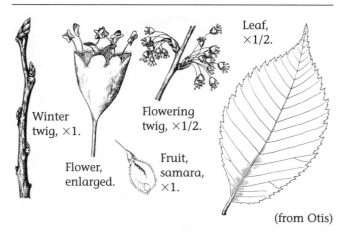

Winter twig, ×1.

Flower, enlarged.

Flowering twig, ×1/2.

Fruit, samara, ×1.

Leaf, ×1/2.

(from Otis)

English elm (*Ulmus procera*)

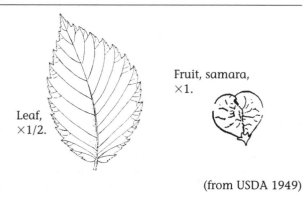

Leaf, ×1/2.

Fruit, samara, ×1.

(from USDA 1949)

Siberian Elm ♦ Chinese Elm   *(Ulmus pumila)*

Leaves: Alternate; simple; elliptic to elliptic-lanceolate; **1" to 3" long**, 1/3" to 1" wide; deciduous; singly serrate margin; acuminate to acute apex; usually nearly equal at base; **dark green and glabrous above**; glabrous or slightly hairy beneath; petiole very short.

Twigs/Buds: Twigs slender; gray; glabrous or slightly hairy. No terminal bud; lateral buds spherical, bud scales tipped with long hairs.

Flowers/Fruit: Fruit a samara; 1/2" long; round; wing as in other elms, **wing margin deeply notched at tip; ripens in spring**.

Bark: Gray; rough; with shallow furrows and long, flat ridges.

Wood: Little information published but similar to American elm.

General: Native to Siberia, China, and Korea. Intermediate shade tolerance.

Landscape Use: Much planted throughout Utah in shelterbelts, yards, and just about anywhere else. Where it has not been planted it often seeds-in aggressively. Commonly, but incorrectly, called Chinese elm (see below). Grows fast and is fairly tough, but has many undesirable features and shouldn't be planted in most cases. Weak wood, diseases, and insects all cause problems for this species. Zones 3-9.

Lacebark Elm ♦ Chinese Elm   *(Ulmus parvifolia)*

Leaves: Alternate; simple; elliptic to ovate or obovate; 3/4" to 2-1/2" long; deciduous; singly serrate margin; acute apex; unequal and rounded at base; dark green and glabrous above; hairy beneath when young; **leathery**.

Twigs/Buds: Twigs slender; gray-brown; glabrous to slightly hairy. Buds small compared to other elms, 1/10" to 1/8" long; brown; slightly hairy.

Flowers/Fruit: Fruit a samara; 1/3" long; oval; wing as in other elms, notched at tip; **ripens in fall**.

Bark: Gray-green with orange and brown; **beautiful interlacing appearance, very characteristic**.

Wood: No information available.

General: Native to northern and central China, Korea, and Japan. This is the true Chinese elm and is not the same as Siberian elm. Intermediate shade tolerance.

Landscape Use: This is a desirable landscape tree that can do well in most of Utah. It has a medium growth rate, a nice crown form, interesting bark and attractive foliage, and is adaptable to a

Siberian elm *(Ulmus pumila)*

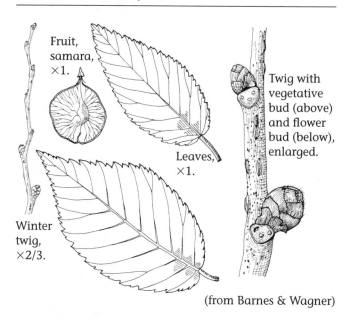

Fruit, samara, ×1.

Leaves, ×1.

Winter twig, ×2/3.

Twig with vegetative bud (above) and flower bud (below), enlarged.

(from Barnes & Wagner)

lacebark elm *(Ulmus parvifolia)*

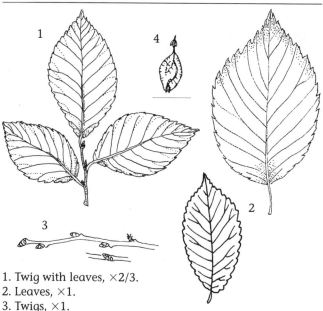

1. Twig with leaves, ×2/3.
2. Leaves, ×1.
3. Twigs, ×1.
4. Fruit, samara, ×1.

(1-3 from Dirr, 4 from USDA 1949)

127

wide variety of sites. It also is resistant to Dutch elm disease. Good examples exist around the Little America Hotel grounds in Salt Lake City. Should be planted more, but make sure you ask for it by its scientific name to avoid confusion. Zones 4-9.

Hackberry   Genus *Celtis*

This genus contains 60 to 70 species found in temperate and tropical regions throughout the world. Five to six tree-sized species are native to North America and one is native to Utah. All have alternate, simple leaves. Small, inconspicuous monoecious or perfect flowers (male, female, and perfect flowers on the same tree) appearing in spring.

❖Netleaf Hackberry   *(Celtis reticulata)*

Leaves: Alternate; simple; broadly ovate; 1" to 3" long and 1" to 2" wide; deciduous; entire margin or with a few teeth; acuminate apex; rounded base; thick; light green and rough or smooth above; lighter beneath with **obvious reticulated or net-like small veins**; petiole 1/8" to 1/2" long.

Twigs/Buds: Twigs slender; gray-brown. No terminal bud; lateral buds small, pointed, pressed against the twig.

netleaf hackberry *(Celtis reticulata)*

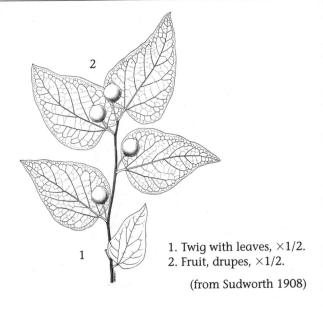

1. Twig with leaves, ×1/2.
2. Fruit, drupes, ×1/2.

(from Sudworth 1908)

Flowers/Fruit: Fruit a drupe; 1/4" in diameter; round; **yellow to orange-red**; one per stem; on stalks 1/2" to 3/4" long; ripen in fall.

Bark: Thick, red-brown to gray-brown; smooth when young; develops short ridges somewhat like common hackberry when older.

Wood: Little known or used; ring-porous; likely similar to common hackberry.

General: Native to scattered areas of the West and Southwest, including much of Utah. Found on dry foothill or valley sites. Shade tolerant.

Landscape Use: This native hackberry is rarely planted in Utah and is not easy to obtain. It would be a good candidate where little supplemental water will be available and where a large tree is not needed. Expect a slow to moderate growth rate. Zones 5(4?)-9.

Hackberry ♦ Common Hackberry
(Celtis occidentalis)

Leaves: Alternate; simple; ovate to ovate-lanceolate; 2" to 4" long; deciduous; serrate margin; long acuminate apex; base uneven; glabrous or slightly rough above; glabrous beneath; light, dull green; "nipple galls" or green bumps often occur on underside of leaves; petiole up to 1/2" long.

hackberry (*Celtis occidentalis*)

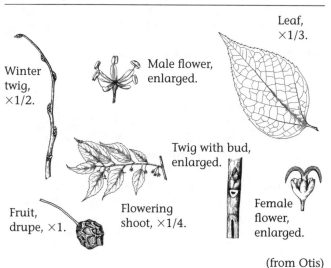

Leaf, ×1/3.

Winter twig, ×1/2.

Male flower, enlarged.

Twig with bud, enlarged.

Fruit, drupe, ×1.

Flowering shoot, ×1/4.

Female flower, enlarged.

(from Otis)

Twigs/Buds: Twigs slender; zigzag; red-brown; pith chambered. No terminal bud; lateral buds small, pointed, pressed against the twig.

Flowers/Fruit: Fruit a drupe; 1/4" in diameter; round; **dark-purple**; one per stem; on stalks 1/2" to 3/4" long; flesh edible; ripen in September or October.

Bark: Gray-brown; smooth when young; develops characteristic **corky warts or ridges when older**; eventually becomes scaly.

Wood: Moderately important; sapwood pale yellow to green-yellow; heartwood yellow to light brown; growth rings distinct; ring-porous; rays visible to the naked eye; often sold as elm.

General: Native from the Great Plains east through most of the eastern U.S., excluding the extreme southeast; not Utah. Prefers moist, rich soils. Intermediate shade tolerance and will survive partial shade from other trees.

Landscape Use: This is one of the best introduced trees for planting throughout Utah. It has a medium-fast growth rate, a very nice crown form, unusual bark, and is adapted to moderate drought, heat, wind, and high soil pH. Fruit is not a problem since it dries or is eaten by birds before dropping and trees do not bear heavily. Often used in windbreaks but also good as a large landscape tree for specimen use, in parks, or along streets. Has proven itself in Utah and should be planted much more; becoming easier to get. Zones 2-9.

Zelkova   Genus *Zelkova*

This genus contains several species native to Japan and China. One of those species is occasionally planted in Utah. Monoecious flowers.

Japanese Zelkova   *(Zelkova serrata)*

Leaves: Alternate; simple; ovate to oblong-ovate; 1" to 5" long and 1" to 2" wide; deciduous; sharply serrate margin; acuminate apex; fairly even, rounded base; dark green and rough above; 8 to 14 vein pairs; glabrous beneath; very short petiole.

Twigs/Buds: Twigs slender; zig-zag; pubescent when young, glabrous later; brown. No terminal bud; lateral buds 1/4" long, ovoid, angled out from twig, with many brown, overlapping scales.

Flowers/Fruit: Flowers inconspicuous, appearing in spring. Fruit a **small, fairly firm, dry drupe**; 1/4" or less in diameter; green to brown; ripens in fall.

Bark: Smooth and gray when young with **horizontal ridges or lenticels**; becomes more lacy like Chinese elm bark when older; distinctive.

Japanese zelkova (*Zelkova serrata*)

Leaf,
1/4.

Twig with
bud, ×2.

Fruit, drupe,
×2.

(from Farrar)

Wood: No information available.

General: Native to Japan and parts of Asia. Intermediate shade tolerance.

Landscape Use: The vase-shaped crown and medium size of this tree make it a possible replacement for American elms, though I think it is somewhat coarse. Quite tolerant of drought and high soil pH. Interesting bark and yellow-orange to red fall color. Tends to have poorly attached branches due to included bark. Zones 5-8.

MORACEAE

Mulberry family. Contains about 70 genera and over 1,500 species. Widely distributed around the world, especially in warmer areas. The **sap is milky** and in some species can be a source of rubber.

Mulberry   Genus *Morus*

This genus contains 12 to 15 species, with two native to the U.S. and two naturalized and none native to Utah. The **blackberry-like frui**t is liked by birds and, in some species, by humans. Flowers monoecious or dioecious within the same species.

Red Mulberry   *(Morus rubra)*

Leaves: Alternate; simple; nearly orbicular; 3" to 5" long; deciduous; variable in shape; **no lobes or up to 3 to 5 lobes**; coarsely serrate margin; acute to acuminate apex; hairy beneath; light yellow fall color; petiole 1/2" to 1" long.

Twigs/Buds: Twigs slender; somewhat zigzag; red-brown to green-brown; showing milky sap when cut. No terminal bud; lateral buds ovoid, pointed, 1/4" long, light brown.

Flowers/Fruit: Flowers small and inconspicuous with no petals. **Multiple fruit of small drupes; resembles a blackberry**; dark purple or nearly black; 1/2" to 3/4" long; juicy; ripening in June or July.

Bark: Thin; dark brown to orange-brown; scaly and furrowed; bark of roots yellow.

Wood: Sapwood yellow; heartwood yellow-brown; growth rings distinct; ring-porous; rays plainly visible to naked eye; little used but excellent firewood.

General: Native to most of the eastern U.S. Usually found on rich, moist sites, but can stand considerable heat. Shade tolerant.

Landscape Use: Mulberries are good city trees that grow fairly rapidly. They need attention to branch structure and attachment to keep them healthy and well-formed. The broad, round crown and shiny, bright green leaves are very attractive. Be sure to plant all-male trees if you do not want fruit. Zones 4-9. **White mulberry (_Morus alba_)**, a native of China, has been widely planted in the U.S. and now is naturalized over much of the country and can be found in Utah, along with red mulberry. Its leaves are similar to red mulberry's but its fruit is white to pinkish-purple when mature. This is the main mulberry that silkworms feed on. Zones 5-9.

Osage-orange   Genus _Maclura_

This genus has one species that is native to Arkansas, Oklahoma, and Texas and has been occasionally planted in Utah in the past. Flowers dioecious.

Osage-orange   (_Maclura pomifera_)

Leaves: Alternate; simple; oblong-lanceolate to ovate; 4" to 5" long; deciduous; entire margin; with a long acuminate apex; dark green and glabrous above; milky juice; petiole 1/2" to 1-1/2" long.

Twigs/Buds: Twigs stout; orange-brown; hairy; **armed with stout, sharp-pointed thorns**. No terminal bud; lateral buds small, round, brown, partially imbedded in bark.

Flowers/Fruit: Flowers small and inconspicuous with no petals. Fruit a **pale green, orange-like structure**; 4" to 5" in diameter; containing a bitter, milky juice; becoming woody; called a "hedge-apple" by some and thought to have moth repelling properties if stored with clothing.

Bark: Thin; dark orange-brown; furrowed with flat ridges.

Wood: Moderate importance in some areas; characteristic bright orange color; very hard and dense; ring-porous; yields a yellow dye; used to make bows, thus the tree is sometimes called "bois d'arc" (pronounced bwadark) or "bow wood"; excellent firewood.

red mulberry (*Morus rubra*)

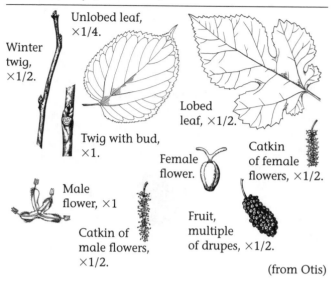

Winter twig, ×1/2.

Unlobed leaf, ×1/4.

Twig with bud, ×1.

Lobed leaf, ×1/2.

Female flower.

Catkin of female flowers, ×1/2.

Male flower, ×1

Catkin of male flowers, ×1/2.

Fruit, multiple of drupes, ×1/2.

(from Otis)

white mulberry (*Morus alba*)

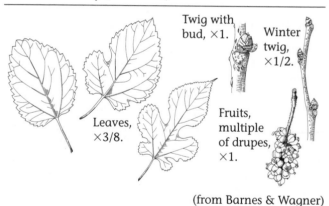

Twig with bud, ×1.

Winter twig, ×1/2.

Leaves, ×3/8.

Fruits, multiple of drupes, ×1.

(from Barnes & Wagner)

General: Native to Arkansas, Oklahoma, and Texas. Shade intolerant.

Landscape Use: Was extensively planted as a hedge (the species is sometimes called hedge) or windbreak by early settlers in the eastern Great Plains and elsewhere, and a few old windbreak trees still exist in Utah as far north as Weber County. Typical height is less than 30 feet. Very tough tree with very interesting wood.

133

Osage-orange (*Maclura pomifera*)

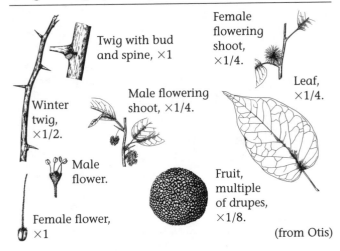

Twig with bud and spine, ×1

Female flowering shoot, ×1/4.

Leaf, ×1/4.

Winter twig, ×1/2.

Male flowering shoot, ×1/4.

Male flower.

Female flower, ×1

Fruit, multiple of drupes, ×1/8.

(from Otis)

Fruitless (male) and thornless cultivars are becoming available and should make this a good landscape tree. I like it even with fruit and thorns. Yellow fall color. Zones 4-9.

CERCIDIPHYLLACEAE

Katsuratree family. Contains one genus, *Cercidiphyllum* (meaning "with *Cercis* or redbud-like leaves") with one species. Native to eastern Asia. Dioecious.

Katsuratree (*Cercidiphyllum japonicum*)

Leaves: **Opposite or sub-opposite**; simple; 2" to 4" long and wide; deciduous; **nearly orbicular to broad-ovate, cordate at base, similar shape to redbud (*Cercis*)**; margin with rounded (crenate) teeth; 3 to 5 main veins extending out from the petiole; obtuse or rounded apex; glabrous above, slightly waxy underneath; purple color in spring, dark blue-green in summer, yellow to orange to red in fall.

Twigs/Buds: Twigs slender; swollen at nodes where leaves attach; brown; spur shoots form in the second year at each node that each bear one leaf and flowers. No terminal bud; lateral buds reddish, covered with two scales, fairly small, appressed.

Flowers/Fruit: Flowers small and inconspicuous, appearing in spring before the leaves. Fruit a small, 1/2" to 1" long pod that splits to reveal thin, winged seeds; matures in fall.

Bark: Brown; shaggy and distinctive when older.

Katsuratree (*Cercidiphyllum japonicum*)

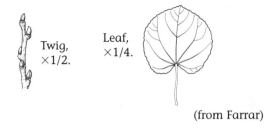

Twig,
×1/2.

Leaf,
×1/4.

(from Farrar)

Wood: No information available.

General: Native to eastern Asia. Likes plenty of water, especially when young. Also prefers rich, well-drained soils. Intermediate shade tolerance.

Landscape Use: This tree grows fairly quickly and has great foliage color through the year, especially the red to yellow fall color with falling leaves exuding a spicy odor. Make sure to give it plenty of water when young. Grows fairly quickly and can get quite large. Pyramidal when young and more flat-topped when older. Fairly free of problems, but suffers if exposed to high temperatures and low humidity. Shade from a building or other trees later in the day can help. Zones 4-8.

MAGNOLIACEAE

Magnolia family. Contains 8 to 12 genera and about 210 species. Distributed throughout southeast Asia, the eastern U.S., central America, and the West Indies to eastern Brazil. Most have **large, conspicuous flowers**. Two genera are occasionally planted in Utah.

Magnolia   Genus *Magnolia*

This genus includes 70 to 80 species known primarily for their **large, distinctive flowers**. Eight species are native to North America with none found naturally west of east Texas and Oklahoma. Many are planted, however. Flowers perfect, often with petal-like sepals. Twigs encircled at each bud by a line formed by scars where stipules (leaf like appendages at the base of each petiole) were attached. Twigs often fragrant when crushed.

Saucer Magnolia   (*Magnolia soulangiana*)

Leaves: Alternate; simple; obovate to broadly oblong; **3" to 6" long; 1-1/2" to 3" wide**; deciduous; entire margin with narrow, pointed apex; glabrous; dark green above.

135

saucer magnolia (*Magnolia* × *soulangiana*)

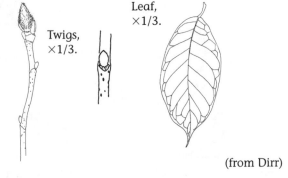

Twigs,
×1/3.

Leaf,
×1/3.

(from Dirr)

Twigs/Buds: Twigs fairly stout; brown; glabrous; fragrant when crushed. Terminal buds 1/2" to 3/4" long, silky; lateral buds smaller.

Flowers/Fruit: **Large (5" to 10"), showy, white to pink to purplish flowers** that open in spring before the leaves; flowers often whitish inside and pink to purple outside. Fruit an aggregate of follicles; held upright; matures in August-September.

Bark: Gray on older trunks, usually smooth.

Wood: No information available.

General: This species is a hybrid of lily magnolia (*M. quinquepeta*) and Yulan magnolia (*M. heptapeta*), both natives of China. Shade intolerant.

Landscape Use: Attractive tree with beautiful flowers that does well throughout the much of Utah. This is a **small to medium-sized, spreading tree.** Flowers are very attractive, but flower buds are sometimes injured by late frosts. I have seen several examples of this tree doing well and blooming in Logan. Zones 4-9.

Other Magnolias
(All have alternate, simple leaves with entire margins)

Star Magnolia (*Magnolia stellata*)

Leaves: Obovate or narrow-elliptical; 2" to 4" long; 1" to 2" wide; deciduous; rounded apex; dark green and glabrous above; paler and mostly glabrous beneath; short petiole.

Twigs/Buds: Twigs slender; glabrous; brown. Flower buds about 1/3" to 1/2" long, covered with hairs; other buds smaller.

Flowers/Fruit: Dramatic, **3" to 4" diameter white flowers with many narrow, fairly long petals**; appear early before the leaves emerge. Fruit an aggregate of follicles; 2" long.

star magnolia (*Magnolia stellata*)

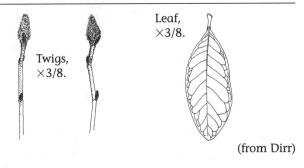

Twigs,
×3/8.

Leaf,
×3/8.

(from Dirr)

Loebner magnolia (*Magnolia × loebneri*)

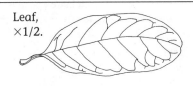

Leaf,
×1/2.

(from Dirr)

General: Native to Japan. Shade intolerant.

Landscape Use: Fairly popular in Utah. A small tree with dramatic white flowers. Though shade intolerant, plant it where with protection from warm winter sun, like near the north side of a building or with evergreens to the south and southwest. Zones 4-9. **Loebner Magnolia** (*Magnolia × loebneri*) is a hybrid of star magnolia and Kobus magnolia (see description below); produces a medium-sized tree with a rounded crown and 5" to 8" diameter flowers with white to pink petals. This is a very desirable tree that deserves more attention in Utah. Zones 3-8.

Cucumbertree ♦ Cucumber Magnolia
(*Magnolia acuminata*)

Leaves: Broadly elliptic to ovate; **6" to 10" long; 4" to 6" wide**; deciduous; acuminate apex; yellow-green and glabrous above; paler and glabrous or slightly hairy beneath; thin; petiole 1" to 1-1/2" long.

Twigs/Buds: Twigs fairly stout; glossy; brown to red-brown; spicy odor when crushed. Terminal buds about 1/2" to 3/4" long, **covered with silvery, silky hairs**; lateral buds smaller.

Flowers/Fruit: Flowers **2" to 3" wide, non-showy, yellow-green;** appearing in May or June after the leaves open. Fruit an aggregate of follicles; 2" to 3" long; held upright; seeds red, about 1/2" long, suspended from slender threads at maturity.

Bark: Brown; furrowed into narrow flaky ridges.

General: Native to the Appalachian region and the lower Mississippi and Ohio River valleys. Shade intolerant.

Landscape Use: Can be planted in Utah but seldom is. Fairly large tree with attractive flowers. Zones 3-8.

Southern Magnolia *(Magnolia grandiflora)*

Leaves: Oval to ovate; 5" to 10" long; 2-1/2" to 4" wide; evergreen in warm climates (leaves live two years), but will sometimes turn brown and fall off in colder climates (generally zones 5 and colder); entire margin; acute to acuminate apex; dark green and shiny above; **densely red-hairy beneath**; thick and leathery; petiole 1" to 2" long.

Twigs/Buds: Twigs stout; green; covered with red hairs or glabrous. Terminal buds about 1 to 1-1/2", covered with white or red silky hairs; lateral buds smaller.

Flowers/Fruit: **Flowers 6" to 10" diameter, white, fragrant**, open in May to June and have 6 to 12 petals. Fruit similar to cucumbertree, but 3" to 4" long and woolly red.

Bark: Thin; brown to gray; smooth when young and flaky on old trees.

General: Native to the extreme southeastern U.S. from southeast Texas to eastern North Carolina. Intermediate shade tolerance.

Landscape Use: Seldom planted in Utah but can do well on warm enough sites. Large shiny leaves, strong pyramidal to oval habit, and dramatic flowers make this a very desirable tree where it is hardy. Prefers rich, well-drained soil. Needs winter wind and sun protection in colder northern sites. Zones 7(6?)-9.

Kobus Magnolia *(Magnolia kobus)*

Leaves: Broadly obovate to ovate; 3" to 6" long; deciduous; pointed apex; dark green and glabrous above; paler and glabrous or slightly hairy on veins beneath; inconspicuous fall color; petiole 1/2" to 3/4" long.

Twigs/Buds: Twigs moderately stout; glabrous; brown. Terminal buds large and **covered with silvery, silky hairs**; lateral buds smaller.

Flowers/Fruit: Flowers are **4" to 5" diameter, white, and appear in March or April**. Fruit an aggregate of follicles; 3" to 5" long; held upright.

cucumbertree (*Magnolia acuminata*)

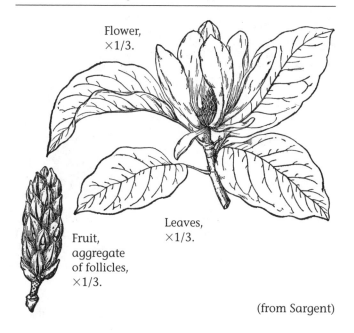

Flower,
×1/3.

Leaves,
×1/3.

Fruit,
aggregate
of follicles,
×1/3.

(from Sargent)

southern magnolia (*Magnolia grandiflora*)

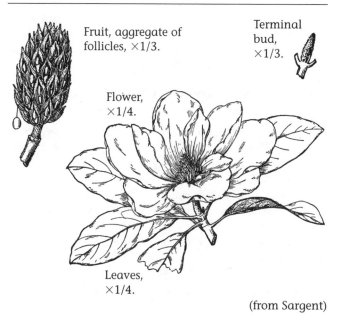

Fruit, aggregate of
follicles, ×1/3.

Terminal
bud,
×1/3.

Flower,
×1/4.

Leaves,
×1/4.

(from Sargent)

Kobus magnolia (*Magnolia kobus*)

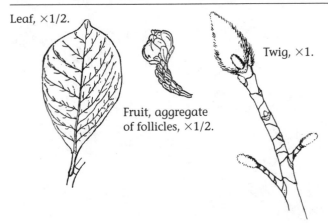

Leaf, ×1/2.

Twig, ×1.

Fruit, aggregate of follicles, ×1/2.

Leaf and fruit from Apgar, twig from Dirr)

Bark: Brown to gray.

General: Native to Japan. Shade intolerant.

Landscape Use: Shrub to large tree (cultivar dependent) that is rarely seen in Utah but worth trying. More cold hardy than most magnolias, and tolerant of a wide range of soil conditions. Zones 3-8.

Yellow-poplar   Genus *Liriodendron*

This genus contains only 2 species worldwide, with one in China and the other in the eastern U.S. Flowers perfect.

Yellow-poplar ♦ Tuliptree ♦ Tulip-poplar (*Liriodendron tulipifera*)

Leaves: Alternate; simple; 4" to 6" across; deciduous; **usually 4-lobed; leaf base and tip flat, leaf shape very distinctive**; entire margin; glabrous; bright green with nice yellow fall color; petiole 2" to 4" long.

Twigs/Buds: Twigs fairly stout; red-brown; pith divided into chambers. Terminal buds about 1/2" long, covered with 2 duck-bill like scales; lateral buds much smaller.

Flowers/Fruit: Has **large, green-yellow flowers** that appear in May or June after the leaves are open. Fruit an aggregate of deciduous samaras; 2-1/2" to 3" long; held upright.

Bark: Dark green and smooth on young stems; becoming thick, ash-gray, furrowed, with rough ridges.

yellow-poplar (*Liriodendron tulipifera*)

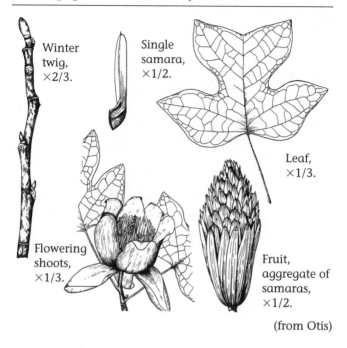

Winter twig, ×2/3.

Single samara, ×1/2.

Leaf, ×1/3.

Flowering shoots, ×1/3.

Fruit, aggregate of samaras, ×1/2.

(from Otis)

Wood: Very important; light yellow sapwood; light yellow to dark brown heartwood; even-textured; diffuse-porous; used for furniture, interior finish, boxes, pallets, crates, plywood, etc.; commonly available in lumber yards where it is usually called poplar.

General: Native to the southeastern U.S. as far north as southeast Missouri, and as far northeast as Vermont. Not a true poplar. Shade intolerant.

Landscape Use: Large tree that is not common in Utah but has been planted enough to have proven itself. Has a good, strong, pyramidal habit and bright green, unusually shaped leaves, and nice fall color that make the tree very attractive. The flowers and fruit are interesting but the seeds can be messy. Zones 4-9.

HAMAMELIDACEAE

Witch-hazel family. Contains 23 genera and about 100 species of trees and shrubs. Found throughout the forested regions of eastern North America to Mexico and Central America; South Africa, Madagascar, Asia, and Australia. Several species have resins that are used in soaps, perfumes, and medicines.

Sweetgum   Genus *Liquidambar*

This genus contains about 6 species worldwide, with one native to North America and the rest in Asia.

Sweetgum ◆ American Sweetgum
(Liquidambar styraciflua)

Leaves: Alternate; simple; 6" to 7" wide; **star-shaped with 5 to 7 palmately arranged lobes**; finely serrate margins; bright green and glossy above; hairy where veins meet below; petioles long and slender; fall color yellow to purple to red.

Twigs/Buds: Twigs slender to stout; green to yellow-brown; round or slightly angled and **may develop corky wings**; glossy; pith star-shaped in cross-section. Terminal buds 1/4" to 1/2" long, with several orange-brown scales; lateral buds similar but smaller.

Flowers/Fruit: Flowers small and inconspicuous, in small heads; no petals; bloom in April to May; monoecious. Fruit a **globose head of 2-celled, beaked capsules**; 1" to 1-1/2" in diameter; woody; brown; held on a long, slender stalk; persists on trees into winter.

Bark: Thick; gray-brown; deeply furrowed into narrow, tight ridges.

Wood: Very important; light colored sapwood; reddish-brown heartwood; moderately heavy, hard, and strong; diffuse-porous; used for lumber for furniture and boxes, veneer, railroad ties, and pulp.

sweetgum (*Liquidambar styraciflua*)

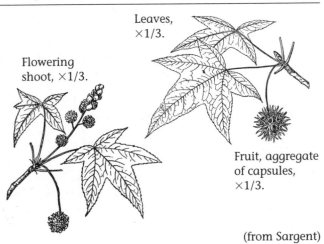

Leaves,
×1/3.

Flowering
shoot, ×1/3.

Fruit, aggregate
of capsules,
×1/3.

(from Sargent)

General: Native to the southern two-thirds of the eastern U.S., extending west to southeastern Missouri, eastern Oklahoma, and eastern Texas. Shade intolerant.

Landscape Use: A large tree that can be planted in Utah, but may winter-kill in colder areas and will not do well in our highest pH soils; otherwise a desirable landscape tree with beautiful fall color. I have not seen these in Utah, but I'm told they do quite well. The strong, pyramidal habit is very appealing and the leaf shape is interesting. Zones 5-9.

PLATANACEAE

Sycamore family. Contains 1 genus, *Platanus*, and 7 to 10 species. Found in North America and southeastern Europe east to India.

American Sycamore ◆ American Planetree
(Platanus occidentalis)

Leaves: Alternate; simple; 3" to 8" wide; deciduous; more or less deeply 3 to 5 lobed; margin of lobes coarsely serrate; bright green and glabrous above; paler and hairy along veins beneath; petioles 2" to 3" long, hollow at the base.

Twigs/Buds: Twigs moderately slender; orange-brown; zigzag. No terminal bud; lateral buds conical, resinous, covered by a single cap-like scale and hidden under hollow petiole base.

Flowers/Fruit: Flowers small in small round heads, appearing in spring; monoecious. Fruit a round, **yellow-brown head or ball** about 1" in diameter that hangs from slender, 3" to 6" long stem; heads usually occur singly; often persists through the winter.

Bark: Brown on younger branches; soon becomes mottled (brown and white) as brown outer bark peels off, showing the **creamy-white, smooth inner bark**; bark on lower trunk of older trees brown and scaly; very distinctive.

Wood: Somewhat important; sapwood light yellow; heartwood light to dark brown; growth rings distinct; diffuse-porous; rays conspicuous to naked eye; used for boxes, furniture, railroad ties.

General: Native to most of the eastern U.S. and as far west as the eastern Great Plains. Usually found naturally along streams. Can get very large. Very shade intolerant.

Landscape Use: This is a large tree that is planted in Utah but is easily confused with the London Planetree (see below), which is more common. Has a strong, pyramidal crown when young with beautiful bark. The fruit can be messy. Zones 4-9. The **London planetree** (*Platanus* × *acerifolia*), a cross between American sycamore and Oriental planetree (*P. orientalis*), often is planted in

Utah (more in the past than now). The main streets of Brigham City and Farmington are good examples. Easily overgrows a site and breaks sidewalks and curbs, but it's a beautiful tree for a large site. Its appearance is similar to that of sycamore, though its fruit heads usually occur 2 or 3 to a stalk. Anthracnose is a fungal disease that can affect both of these species, causing early season leaf drop or twig dieback. Trees grow new leaves, however, and usually are not severely affected. Zones 4-9.

American sycamore (*Platanus occidentalis*)

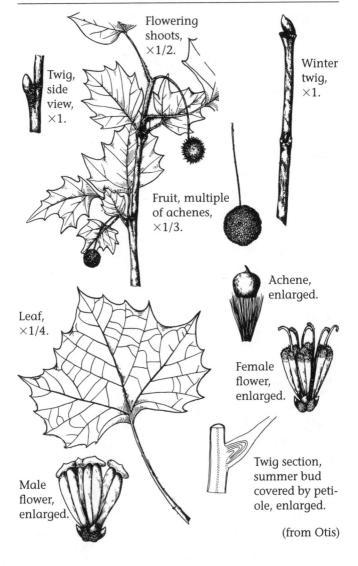

Flowering shoots, ×1/2.

Twig, side view, ×1.

Winter twig, ×1.

Fruit, multiple of achenes, ×1/3.

Achene, enlarged.

Leaf, ×1/4.

Female flower, enlarged.

Male flower, enlarged.

Twig section, summer bud covered by petiole, enlarged.

(from Otis)

London planetree (*Platanus* × *acerifolia*)

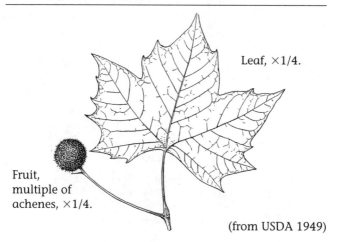

Leaf, ×1/4.

Fruit, multiple of achenes, ×1/4.

(from USDA 1949)

ROSACEAE

Rose family. This is a broad-ranging and diverse family that contains about 120 genera and 3,300 species. Widely distributed around the world, but more common in temperate climates. This family is relatively unimportant from a forestry standpoint, but is very important to agriculture and horticulture and many provide good wildlife habitat.

Cherry, Plum, Peach Genus *Prunus*

An important genus from a horticultural standpoint, with 200 to 400 species reported, depending on the source, fruit and 25 to 30 species native to the U.S. Known for their fruit and flowers, though an important timber tree in this genus is black cherry (*Prunus serotina*), which is prized for its beautiful wood, though seldom grown in the western U.S. Flowers perfect and often showy, and **fruit a one-seeded dry or fleshy drupe**. Buds have many pairs of overlapping scales.

❖Common Chokecherry (*Prunus virginiana*)

Leaves: Alternate; simple; oval to obovate; 2" to 4" long and two-thirds as wide; deciduous; dark green and glabrous above, paler beneath; sharply, finely serrate margin with spreading (mostly not in-curving) teeth; petiole 1/2" long with **small, conspicuous gland or bump on each side at base of leaf blade**.

Twigs/Buds: Twigs slender to medium-stout; new twigs somewhat downy, otherwise glabrous with a few small round lenticels;

red-brown when young turning patchy silver-gray when older; twigs often infected with black growth from black-knot disease. Terminal buds 1/4" to 1/3" long, scaly, red-brown to brown like twig; lateral buds same size or slightly smaller.

Flowers/Fruit: Small white flowers appear in elongated bunches in May. Fruit a drupe; black; round; about 1/3" in diameter; edible; sour.

Bark: On young stems smooth, red-brown; on older stems turning gray-black and remaining fairly smooth with obvious **lenticels that do not extend horizontally** like many other *Prunus* species.

Wood: Not important and little known.

General: Native to most of the continental U.S., including Utah, and to much of Canada. Large shrub to small tree, usually with a multi-stemmed habit. Likes fairly moist locations with rich soils, but will do well on poorer sites. Shade intolerant.

Landscape Use: Attractive flowers and small size potentially make it a useful tree. Good for wildlife habitat plantings and windbreaks, and fruit can be used in jams and jellies. Black knot disease reduces attractiveness and vigorous sucker-sprouting can be a problem. Most commonly found in the landscape as **'Schubert'** or **'Canada Red'** cultivar, known for its purple-red foliage and more upright, single-stemmed habit. Zones 2-6.

common chokecherry (*Prunus virginiana*)

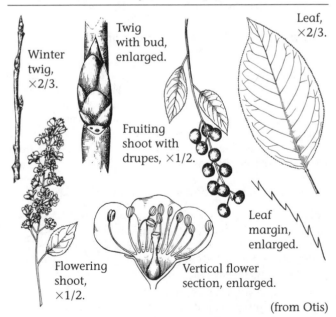

Winter twig, ×2/3.

Twig with bud, enlarged.

Leaf, ×2/3.

Fruiting shoot with drupes, ×1/2.

Leaf margin, enlarged.

Flowering shoot, ×1/2.

Vertical flower section, enlarged.

(from Otis)

Purpleleaf Plum ◆ Cherry Plum ◆ Myrobalan Plum *(Prunus cerasifera)*

Leaves: Alternate; simple; ovate to obovate; 1-1/2" to 2-1/2" long and half as wide; deciduous; usually **purple-green to dark purple**, occasionally dark green; glabrous above and beneath except for hairs along veins beneath; finely serrate margin; may have glands where petiole attaches to blade.

Twigs/Buds: Twigs slender; glabrous; silver-gray when young, dark gray when older. Buds 1/4" long, scaly, dark purple-gray.

Flowers/Fruit: Flowers pink or white; 3/4" to 1" in diameter; appearing in early spring. Fruit a **one-seeded round drupe (plum) about 1" in diameter; dark purple**; usually present in small numbers; sweet and edible; maturing in mid-summer.

Bark: Shiny smooth and dark purple at first with small horizontal lenticels, roughening with age with small vertical cracks and enlarging brown lenticels.

Wood: Not important and essentially unknown; dark heartwood.

General: Native to western Asia and cultivated for centuries. Fairly adaptable to different sites, but also pest-prone like many *Rosaceae*. Shade intolerant.

Landscape Use: A small tree widely used in the landscape, in Utah mostly as the purple-leaved cultivar 'Newport'. I have had two of these trees in my yard in Logan and I am not impressed. Included bark and weak branch attachments are common, flowers are alright but not great, and I can't stand purple-leaved trees. Reputed to lack cold-hardiness, but mine survived the cold, only to succumb to branch breakage and trunk decay. There definitely are better small flowering trees than this. Zones 5(4?)-8.

purpleleaf plum *(Prunus cerasifera)*

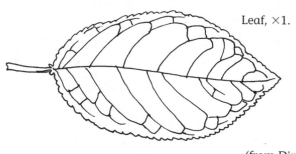

Leaf, ×1.

(from Dirr)

Canada plum (*Prunus nigra*)
for
common plum (*Prunus domestica*)

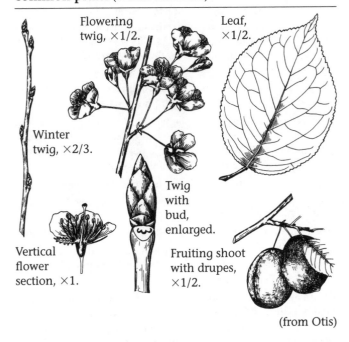

Flowering twig, ×1/2.

Leaf, ×1/2.

Winter twig, ×2/3.

Twig with bud, enlarged.

Vertical flower section, ×1.

Fruiting shoot with drupes, ×1/2.

(from Otis)

Common plum (*Prunus domestica*) also is widely planted in Utah for its fruit in varieties and forms too numerous to mention here. Shiny silver-gray bark with prominent horizontal lenticels is a key identifying characteristic, as well as the fruit. Zones 4-9.

Other *Prunus:*
(All have alternate, simple, oval to obovate, deciduous, serrate-margined leaves)

European Bird Cherry ♦ May Day Tree
(Prunus padus)

Leaves: Two or more glands or bumps on petiole.

Flowers/Fruit: Fragrant 1/2" white flowers in **elongated, drooping bunches** appearing in early May. Fruit is a 1/4" to 1/3" diameter black drupe maturing in mid to late summer.

General: Small to medium sized tree, depending on cultivar, native to Europe, Asia, and Japan. Shade intolerant.

Landscape Use: Black knot disease is a problem. Various crown and inflorescence sizes and foliage colors are available. Zones 3(2?)-7.

148

European bird cherry (*Prunus padus*)

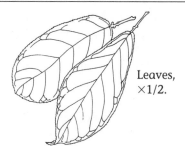

Leaves,
×1/2.

(from Dirr)

sour cherry (*Prunus cerasus*)

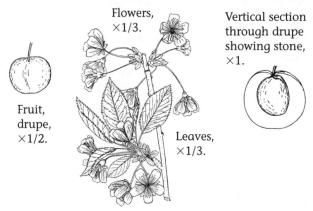

Flowers,
×1/3.

Vertical section
through drupe
showing stone,
×1.

Fruit,
drupe,
×1/2.

Leaves,
×1/3.

(from Britton & Brown Vol. II)

Sour Cherry   (*Prunus cerasus*)

Leaves: Doubly serrate; 2" to 3" long, slightly pubescent beneath; **no glands on petiole**.

Flowers/Fruit: White, 1/3" to 1/2" flowers in small clusters. Fruit a **large, bright red drupe**; juicy; typical pie cherry.

Bark: Shiny and layered with **prominent horizontal ridges or lenticels**.

General: Small tree native to Europe and Asia, but long cultivated around the world. Intermediate shade tolerance.

Landscape Use: Commonly planted orchard tree grown for "pie cherries". Avoid unless fruit is important. Better species are available for ornamental purposes. Zones 3-9.

149

Sweet Cherry ◆ Mazzard   *(Prunus avium)*

Leaves: Doubly serrate; 2" to 6" long, pubescent beneath; **2 prominent glands on petiole near blade**.

Flowers/Fruit: White, fragrant, 1" flowers in small clusters present in April. Fruit a **large, dark red drupe**; juicy; typical sweet cherry.

Bark: Shiny and layered with **prominent horizontal ridges or lenticels**.

General: Small tree native to Europe and Asia, but commonly grown around the world for its fruit. Shade intolerant.

Landscape Use: Typical sweet cherry orchard tree. Again, better ornamental species are available for the landscape if fruit is not important. Zones 3-8.

Sargent Cherry   *(Prunus sargentii)*

Leaves: Leaves 3" to 5" long; glabrous beneath; **two to four prominent glands on petiole near blade**.

Flowers/Fruit: **Pink**, 1" to 1-1/2" flowers in small clusters present in late April or early May. Fruit a 1/3" diameter purple to black drupe.

Bark: Shiny reddish-brown with **prominent horizontal ridges or lenticels**.

General: Medium-sized tree native to Japan. Shade intolerant.

Landscape Use: Good landscape tree that should be used more. Bark very attractive. Good fall color. Zones 4-7.

Japanese Flowering Cherry ◆ Oriental Cherry
(Prunus serrulata)

Leaves: Long, pointed tip; teeth often bristle-tipped; 2" to 5" long; glabrous beneath; **2 to 4 glands on petiole near blade**.

Flowers/Fruit: **Pink** (some cultivars white), 1/2" to 2-1/2" single or doubled flowers in small clusters present in April as leaves form. Fruit a small black drupe (cherry); often fruitless or nearly so.

Bark: Shiny, gray-brown, and peeling horizontally.

General: Native to China, Japan, and Korea, with many cultivars that are commonly grown around the world for their flowers. Shade intolerant.

Landscape Use: Oriental cherry prized for its beautiful flowers. 'Kwanzan' is a popular cultivar famous for its spring floral display in Washington D.C. Usually grafted several feet above the ground on a sweet cherry rootstock; does better on its own roots, but may get larger. Good bronze to red fall color. Ornamental cherries have some very good characteristics, and the *Prunus* genus is important in the

sweet cherry (*Prunus avium*)

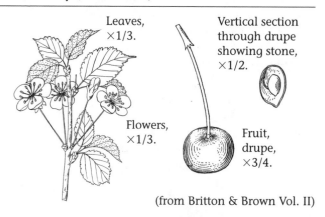

Leaves, ×1/3.

Flowers, ×1/3.

Vertical section through drupe showing stone, ×1/2.

Fruit, drupe, ×3/4.

(from Britton & Brown Vol. II)

Sargent cherry (*Prunus sargentii*)

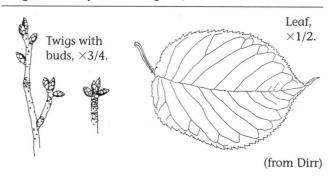

Twigs with buds, ×3/4.

Leaf, ×1/2.

(from Dirr)

Japanese flowering cherry (*Prunus serrulata*)

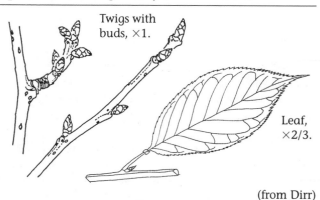

Twigs with buds, ×1.

Leaf, ×2/3.

(from Dirr)

wild for wildlife. However, in cultivated landscapes *Prunus* species tend to have a fair amount of problems, especially with various diseases. So plant what you like, but keep this in mind. Zones 5-9.

Higan Cherry   *(Prunus subhirtella)*

Leaves: Usually doubly serrate; 1" to 4" long; hairy on veins beneath; **glands on petiole near blade**.

Flowers/Fruit: Pink or white, single or double flowers in small groups that open in March or April before the leaves. Fruit a 1/3" diameter drupe (cherry); red at first, then black when mature.

General: Small to medium-sized tree; native to Japan. Shade intolerant.

Landscape Use: Weeping form is common and usually is grafted several feet above the ground. Should be a fairly good, reliable tree in the landscape, but know what you are getting since cultivars vary widely. Zones 4-9. A common hybrid is **Yoshino cherry** (*Prunus yedoensis*), probably a hybrid or hybrids of *P. serrulata* and *P. subhirtella*. Zones 5-8.

Peach   *(Prunus persica)*

Leaves: Oblong-lanceolate; 3" to 6" long, 3/4" to 1-1/2" wide; glabrous; serrate; short petiole with glands.

Flowers/Fruit: Pink to white, single or double flowers 2" to 2-1/2" wide. Fruit a **hairy, large red to yellow drupe (common peach)** with a groove down one side and a hard, wrinkled pit.

General: Native to China and long-cultivated. Very prone to pest damage. Shade intolerant.

Landscape Use: Should only be grown for fruit. Pests are a severe problem. Also not very cold-hardy, and trees planted as far north as Brigham City regularly get knocked back. Be sure not to water excessively. Many cultivars. Zones 5-9.

Apricot   *(Prunus armeniaca)*

Leaves: Ovate leaves **broader than in peach**.

Flowers/Fruit: Pink to white flowers 1" wide. Fruit similar to peach but **smaller and nearly glabrous with a smooth pit**.

General: Native to Asia and long-cultivated. Shade intolerant.

Landscape Use: Generally only grown for fruit, and I have not seen that many well-kept apricots. However, Dr. Phil Allen at BYU feels that apricot makes a good specimen tree with a nice branch structure. Pests can be a problem. More cold-hardy than peach and quite drought hardy. Many cultivars. Zones 4(3?)-9.

Higan cherry (*Prunus subhirtella*)

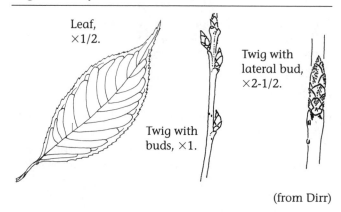

Leaf,
×1/2.

Twig with
buds, ×1.

Twig with
lateral bud,
×2-1/2.

(from Dirr)

Yoshino cherry (*Prunus × yedoensis*)

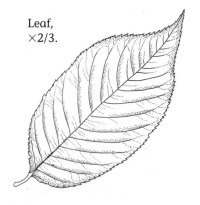

Leaf,
×2/3.

(from Dirr)

peach (*Prunus persica*)

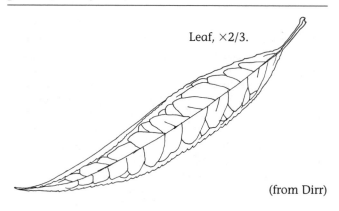

Leaf, ×2/3.

(from Dirr)

153

Apple   Genus *Malus*

Another important horticultural genus, with about 25 species worldwide grown for their fruit and flowers. Flowers perfect and showy, fruit a **fleshy pome** with several seeds, and twigs often have short, spiny spur shoots.

Apple   *(Malus pumila)*

Leaves: Alternate; simple; ovate; deciduous; serrate margin; white hairy beneath.

Twigs/Buds: Twigs red-brown; somewhat woolly; characteristic sweet taste. Terminal bud **woolly (particularly at tip)**, blunt; lateral buds similar but smaller.

Flowers/Fruit: Flowers 1" wide and showy; white to pink. Fruit a **pome or apple**; red, yellow, or green.

Bark: Thin; red-brown to gray-brown; divided by shallow furrows into wide, scaly ridges.

Wood: Not generally used for wood products other than fuel; hard; good firewood.

General: Not native to Utah; cultivated apples are of European or Asiatic origin. Fairly adaptable and tough, but prone to many minor and major pests. Shade intolerant.

Landscape Use: Not a good landscape tree unless fruit is desired. Perfect fruit involves extensive pesticide use. Most eating apples are cultivars or varieties that are grafted. Zones 3-9.

Crabapple   *(Malus species)*
*See also **Apple** description and illustrations*

Leaves: Similar to apple, but some species/cultivars have lobed leaves and undersides of leaves may or may not be hairy.

Flowers/Fruit: Flowers similar to apple; sometimes doubled (with extra sets of petals); cultivars available with white, pink, red, or purplish flowers. Fruit a red, yellow, orange, or green pome; mostly **smaller than apple**, 1/4" to 2" diameter, depending on cultivar.

General: Crabapples are a confusing group of trees from a horticultural or botanical standpoint. They consist of several species and hundreds of cultivars from all over the world. The most concise definition I have seen, by Michael Dirr, is that if the fruit is 2" in diameter or less it is a crabapple; if more than 2" it is an apple. Shade intolerant.

Landscape Use: Crabapples are extremely valuable from an ornamental standpoint, making excellent small to medium-sized landscape trees. They vary widely, however, in their disease resistance, ornamental characteristics, and size. For a very complete

apple (*Malus pumila*)

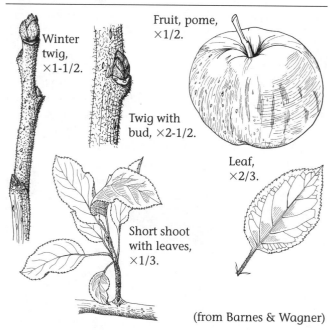

Winter twig, ×1-1/2.

Twig with bud, ×2-1/2.

Fruit, pome, ×1/2.

Leaf, ×2/3.

Short shoot with leaves, ×1/3.

(from Barnes & Wagner)

crabapple (*Malus* spp.)

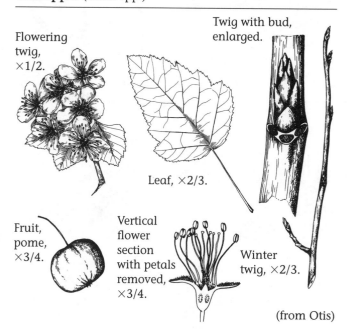

Flowering twig, ×1/2.

Twig with bud, enlarged.

Leaf, ×2/3.

Fruit, pome, ×3/4.

Vertical flower section with petals removed, ×3/4.

Winter twig, ×2/3.

(from Otis)

155

discussion of crabapples, see Dirr (1990). Zones 3-9. The crabapple selection guide in this volume lists some highly-rated crabapple species/cultivars and their characteristics.

Pear   Genus *Pyrus*

Another genus known for its fruit and flowers; about 25 species native to Europe, Asia, and northern Africa. Flowers perfect and showy; fruit a fleshy, often elongated pome with several seeds.

Callery Pear   *(Pyrus calleryana)*

Leaves: Alternate; simple; broadly ovate to ovate; 1-1/2" to 3" long and nearly as wide; deciduous; rounded teeth on margin; **leaf base flat across or somewhat cordate**; glabrous; dark green; glossy; turning orange, yellow, red, or purple in fall.

Callery pear *(Pyrus calleryana)*

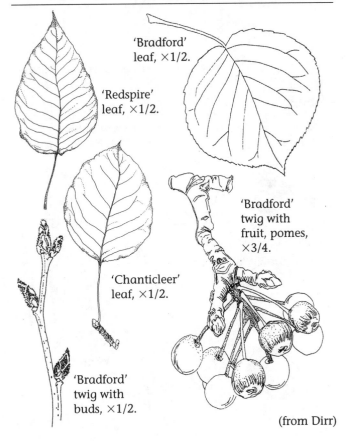

'Bradford' leaf, ×1/2.

'Redspire' leaf, ×1/2.

'Chanticleer' leaf, ×1/2.

'Bradford' twig with fruit, pomes, ×3/4.

'Bradford' twig with buds, ×1/2.

(from Dirr)

Twigs/Buds: Twigs brownish-green; glabrous and glossy when mature. Terminal bud 1/4" to 1/2" long, **very wooly**, gray-brown; lateral buds similar in size and appearance.

Flowers/Fruit: Flowers showy, white; 1/2" to 1" in diameter. Fruit a **pome; rounded; 1/2" across or less; reddish-brown**; production is uneven and many trees may have no fruit.

Bark: Gray-brown; smooth on younger stems breaking vertically into wide, flat plates.

Wood: No information available.

General: Native to China. Fairly tough and withstands high soil pH quite well. Shade intolerant.

Landscape Use: This small to medium-sized tree with a nice, conical crown has been widely planted throughout the U.S., mainly as the cultivar 'Bradford'. Its white flowers in early spring and its fall color are outstanding. It has several problems, however, including a size that eventually is bigger than most people expect, occasional winter kill of buds and possibly cambium in colder locations, poor branch attachment due to included bark, and a flower odor that is objectionable to some. Other selections of *Pyrus calleryana* that may have less problems include "Aristocrat", "Chanticleer", and "Redspire". Zones 5(4?)-9. **Common pear** (*Pyrus communis*) has more elongated leaves and less dramatic flowers with a much larger yellow to red to purple fruit; should only be grown where fruit is desired. Zones 4-9. **Ussurian pear** (*Pyrus ussuriensis*) is a cold-hardy pear also worth trying in Utah, with good white flowers, shiny dark green leaves, and red-purple fall color. Zones 3-7.

common pear (*Pyrus communis*)

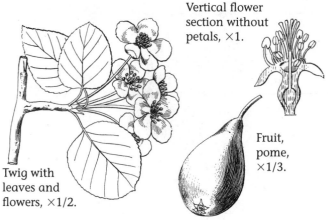

Vertical flower section without petals, ×1.

Fruit, pome, ×1/3.

Twig with leaves and flowers, ×1/2.

(from Britton & Brown Vol. II)

Mountain-ash, Rowan   Genus *Sorbus*

This genus includes about 80 species native throughout the Northern Hemisphere and 4 trees native to North America. Flowers are perfect and showy, and fruit is a fleshy, round pome. Not true ashes (family Oleaceae, genus *Fraxinus*).

European Mountain-ash ◆ Rowan
(Sorbus aucuparia)

Leaves: Alternate; once pinnately compound; 5" to 9" long; deciduous; 9 to 15 leaflets; leaflets 1" to 2" long, oblong, margin sharply serrate; dark green and glabrous above, whitish beneath; hairy; beautiful yellow, red, or purple fall color.

Twigs/Buds: Twigs stout; at first brown and hairy, later becoming gray-brown and glabrous. Buds 1/4" to 3/4" long; red-brown; not sticky; **very hairy**.

Flowers/Fruit: Flowers white, 1/3" diameter, borne in large, flat-topped bunches. Fruit a **berry-like pome**; round; 1/4" to 1/2" diameter; **bright orange-red**; bitter taste; liked by birds.

Bark: Thin; gray-brown; smooth or slightly scaly.

Wood: Unimportant; sapwood light colored, thick; heartwood light brown; light; soft; weak; diffuse-porous.

European mountain-ash *(Sorbus aucuparia)*

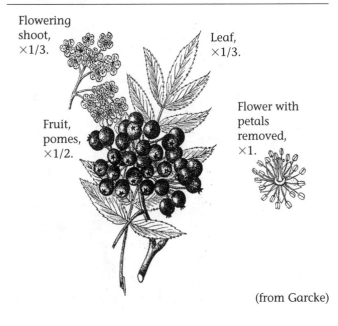

Flowering shoot, ×1/3.

Leaf, ×1/3.

Fruit, pomes, ×1/2.

Flower with petals removed, ×1.

(from Garcke)

General: Native from Europe to western Asia and Siberia and naturalized in some parts of the northern U.S. and Canada. A small, slow-growing, short-lived tree that prefers cool, moist sites. Shade intolerant.

Landscape Use: Often planted in Utah and elsewhere because of its small size, great fall color, and attractive fruit. Subject to many pests, however, including fireblight and borers, and old trees rarely look good. Zones 3-7. ❖**Greene mountain-ash** (*Sorbus scopulina*) is a shrub or small tree with smaller leaves native to cool, moist canyon sites in Utah and rarely planted. Zones 2-6. **American mountain-ash** (*S. americana*) is an eastern U.S. native similar to European

Greene mountain-ash (*Sorbus scopulina*)

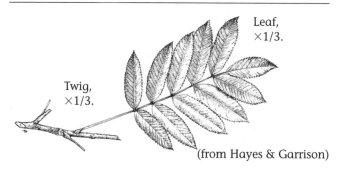

Leaf, ×1/3.

Twig, ×1/3.

(from Hayes & Garrison)

American mountain-ash (*Sorbus americana*)

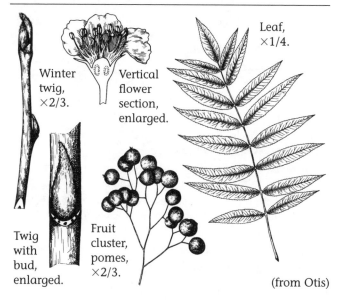

Winter twig, ×2/3.

Vertical flower section, enlarged.

Leaf, ×1/4.

Twig with bud, enlarged.

Fruit cluster, pomes, ×2/3.

(from Otis)

159

Korean mountain-ash (*Sorbus alnifolia*)

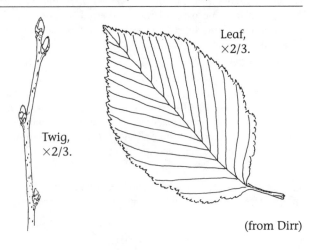

Leaf,
×2/3.

Twig,
×2/3.

(from Dirr)

mountain-ash but with sticky, nearly hairless buds and longer leaflets (up to 2-1/2" long). Less available than European, but could be planted in Utah. Zones 3-6. **Korean mountain-ash** (*Sorbus alnifolia*) has simple leaves similar to beech and nice fall color; otherwise similar to European mountain-ash but is a superior species that should be planted more often. Zones 3-7.

Serviceberry, Shadbush   Genus *Amelanchier*

This genus includes about 25 species, with 18 native to the U.S. and one native to Utah. Flowers are perfect and showy, and fruit is a small, berry-like pome.

❖Saskatoon ◆ Western Serviceberry
(Amelanchier alnifolia)

Leaves: Alternate; simple; broad oval to round; 1" to 2" long; deciduous; coarsely serrate margin; dark green above, paler beneath; petiole 3/8" to 3/4" long.

Twigs/Buds: Twigs slender; red-brown to gray-brown; hairy at first, later becoming glabrous.

Flowers/Fruit: Flowers similar to downy serviceberry (below), but in **1" long clusters**. Fruit also similar to downy serviceberry; sweet, juicy, edible.

Bark: Thin; brown to gray; smooth.

Wood: Unimportant; similar to downy serviceberry; diffuse-porous.

Saskatoon (*Amelanchier alnifolia*)

Leaves, ×1/2.

Fruit, pomes, ×1/2.

Twig with buds, ×1/2.

(from Sudworth 1908)

Utah serviceberry (*Amelanchier utahensis*)

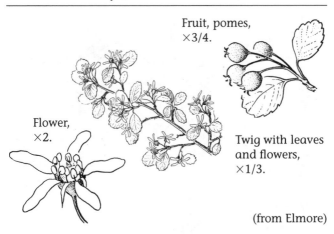

Fruit, pomes, ×3/4.

Flower, ×2.

Twig with leaves and flowers, ×1/3.

(from Elmore)

General: A large shrub or small tree native to most of the north-western U.S. and western Canada on fairly cool, moist sites. In Utah found in protected, cool canyon locations. Often found in groups due to sprouting from underground stems. Shade tolerant.

Landscape Use: Seldom planted in cultivated landscapes. Zones 3-8. ❖**Utah serviceberry** (*Amelanchier utahensis*) is another Utah native serviceberry that could be planted but is not. Its leaves are covered with fine hairs and the fruit is not juicy, but is sweet and edible. Also a mountain canyon species. Zones 3-8.

161

Other Serviceberries

Downy Serviceberry *(Amelanchier arborea)*

Leaves: Alternate; simple; oblong-ovate to oval; 2" to 4" long; deciduous; finely serrate margin; pointed tip; dark green and glabrous above, pale beneath; fall color yellow, orange, or red; petioles thin, 3/8" to 1-1/4" long.

Twigs/Buds: Twigs slender; red-brown to dark gray; bitter almond taste. Terminal bud 1/4" to 1/2" long, conical, pointed, chestnut-brown.

Flowers/Fruit: Attractive **white flowers with narrow, strap-like petals; borne in small bunches 2" to 4" long**; appearing early, before leaves. Fruit a **berry-like pome**; round; 1/4" to 1/2" diameter; dark red to purple; more or less with a gray to white waxy coating; sweet, dry, edible.

Bark: Thin; gray, often streaked with darker lines; smooth or slightly furrowed with scaly ridges.

downy serviceberry *(Amelanchier arborea)*

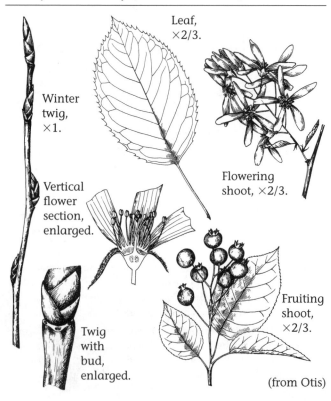

Leaf, ×2/3.

Winter twig, ×1.

Vertical flower section, enlarged.

Flowering shoot, ×2/3.

Twig with bud, enlarged.

Fruiting shoot, ×2/3.

(from Otis)

162

Wood: Unimportant; sapwood light colored, thick; heartwood light brown; heavy; hard; close-grained; diffuse-porous.

General: Native to most of the eastern U.S., where it often is found as a small understory tree in mixed hardwood forests. Shade tolerant.

Landscape Use: Seldom planted, but should be more often as cultivars become more available. Shade tolerance, attractive flowers, relatively small size, and good fall color make it a desirable tree. Fairly tough and pest-free. Zones 4-9.

Cliffrose   Genus *Cowania*

This genus of evergreen shrubs contains about 4 species native to the southwestern U.S. and Mexico. Two species are native to Utah. Flowers are perfect.

❖Cliffrose ◆ Quininebush   (*Cowania mexicana*)

Leaves: Alternate; simple; 3- to 5-lobed; 1/4" to 1/2" long; **evergreen, leaves persistent for two years; thick; dark green and glandular above**, paler and hairy beneath.

Twigs/Buds: Twigs slender; stiff; reddish. Buds small and inconspicuous, scaly.

cliffrose (*Cowania mexicana*)

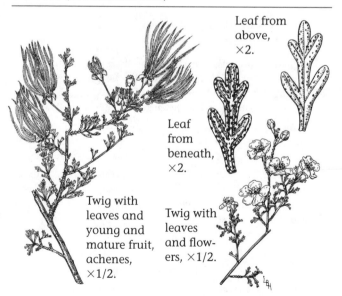

Leaf from above, ×2.

Leaf from beneath, ×2.

Twig with leaves and young and mature fruit, achenes, ×1/2.

Twig with leaves and flowers, ×1/2.

(from Benson & Darrow)

Flowers/Fruit: Flowers creamy-white, rose-like with 5 petals; 1" in diameter; appear in April to May. Fruit is a small achene, with 5 to 8 grouped at each flower, tipped by a **2" long, white, hairy plume** (a persistent style from the flower).

Bark: Thin; red-brown to gray; breaking into long, narrow strips.

Wood: Unimportant and little known; heartwood dark red-brown; hard and dense; makes good firewood; diffuse-porous.

General: Native to the from southwestern Colorado to eastern California and Mexico, including southwest Utah, where it is found on dry sites. This species usually is shrubby, but can reach 25' tall. The leaves are bitter, but are browsed by wildlife. Shade intolerant. Welsh *et al.* call this species *Purshia mexicana*.

Landscape Use: This species is seldom planted, but could be used on dry sites. It is very drought resistant and tough, and the flowers are quite ornamental. The fruit also is interesting. Zones 5-9.

Mountain-mahogany   Genus *Cercocarpus*

A shrubby genus with about 20 species native to the western U.S. and Mexico. Three species are native to Utah, with only one reaching tree size. The two smaller, shrubbier species are birchleaf mountain-mahogany (*Cercocarpus montanus*) and dwarf mountain-mahogany (*Cercocarpus intricatus*). Flowers are perfect, but without petals, and fruit is a small achene with a long, twisted plume.

❖Curlleaf Mountain-mahogany
(Cercocarpus ledifolius)

Leaves: Alternate, with several borne on short spur-shoots; simple; lanceolate; 1/2" to 1" long; **evergreen, leaves persistent for two years; margin entire and edges are rolled under; leathery**; shiny dark green above, paler and finely hairy beneath; petiole short.

Twigs/Buds: Twigs stout; stiff; early-on pubescent and red-brown; becoming glabrous and brown or silvery; with short spur-shoots that hold leaves and flowers. Buds small, scaly, and hairy.

Flowers/Fruit: Flowers are small and inconspicuous, with no petals; solitary or in 2's or 3's. Fruit is a 1/4" long, dry achene with a **2" to 3" long, hairy, corkscrew-twisted tail or plume** attached (a persistent style from the flower).

Bark: Thick; red-brown; very firm; furrowed.

Wood: Unimportant and little known; heartwood dark red-brown; hard and dense; makes good firewood; diffuse-porous.

General: Native to much of the interior western U.S., including most of Utah, where it is found in higher, open mountain locations.

curlleaf mountain-mahogany (*Cercocarpus ledifolius*)

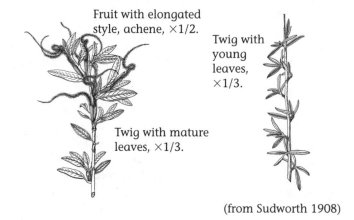

Fruit with elongated style, achene, ×1/2.

Twig with young leaves, ×1/3.

Twig with mature leaves, ×1/3.

(from Sudworth 1908)

Shrubby, but can get quite large, with a broad, rounded crown. Long-lived and slow-growing, probably needing fire or disturbance to regenerate naturally from seed. An important species for wildlife. Shade intolerant.

Landscape Use: Mountain-mahoganies are rarely used in cultivated landscapes, but could be used more. Availability would be mostly as seedlings through conservation nurseries or those specializing in native plants. They are fairly drought resistant and tough, and are potentially good choices for xeriscapes. Fruit is very interesting. Zones 3(2?)-8.

Hawthorn   Genus *Crataegus*

There are between 300 and 1,000 species of hawthorns worldwide, with over 100 species native to North America and one native to Utah. Most hawthorns are small trees or large shrubs, and they readily hybridize, making identification difficult at times. As with most *Rosaceae*, flowers are perfect and showy; appear in mid-May to early June. The fruit is a small, apple-like pome.

❖Black Hawthorn ◆ Douglas Hawthorn (*Crataegus douglasii*)

Leaves: Alternate; simple; oval; 1" to 3" long; deciduous; margin sharply **doubly serrate or shallowly lobed, especially on the upper half**; glabrous or nearly so; dark green above; petiole 1/2" long.

Twigs/Buds: Twigs more or less zig-zag; usually with stiff, sharp, 1" long thorns. Terminal bud small, round, scaly, and shiny brown; lateral buds similar.

Flowers/Fruit: Flowers showy, white, 5-petalled, 1/2" to 3/4" in diameter; appear in small groups at the ends of the branches in spring. Fruit a small pome; round; 1/3" to 1/2" diameter; flesh dry and mealy, but edible; red at first and **black when mature** in fall, often persisting into winter.

Bark: Dark gray; scaly or slightly furrowed.

Wood: Unimportant; sapwood light colored, thick; heartwood red-brown; heavy; hard; close-grained; diffuse-porous.

General: Black hawthorn is native throughout the West and in the mountains throughout Utah. A small, slow growing tree that can be shrubby. Shade intolerant.

Landscape Use: This native hawthorn is rare in cultivated landscapes. It could be used more in naturalized landscapes and would be good for wildlife habitat plantings. Zones 2-8.

Other Hawthorns
(All have alternate, simple, deciduous, serrate-margined or lobed leaves; fruit a small pome that usually persists into winter. See Dirr (1990) for a more complete discussion of hawthorns.)

Cockspur Hawthorn   *(Crataegus crusgalli)*

Leaves: Oval; 1" to 4" long and 1/3 as wide; finely serrate margin, seldom lobed; glabrous; shiny above; leathery; purple-red fall color.

Twigs/Buds: Longer thorns than *C. douglasii*, 1-1/2" to 3" long, though one common cultivar, var. *inermis*, is thornless.

Flowers/Fruit: Flowers white; 1/2" diameter; similar to *C. douglasii*. Fruit a 3/8" to 1/2" diameter pome, **deep orange-red when mature**.

General: Native to much of the eastern U.S. Fairly tough and drought tolerant; pH adaptable. Shade intolerant.

Landscape Use: A nice small tree with good fall color, attractive persistent fruit in winter, and thornless if var. *inermis* is used. Is being planted some in Utah and some nurseries are carrying it. Should be planted more. Zones 3-8.

Washington Hawthorn   *(Crataegus phaenopyrum)*

Leaves: **Nearly deltoid or triangular;** 1" to 3" long and nearly as wide; serrate margin with several small lobes; glabrous; dark green and glossy above; thin; orange to red fall color; petiole 1" long.

black hawthorn *(Crataegus douglasii)*

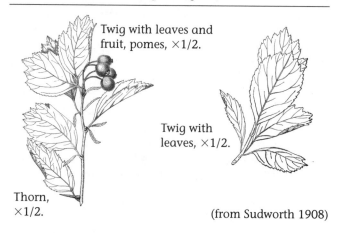

Twig with leaves and fruit, pomes, ×1/2.

Twig with leaves, ×1/2.

Thorn, ×1/2.

(from Sudworth 1908)

cockspur hawthorn *(Crataegus crusgalli)*

Flowering shoot, ×1/3.

Fruiting shoot with thorns, ×1/3.

(from Sargent)

Washington hawthorn *(Crataegus phaenopyrum)*

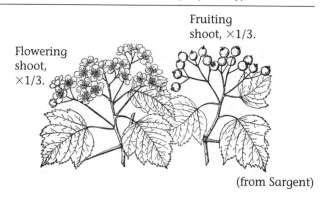

Fruiting shoot, ×1/3.

Flowering shoot, ×1/3.

(from Sargent)

Twigs/Buds: First year twigs dark green-red; turning light gray in later years. Numerous 1" to 3" long, slender thorns. Buds small, round, dark red.

Flowers/Fruit: Flowers white; 1/2" diameter; similar to *C. douglasii*. Fruit a 1/4" diameter pome, **bright orange-red when mature, glossy**; persistent into winter.

General: Native to much of the eastern U.S. Also fairly tough, drought tolerant and pH adaptable. Shade intolerant.

Landscape Use: This is one of the best hawthorns where its long thorns won't cause safety problems. It has beautiful flowers, great fall color, attractive fruit that is liked by birds, and a small size. It is being planted quite a bit in Utah, and more planting is warranted. Zones 3-8.

Lavalle Hawthorn   *(Crataegus × lavallei)*

Leaves: Elliptic to obovate; 2" to 4" long and half as wide; upper 2/3's of margin serrate with no lobes; shiny dark green and glabrous above when mature; densely, **finely pubescent beneath**, especially on veins; thick; stay on late in fall and turn dark purple, bronze, or brown.

Twigs/Buds: Twigs stout; greenish, with **many hairs at first**, turning glabrous and gray-green as they age; thorns are fairly short and stout, may have buds, relatively few thorns present.

Flowers/Fruit: Flowers white; 3/4" diameter; similar to *C. douglasii*. Fruit fairly large; a **5/8" to 3/4" diameter** pome, bright orange-red when mature, somewhat glossy; persistent into winter.

General: A hybrid of *C. crusgalli* and probably *C. pubescens*. Maybe not as tough as some other hawthorns, though pH adaptable. Shade intolerant.

Landscape Use: A small, dense-crowned tree with an often lop-sided appearance. It has nice flowers, attractive fruit, and dark-green leaves. Though supposedly cold-hardy, I have seen what appears to be cold damage on these trees in Logan. Zones 4-8.

English Hawthorn   *(Crataegus laevigata)*

Leaves: Broad ovate; 1" to 2-1/2" long and nearly as wide; fairly flat across the bottom, with 3 to 5 finely toothed, distinct lobes; dark green and glabrous in summer, turning brown in fall; petiole 1/4" to 3/4" long.

Twigs/Buds: Twigs greenish; glabrous; thorns are fairly short, 1/2" to 1" long, and may not be present.

Flowers/Fruit: Flowers sometimes white, but often **pink, or red**, depending on cultivar; 5/8" diameter; often doubled. Fruit a 1/4"

Lavalle hawthorn (*Crataegus × lavallei*)

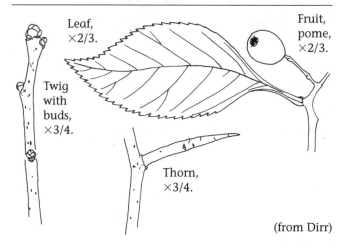

Leaf,
×2/3.

Fruit,
pome,
×2/3.

Twig
with
buds,
×3/4.

Thorn,
×3/4.

(from Dirr)

English hawthorn (*Crataegus laevigata*)

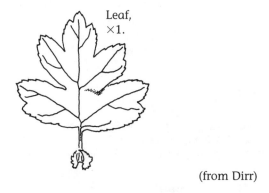

Leaf,
×1.

(from Dirr)

to 1/2" diameter pome, orange-red to deep red when mature, fairly dull; persistent into winter.

General: Native to Europe and northern Africa. Also called *C. oxyacantha* by some. Seems to be adaptable to a variety of sites. Shade intolerant.

Landscape Use: A small tree up to about 20' tall, with a rounded crown. Often seen in a pink to nearly red-flowered form; very beautiful. Older trunks of the trees I have seen in Logan **split into longitudinal segments**, almost like a twisted bundle of 1" to 2" diameter stems. Zones 4-8.

Green Hawthorn   *(Crataegus viridis)*

Leaves: Elliptic to ovate; 1-1/2" to 3" long and 2/3's as wide; margin serrate and shallowly lobed near the tip; shiny dark green and glabrous above; lighter beneath with some hair on veins; purple to red fall color; petiole 1/2" to 1-1/2" long.

Twigs/Buds: Twigs gray-brown; glabrous; thorns 1-1/2" long, often absent.

Flowers/Fruit: Flowers white; 3/4" diameter. Fruit a **1/4" to 1/3" diameter** pome, bright red when mature; persistent into winter.

General: Native to the eastern U.S. Shade intolerant.

Landscape Use: Another attractive hawthorn with nicely colored fruit. Seldom planted in Utah, but worth trying. Zones 4-8.

FABACEAE

Legume family. Contains about 550 genera and 15,000 species that are widely distributed around the world. Second only to the grass family in economic importance worldwide, though the woody species in this family are less important than some of the herbaceous species (beans, peas, alfalfa, clover, etc.). Most of the species in this family have root nodules with bacteria in them that can fix nitrogen, though many of the trees do not. **The fruit is a legume**.

Mesquite   Genus *Prosopis*

This genus of tough, drought-hardy trees and shrubs with spiny branches is found mainly in the southwestern U.S. and Mexico. Only one species commonly reaches tree size in Utah.

❖Honey Mesquite   *(Prosopis juliflora)*

Leaves: Alternate; twice (sometimes three to four times) pinnately compound; pinnae (the smallest branches of the leaf that hold the leaflets) each with 12 to 30 small leaflets; deciduous; leaflets linear to oblong, 1/2" to 2" long, margins entire, glabrous; petiole tipped with a spine; no notable fall color.

Twigs/Buds: Twigs glabrous; smooth; with 1/2" to 2" long spines at each leaf. No terminal bud; lateral buds small, round, brown.

Flowers/Fruit: Flowers perfect, **yellow, fragrant**, small; appear throughout the summer. **Fruit a thin, flat to round legume**; yellowish; 4" to 9" long and 1/4" to 1/2" wide; constricted between 1/4" long, brown seeds; edible.

green hawthorn (*Crataegus viridis*)

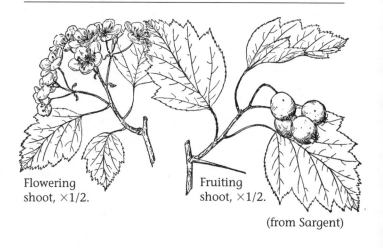

Flowering
shoot, ×1/2.

Fruiting
shoot, ×1/2.

(from Sargent)

honey mesquite (*Prosopis glandulosa*)

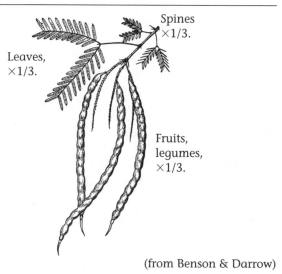

Spines
×1/3.

Leaves,
×1/3.

Fruits,
legumes,
×1/3.

(from Benson & Darrow)

Bark: Thick; dark red to brown; scaly and furrowed.

Wood: Very hard, heavy; used for lumber, firewood; heartwood brown, sapwood yellow; ring-porous.

General: Native throughout much of the southwestern U.S. south into Mexico, including extreme southwest Utah. This shrub to small tree is well adapted to desert sites with a deep, extensive

171

root system. It tolerates heat, drought, high soil pH, and salinity and is quite long-lived. Shade intolerant.

Landscape Use: This tough tree is seldom planted and likely is not very cold hardy, but it could be used in natural landscapes in Washington County. Zones 7(?)-10.

Mimosa   Genus *Albizia*

This genus contains about 25 tropical and subtropical species native to Asia, Africa, and Australia, with one native to Mexico and one planted in warmer parts of Utah. All are deciduous, have twice pinnately compound leaves, and a long thin pod or legume for a fruit.

Mimosa ♦ Silk-tree ♦ Albizia   *(Albizia julibrissin)*

Leaves: Alternate; twice pinnately compound; 10 to 25 pinnae (the smallest branches of the leaf that hold the leaflets), each with 40 to 60 small, leaflets; deciduous; leaflets sickle-shaped and oblong, uneven at the base, 1/4" to 1/2" long, margins entire, slightly hairy on midribs beneath; dark green with no notable fall color; leaves emerge in May or June.

Twigs/Buds: Twigs glabrous; angled; green; with many small lenticels. No terminal bud; lateral buds small, round, brown.

Flowers/Fruit: Flowers perfect, **pink, with many pink stamens 1" long or more**; flowers arranged in small heads at ends of branches, emerging continuously from May to August. **Fruit a thin, flat, strap-shaped legume**; gray-brown; 4" to 6" long and 1" wide; matures in September and October and persists through the winter, often in large numbers.

Bark: Smooth and gray-brown.

Wood: Little known and unimportant; ring-porous.

General: Native from China to Iran, but heavily planted and naturalized in the southeastern U.S. Small to medium sized with a broad, flat-topped crown. Fairly susceptible to pests in the southeastern U.S., but less problems here in Utah. Tolerant of heat, dryness, high soil pH and salinity. Shade intolerant.

Landscape Use: This tree is popular because of its fine texture and showy pink flowers present through much of the summer, though litter can be a problem. It is damaged by temperatures below about -5°F and shouldn't be planted in colder locations, but may do well on warmer sites along the Wasatch Front, as well as in the St. George area. I have seen a mimosa planted in Logan that looks like it grows well but dies to the ground most years. Zones 6-9.

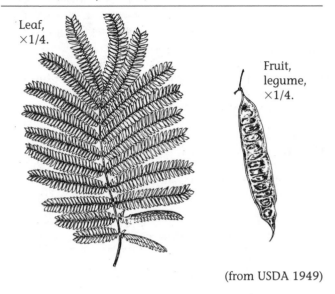

Leaf, ×1/4.

Fruit, legume, ×1/4.

(from USDA 1949)

Redbud   Genus *Cercis*

This is a small genus with 7 species worldwide, mostly in southern Europe and Asia, and with two species native to North America and one to Utah. All are deciduous, have simple leaves, and a thin pod or legume for a fruit.

Eastern Redbud ♦ Judas-tree   *(Cercis canadensis)*

Leaves: Alternate; simple; **heart-shaped**; 3" to 5" wide; deciduous; entire margin; angled or pointed at the tip; usually glabrous; purple when young, turning dark green when mature; nice yellow fall color; petiole long, slender.

Twigs/Buds: Twigs usually zigzag; bark on twigs glossy brown. No terminal bud; lateral buds small, blunt, scaly, chestnut-brown, possible with another, smaller bud present just below it.

Flowers/Fruit: **Beautiful purple-pink, pea-like flowers** (white on one cultivar) that appear before the leaves in April; perfect; flowers buds round and borne in groups on stalks. Fruit a legume; short-stalked; flat; brown; 2" to 4" long; 1/2" wide; pointed on both ends; contains 8 to 12 brown, hard seeds.

Bark: Thin; gray; becoming scaly on old trunks with attractive cinnamon-red inner bark.

Wood: Little information published; hard; brown.

173

General: Native to most of the eastern U.S. (not Utah), where it often grows naturally as a small understory tree in the partial shade from larger overstory trees. Never gets very large. Shade tolerant.

Landscape Use: Very nice tree that can be difficult to get started, but does well and is quite adaptable once established. Beautiful flowers that appear very early in the spring, nice leaves and bark, and small size all make it very worthwhile. Best grown in full to partial shade under other trees or on the north or east sides of a building. Sun-grown trees will have more compact, rounded crowns and may not do well in very hot, dry areas. Zones 3-9. **California redbud** or **western redbud** (*Cercis occidentalis*), native to southern Utah, Arizona, Nevada, and California, is a shrub to small tree similar to *C. canadensis* but with smaller leaves that are not pointed at the tip. Worth trying in warm locations. Zones 7-9.

eastern redbud (*Cercis canadensis*)

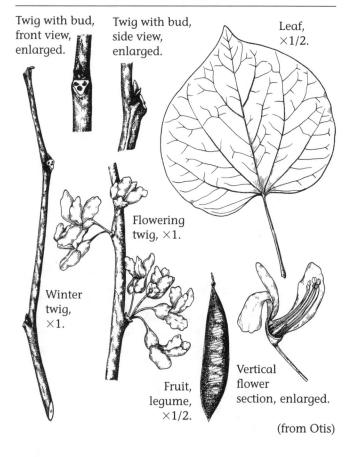

Twig with bud, front view, enlarged.

Twig with bud, side view, enlarged.

Leaf, ×1/2.

Flowering twig, ×1.

Winter twig, ×1.

Fruit, legume, ×1/2.

Vertical flower section, enlarged.

(from Otis)

California redbud (*Cercis occidentalis*)

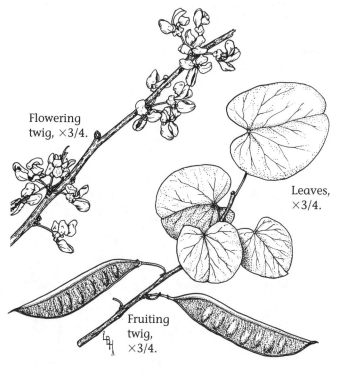

Flowering twig, ×3/4.

Leaves, ×3/4.

Fruiting twig, ×3/4.

(from Benson & Darrow)

Honeylocust   Genus *Gleditsia*

About 12 species of *Gleditsia* exist in North America, Asia, tropical Africa, and South America. All are deciduous, have compound leaves, a pod or legume for a fruit, and most are armed with thorns in nature.

Honeylocust   *(Gleditsia triacanthos)*

Leaves: Alternate; both **once and twice pinnately compound**; once pinnately compound leaves with 15 to 30 nearly stalk-less leaflets; deciduous; twice pinnate leaves with 4 to 7 pairs of 6" to 8" long, lateral "branches"; leaflets ovate to ovate-lanceolate, up to 1-1/2" long by 3/4" wide, margins with fine, rounded teeth, leaflet tip pointed or rounded, glabrous; bright green; nice yellow color in fall.

Twigs/Buds: Twigs stout to slender; glabrous; glossy; zigzag; native trees having stiff, sometimes branched, brown to red thorns

175

from 3" to 12" long; thornless varieties are more often planted. No terminal bud; lateral buds small, nearly hidden by bark, 3 or more at each leaf scar.

Flowers/Fruit: Flowers dioecious (some are perfect), small, greenish-white or yellow; not showy; appearing after leaves open. **Fruit a flat, strap-shaped legume**; green at first, maturing red-brown; twisted; 12" to 18" long; containing 12-14 dark brown, oval seeds; many cultivars do not bear fruit.

honeylocust (*Gleditsia triacanthos*)

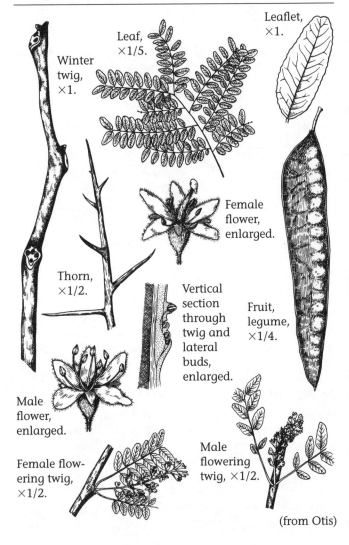

Leaflet, ×1.

Leaf, ×1/5.

Winter twig, ×1.

Female flower, enlarged.

Thorn, ×1/2.

Vertical section through twig and lateral buds, enlarged.

Fruit, legume, ×1/4.

Male flower, enlarged.

Female flowering twig, ×1/2.

Male flowering twig, ×1/2.

(from Otis)

176

Bark: Smooth and gray on younger branches; on older stems becoming gray-brown to nearly black, and broken by vertical furrows into plates or scaly ridges.

Wood: Slightly important where native; sapwood yellow; heartwood red-brown; growth rings conspicuous; ring-porous; rays conspicuous to naked eye; used for veneer and firewood.

General: Native to most of the eastern U.S. Very hardy and drought resistant; tolerant of salt and high pH. Often invades old fields where native, with trunks covered with red thorns. This species does not fix nitrogen. Shade intolerant.

Landscape Use: A good, large landscape tree because of its relative toughness, its adaptability to a variety of sites, and its fine texture and light shade. Does well even if surrounded by pavement. However, it is over-planted in Utah and is not trouble-free. *Thyronectria* and other cankers entering through bark injuries have become problems elsewhere and eventually may cause trouble here. Thornless and fruitless cultivars generally are planted. Zones 3-9.

Coffeetree   Genus *Gymnocladus*

This genus has only 2 species, one in North America and one in China. Both are deciduous, have twice compound leaves, and a pod or legume for a fruit.

Kentucky Coffeetree   *(Gymnocladus dioicus)*

Leaves: Alternate; twice pinnately compound; very large, **can be 2' to 3' long**; deciduous; 20 to 40 ovate leaflets, 1-1/2" long, pointed at tip, entire margins, glabrous; dark blue-green; yellow fall color.

Twigs/Buds: Twigs very stout; brown; glabrous or velvety; pith is wide and salmon-pink. No terminal bud; lateral buds deeply sunken in the bark; brown; hairy; 2 at each leaf scar.

Flowers/Fruit: Flowers dioecious (some are perfect), greenish-white, attractive; borne in large groups but not very conspicuous. **Fruit a flat legume; red-brown; leathery; pointed; 4" to 6" long by 1-3/4" wide**; remaining closed until or through winter; contains 4 to 8 olive-brown, 1/2" diameter, flat, very-hard seeds imbedded in a sweet pulp.

Bark: Smooth and brown to gray on younger branches; on older stems turning gray, furrowed, with curved scales.

Wood: Unimportant; sapwood yellow; heartwood red; growth rings conspicuous; ring-porous; rays not conspicuous to naked eye.

General: A fairly large tree native to most of the central-eastern U.S. Never very common naturally. Seeds ground and used as a

Kentucky coffeetree (*Gymnocladus dioicus*)

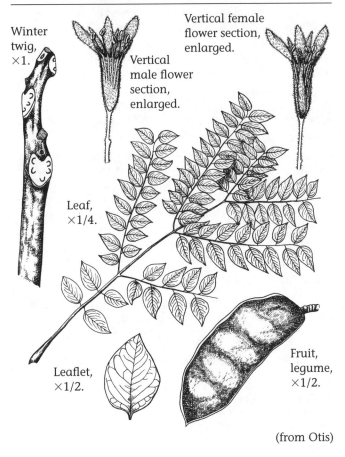

Winter twig, ×1.

Vertical male flower section, enlarged.

Vertical female flower section, enlarged.

Leaf, ×1/4.

Leaflet, ×1/2.

Fruit, legume, ×1/2.

(from Otis)

coffee substitute by early settlers where native. Well-adapted to a variety of climates and soils. Shade intolerant.

Landscape Use: An excellent landscape tree that is seldom planted, but should be more often. Its stout twigs give it an interesting coarse texture in winter, and the dark blue-green foliage is very nice. The bark also is very attractive. The pods make it somewhat messy, but usually are not abundant. Zones 3-8.

Yellowwood   Genus *Cladrastis*

Another small genus, with 3 species native to eastern Asia and one to North America. All have deciduous, compound leaves, and a pod or legume for a fruit.

Yellowwood *(Cladrastis lutea or C. kentuckea)*

Leaves: Alternate; **once pinnately compound; 8" to 12" long; deciduous; 5 to 11 elliptic leaflets, 2" to 4" long** (terminal leaflet the largest), pointed apex, entire margins, glabrous; bright green; yellow fall color; petiole base swollen, covering bud.

Twigs/Buds: Twigs slender; zig-zag; red-brown; glabrous. No terminal bud; several lateral buds at each leaf scar packed into a brown, hairy cone, covered by the leaf base and nearly surrounded by the leaf scar.

Flowers/Fruit: Flowers perfect, white, 1" to 1-1/4" long, pea-like, attractive, fragrant; borne in large, drooping groups in May to early June; very attractive. **Fruit a 2" to 4" long, 1/2" wide legume; brown;** maturing in October; contains 4 to 6 brown, flat, very hard seeds.

Bark: Very smooth and gray on young and old branches.

Wood: Unimportant; named for yellow heartwood; growth rings conspicuous; ring-porous.

General: Native to the southeastern U.S. and parts of the Midwest. Not common even where native. Likes well-drained, rich soil. Fixes nitrogen. Shade intolerant.

Landscape Use: This is a good, medium-sized landscape tree that is seldom planted, but should be more often because of its nice flowers and foliage. Weak branch attachments due to included bark can be a problem. Zones 4-8.

yellowwood *(Cladrastis lutea)*

Flowering twig with leaves, ×1/3.

Twig with fruit, legumes, ×1/3.

(from Sargent)

179

Scholar-tree   Genus *Sophora*

This genus has about 20 species native to Asia and North America. They are deciduous or evergreen and sometimes herbaceous, have compound leaves, and a pod or legume for a fruit.

Japanese Pagodatree ♦ Scholar-tree
(Sophora japonica)

Leaves: Alternate; once pinnately compound; 6" to 10" long; deciduous; 7 to 17 ovate to ovate-lanceolate leaflets, 1" to 2" long, entire margins, rounded at base, bright green and lustrous above, somewhat waxy to hairy beneath.

Twigs/Buds: Twigs slender; glabrous; **green on twigs up to 4 to 5 years old**; pith solid, greenish. No terminal bud; lateral buds blackish, hidden by leaf scar or by base of rachis when leaves are attached.

Flowers/Fruit: Flowers, perfect, **creamy-white, showy**, pea-like; bloom in July or August; borne in large, loose bunches; very attractive. Fruit a yellow-brown legume; 3" to 8" long; containing 3-6 brown seeds.

Bark: Similar appearance to black locust bark; gray-brown.

Wood: No information available.

Japanese pagodatree *(Sophora japonica)*

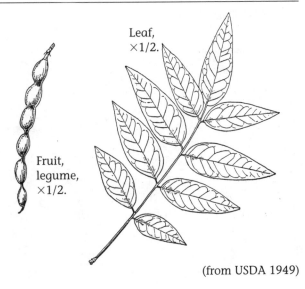

Leaf,
×1/2.

Fruit,
legume,
×1/2.

(from USDA 1949)

General: Native to China and Korea. Prefers rich, moist, well-drained soils. Shade intolerant.

Landscape Use: A good landscape tree that should be planted more. Flowers are very attractive. I have observed several 4" to 6" caliper trees near my office in Logan that are nearly surrounded by pavement. They have grown quickly, sometimes to the point that some of the new growth droops and looks awkward. I also have seen two of these trees killed by what appeared to be a canker. Dr. Frank Santamour of the U.S. National Arboretum has proposed after some genetic studies that the name of this species be changed to *Styphnolobium japonicum*. Zones 4-8.

Laburnum   Genus *Laburnum*

This genus consists of 3 species native to Europe and Asia, 2 of which form a popular hybrid. All are deciduous, have compound, trifoliolate leaves (with 3 leaflets), and a small pod or legume for a fruit.

Goldenchain Tree • Waterer Laburnum
(Laburnum × watereri)

Leaves: Alternate; **compound; trifoliolate** (3 leaflets); leaflets elliptic, oblong to obovate, 1-1/4" to 3" long, with pointed tip, glabrous, entire, attached to rachis/petiole with no stalk; bright green; unremarkable fall color.

goldenchain tree (*Laburnum × watereri*)

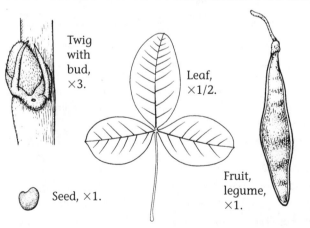

Twig with bud, ×3.

Leaf, ×1/2.

Fruit, legume, ×1.

Seed, ×1.

(from Farrar)

Twigs/Buds: Twigs moderately stout; olive-green, even on older stems; few lenticels; glabrous; older growth has short spur-like shoots. Terminal bud present; small; ovoid; 1/16" to 1/8" long; covered with 2 to 4 silver-haired scales.

Flowers/Fruit: Flowers perfect; **bright yellow; pea-like; in 6" to 10" long, narrow clusters that hang down**; very attractive; blooms in May. Fruit a 1" to 2" long, hairy pod with 6 to 10 small, poisonous seeds; maturing in October.

Bark: Olive-green even on older stems, eventually becoming fissured.

Wood: No information available.

General: A hybrid of Scotch laburnum (*L. alpinum*) and common laburnum (*L. anagyroides*), both of which are native to central, southern, and eastern Europe. Shade intolerant.

Landscape Use: A small tree with a rounded crown that has outstanding flowers. Plant in groups rather than individually. Doesn't like excessive heat or cold, but withstands high pH. Could be fairly short-lived. All plant parts, and especially seeds, contain a poison, so use with care in public areas or where children play. Zones 5-7.

Locust • False Acacia   Genus *Robinia*

This genus contains about 15 to 20 species of trees and shrubs, all native to North America. All are deciduous, have compound leaves, and a pod or legume for a fruit, and most are armed with small spines.

❖New Mexican Locust   (*Robinia neomexicana*)

Leaves: Alternate; once pinnately compound; 6" to 10" long; deciduous; 9 to 21 oblong, oval leaflets, 1" to 1-1/2" long, with entire margins, a bristle tip, and no stalks, **covered with gland-tipped hairs**; dark green in summer; yellow fall color.

Twigs/Buds: Twigs moderately stout; often zigzag; covered with glandular hairs (hairs with small swellings at the tips); generally with **medium-length, stiff spines, 1/2" long, in pairs at bases of leaves**. No terminal bud; lateral buds hidden under cracks of bark near leaf scar.

Flowers/Fruit: Flowers perfect, pink to white, 1" wide, pea-like; arranged in 4" to 8" long groups; attractive and fragrant; blooms in late spring. Fruit a brown, flat legume; 3" to 4" long; containing 4-8 flat brown seeds; covered with bristly hairs.

Bark: Light gray to brown; thin; shallowly furrowed.

Wood: Little information available; unimportant. Growth rings distinct; ring-porous.

New Mexican locust (*Robinia neomexicana*)

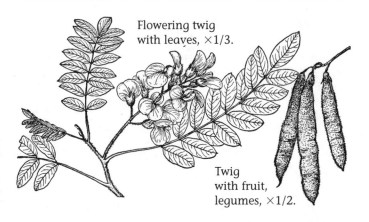

Flowering twig with leaves, ×1/3.

Twig with fruit, legumes, ×1/2.

(from Sargent)

General: A small tree or shrub native to the southwestern U.S., including Utah. Nitrogen fixer. Browsed by wildlife and livestock. Readily produces sucker sprouts. Shade intolerant.

Landscape Use: Seldom used but could be used more, especially in naturalized landscapes and tough situations. Very drought tolerant and able to withstand tough conditions, though susceptible to locust borer damage. Zones 5(4?)-9.

Black Locust (*Robinia pseudoacacia*)

Leaves: Alternate; once pinnately compound; 8" to 14" long; deciduous; 7 to 19 elliptical, ovate-oblong or ovate leaflets, 1-1/2" to 2" long, entire margins, glabrous; dark green in summer; yellow-green fall color.

Twigs/Buds: Twigs moderately stout; often zigzag; generally have **short, stiff spines, 1/4" to 1/2" long, in pairs at bases of leaves**. No terminal bud; lateral buds hidden under cracks of bark near leaf scar.

Flowers/Fruit: Flowers perfect, white, 1" wide, pea-like; arranged in 4" to 8" long groups; very fragrant and attractive; flowers in May to early June. Fruit a dark brown, flat legume; 3" to 5" long; containing 4-8 flat brown seeds.

Bark: Red-brown to nearly black; deeply furrowed into **criscrossing scaly ridges**; inner bark may be poisonous.

Wood: Moderately important; sapwood yellow; heartwood yellow to golden-brown and rot-resistant; growth rings distinct;

black locust *(Robinia pseudoacacia)*

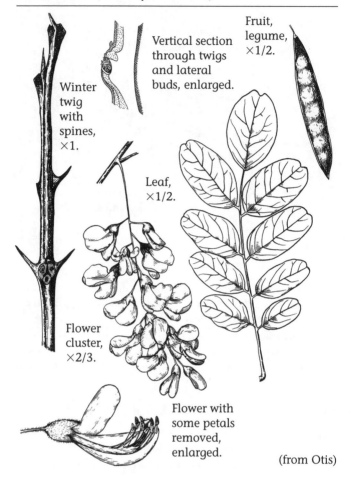

Winter twig with spines, ×1.

Vertical section through twigs and lateral buds, enlarged.

Fruit, legume, ×1/2.

Leaf, ×1/2.

Flower cluster, ×2/3.

Flower with some petals removed, enlarged.

(from Otis)

ring-porous; rays generally visible to the naked eye; used for fence posts, railroad ties, etc.

General: Native to the central-eastern U.S. Widely planted and naturalized east of the Rockies. Fast growing and well-adapted to a wide variety of sites. Nitrogen fixer. Readily produces sucker sprouts. Shade intolerant.

Landscape Use: An old pioneer tree that is not planted much any more, but should be used, especially under tough conditions. An attractive medium to large-sized tree with a narrow crown and an interesting texture, especially in winter. The attractive, fragrant flowers and the foliage are very nice and the bark is interesting. Unfortunately, it is somewhat pest-prone, with the locust borer

especially bad. Zones 3-9. **Idaho flowering locust** (*Robinia* ×
ambigua) probably is a hybrid of *R. pseudoacacia* and bristly locust
(*R. hispida*). It differs from black locust in having pink flowers and a
more open growth habit.

RUTACEAE

Rue or citrus family. Contains 140 genera and about 1,300 species,
most with tissues containing a bitter, aromatic oil. Generally found
in warm and temperate regions. Includes the commercially important *Citrus* genus (orange, lemon, lime, etc.).

Wafer-ash   Genus *Ptelea*

A small genus of 7 to 10 aromatic small trees or shrubs native to
North America. Deciduous, compound leaves; fruit a 2-seeded
samara.

❖Common Hoptree ◆ Wafer-ash ◆ Western Hoptree (*Ptelea angustifolia*)

Leaves: Alternate; once pinnately compound; deciduous; **3
leaflets; dark green; strong odor** when crushed; shiny.

Twigs/Buds: Twigs slender; round; dark brown; shiny. No terminal bud; lateral buds small, hairy.

common hoptree (*Ptelea angustifolia*)

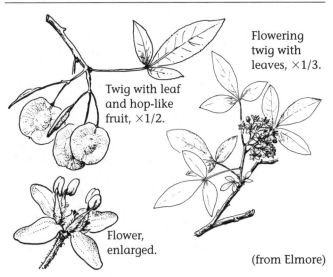

Flowering
twig with
leaves, ×1/3.

Twig with leaf
and hop-like
fruit, ×1/2.

Flower,
enlarged.

(from Elmore)

185

Flowers/Fruit: Flowers polygamo-monoecious, greenish-white, small, fragrant; held in dense clusters; appear in mid-May to early June. Fruit a two-seeded samara that resembles hops or an elm samara; round; 1/2" to 1" diameter; held in drooping clusters that persist after leaves fall; bitter tasting.

Bark: Dark gray to gray-brown; fairly smooth to warty.

Wood: Heavy; hard; ring-porous; not important.

General: Native from western Texas, west to California, and northern Mexico, including southern Utah. Thought by some to be a variant of an eastern U.S. species, *Ptelea trifoliata* var. *angustifolia*. Typically found on rocky slopes at the edge of wooded areas. Intermediate shade tolerance.

Landscape Use: Seldom if ever planted in cultivated landscapes. Small and generally shrubby. Likely fairly drought tolerant and able to withstand harsh soils conditions. Zones 3-9.

Corktree Genus *Phellodendron*

A genus containing 8 or 9 species of trees, all native to eastern Asia. All are deciduous and have pinnately compound leaves, aromatic tissues, and a drupe for a fruit.

Amur Corktree *(Phellodendron amurense)*

Leaves: Opposite; once pinnately compound; 10" to 15" long; deciduous; 5 to 11 ovate to ovate-lanceolate leaflets, 2-1/2" to 4-1/2" long, entire margins, rounded or narrowed at base, dark green and lustrous above, glabrous to slightly hairy along veins beneath; yellow fall color.

Twigs/Buds: Twigs stout; glabrous; orange-yellow to yellowish-gray eventually becoming brown; **inner bark bright yellow-green on young stems**. No terminal bud; **lateral buds silky, red or bronze, hidden by base of rachis when leaves are attached**.

Flowers/Fruit: Flowers dioecious, yellow-green, in small bunches; appear in late May to early June; inconspicuous. Fruit a black drupe; round; 1/2" diameter; strong odor when crushed; ripens in October and may persist into winter; found only on female trees.

Bark: Gray; smooth when young; becoming furrowed in an interlacing pattern on older portions of trunk; thick and corky.

Wood: No information available.

General: Native to northern China, Manchuria, and Japan. Shade intolerant.

Amur corktree (*Phellodendron amurense*)

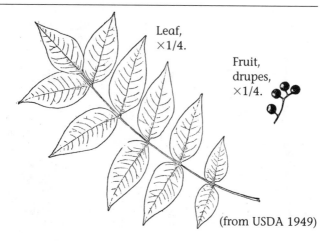

Leaf,
×1/4.

Fruit,
drupes,
×1/4.

(from USDA 1949)

Landscape Use: Good large landscape tree that is rarely planted. Males usually are planted in landscapes to avoid fruit messiness. Fairly pest-free and tolerant of a variety of soil and other site conditions. Zones 3-8.

SIMAROUBACEAE

Quassia family. Contains 32 genera and about 200 species. Chiefly tropical and subtropical.

Ailanthus   Genus *Ailanthus*

A genus containing 8 or 9 species of deciduous trees native Asia and northern Australia. All have alternate, pinnately compound leaves and a samara for a fruit.

Tree-of-heaven ◆ Ailanthus   (*Ailanthus altissima*)

Leaves: Alternate; once pinnately compound; **1' to 2-1/2' long** with 11 to 41 leaflets; deciduous; leaflets ovate-lanceolate, 3" to 6" long, entire margins except typically glandular-lobed near the base; bad smelling when crushed.

Twigs/Buds: Twigs very coarse; velvety or downy; brown pith. No terminal bud; Lateral buds round, brown, normally hairy, relatively small.

Flowers/Fruit: Flowers dioecious (some are perfect), yellow-green, small, 5-petals; arranged in long bunches, blooming in

tree-of-heaven (*Ailanthus altissima*)

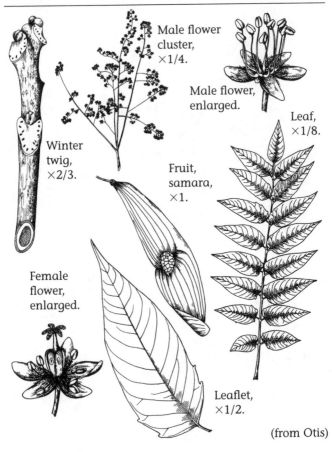

Male flower cluster, ×1/4.

Male flower, enlarged.

Leaf, ×1/8.

Winter twig, ×2/3.

Fruit, samara, ×1.

Female flower, enlarged.

Leaflet, ×1/2.

(from Otis)

June; inconspicuous. Fruit a samara; oblong; spirally twisted wing in center of which is a single, dry seed; yellow-green turning orange-red; in late summer and finally brown in fall; fairly attractive; normally occurs in great abundance.

Bark: **Thin; gray; smooth**; becomes slightly furrowed with age.

Wood: Unimportant; little information is published; light colored; brittle.

General: Native to China, but becoming naturalized in urban areas anywhere it has been planted. Starts readily from seed that is scattered by wind, and from root sprouts. Thrives under almost any type of condition, especially harsh, urban conditions. Resistant to smoke and gases, difficult to get rid of. Shade intolerant.

Landscape Use: A large, tough tree that sprouts readily, grows very fast, is weak-wooded, and is fairly short-lived. Common mainly in cities, where large trees will grow right out of pavement cracks and window wells. Quite attractive, but with a lot of bad habits that make it undesirable except for the worst sites. Zones 4-8.

MELIACEAE

Mahogany family. Contains 40 to 50 genera and 600 to 800 species mostly native to tropical and subtropical regions throughout the world, with only one species native to the U.S. This family includes many important tropical timber trees.

Chinaberry   Genus *Melia*

This genus consists of 10 species native to southern Asia and Australia. All have twice pinnately compound leaves and a fleshy drupe for a fruit.

Chinaberry   *(Melia azedarach)*

Leaves: Alternate; **twice pinnately compound; 12" to 24" long** and half as wide; deciduous; with many ovate to oval leaflets, 1-1/2" to 2" long, with a drawn-out point at their tips, serrate to slightly lobed, glabrous but with some hair when young, deep green; yellow-green fall color.

Twigs/Buds: Twigs stout; olive-green; large round pith; brittle; strong-smell when crushed. No terminal bud; lateral buds small, 1/16" to 1/8" across, round, brown, pubescent; arranged within a shield-shaped leaf scar.

Chinaberry (*Melia azedarach*)

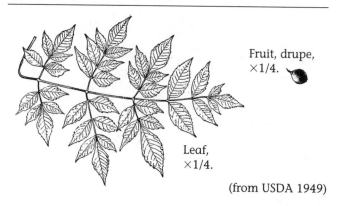

Fruit, drupe, ×1/4.

Leaf, ×1/4.

(from USDA 1949)

Flowers/Fruit: Flowers perfect, light purple, 5/8" to 3/4" across; in a 4" to 8" long cluster; bloom in May; fragrant and showy. Fruit a **yellow drupe; 3/8" to 5/8" diameter**; fleshy; with a hard black seed; ripens in September and persists through the winter.

Bark: Gray-brown; furrowed, with obvious lenticels.

Wood: Little information available; unimportant; soft, weak.

General: A medium-sized tree native to India and China that has been widely planted in the southern U.S. and has become naturalized in some areas. Very adaptable. Shade intolerant.

Landscape Use: This tree is somewhat attractive, but grows quickly and can be weedy, readily sprouting and reproducing from seed. There are many trees better than this. Zones 8-10.

ANACARDIACEAE

Cashew family. This economically important family contains 70 genera and about 600 species of trees and shrubs, mostly native to warmer climates. Many chemicals, dyes, valuable woods, and the well-known cashew, pistachio, and mango fruits come from this family.

Pistachio   Genus *Pistacia*

This genus includes 8 species native to the Mediterranean region, eastern Asia, Mexico, and Texas. Two species are occasionally planted in Utah. The fruit is a drupe.

Chinese Pistache   *(Pistacia chinensis)*

Leaves: Alternate; once pinnately compound; deciduous; 10" long; with 10 to 12 leaflets that are 2" to 4" long and one-fourth as wide, lanceolate, short or no-stalked, entire, apex pointed, glabrous, dark green; good yellow to orange-red fall color.

Twigs/Buds: Twigs stout; **brown with prominent orange lenticels; glabrous; strong odor when crushed**; pith wide, white, solid. Terminal bud 3/8" long, scaly, dark brown to black, glabrous or slightly hairy; lateral buds similar but smaller.

Flowers/Fruit: Flowers dioecious, small, in small groups, green; bloom in April on previous year's wood. Fruit a round, **1/4" diameter drupe; red or blue when ripe** in October, eaten by birds.

Bark: Scaly; shallowly furrowed; gray with orange inner bark exposed when scale flake off.

Wood: No information available.

Chinese pistache (*Pistacia chinensis*)

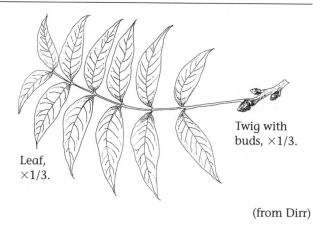

Leaf,
×1/3.

Twig with
buds, ×1/3.

(from Dirr)

General: Native to China. Drought resistant and otherwise very
adaptable. Shade intolerant.

Landscape Use: This is a good, tough, medium to large tree that
should be planted more in warmer locations. Nice fall color and
fairly free of pests. Used as an understock for grafted commercial
pistachios. Zones 6-9. **Pistachio** (*Pistacia vera*), the common pistachio nut, also can be grown in Utah. I have seen several of these
small trees growing on a rocky, windy, south-facing hillside over-
looking the Logan River in Logan. They receive no irrigation or
care at all, yet do quite well and bear good, large fruit. I assume
they are not grafted, since the *P. chinensis* rootstock likely would
not be cold-hardy and these trees seem unaffected by the cold.
The compound leaves are fleshy and the leaves and fruit turn a
nice orange-red in the fall. Zones 4-9.

Smoketree   Genus *Cotinus*

A genus including only 2 species of small, shrubby trees, one
native from southern Europe to China, and the other native to the
south-central and southeastern U.S. They are known for their
attractive foliage and inflorescences.

Common Smoketree ♦ Smokebush
(*Cotinus coggygria*)

Leaves: Alternate; simple; deciduous; oval to obovate; 1" to 3"
long; rounded tip; entire; glabrous; blue-green or purple, depending on cultivar; yellow to red fall color, sometimes very attractive.

191

Twigs/Buds: Twigs stout; purple to brown with whitish waxy coating that rubs off; glabrous; obvious small lenticels; orange-brown, solid pith; strong odor when crushed. Buds small, scaly, red-brown, pointed.

Flowers/Fruit: Flowers dioecious (some are perfect), tiny, yellow, inconspicuous, many do not fully develop; borne on a 6" to 8" long and wide inflorescence in may to June. Fruit a 1/8" to 1/4" wide, dry, drupe. Stalks of flowers and fruit are very showy and smoky looking because of their **hairy, pink or purple stalks**.

Bark: Thin; gray, furrowed and scaly.

Wood: Little information available. Yellow.

General: A small tree or large shrub native from southern Europe to central China, but widely planted. Adapted to a variety of sites. Intermediate shade tolerance.

Landscape Use: A small, shrubby tree with a very interesting appearance due to its hairy flower/fruit stalks; most flowers abort and do not bear fruit. Somewhat awkward, but still attractive; maybe best planted in groups. Flower/fruit stalks can be removed in winter after they lose their appeal. Plant also can be cut back heavily and allowed to sprout to promote vigor and good color. Various foliage and flower/fruit colors available. Zones 4-9. **American smoketree** or **chittamwood** (*Cotinus obovatus*) is a similar species that gets larger, has larger leaves, dioecious flowers, and excellent yellow to red to purple fall color. Worth trying if you can get it. Zones 4(3?)-8.

AQUIFOLIACEAE

Holly family. This family contains 3 genera and over 300 species widely distributed around the world. Many are used as ornamentals, especially for their foliage and fruit. **Leaves are often evergreen**.

Holly   Genus *Ilex*

This genus contains 295 species of trees and shrubs from every continent except Australia. Fifteen hollies are native to the U.S., all in the east.

American Holly   *(Ilex opaca)*

Leaves: Alternate; simple; **evergreen, persisting 3 years**; 2" to 4" long; elliptical; margin with long, sharp, spiny teeth, though some leaves may be nearly entire; thick and leathery; green to dark green above and paler below, with some cultivars glossy dark green; petiole grooved, 1/4" to 1/2" long.

American smoketree (*Cotinus obovatus*)

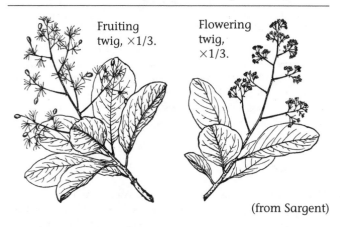

Fruiting twig, ×1/3.

Flowering twig, ×1/3.

(from Sargent)

American holly (*Ilex opaca*)

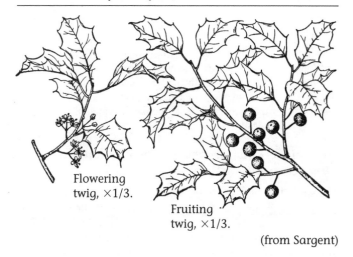

Flowering twig, ×1/3.

Fruiting twig, ×1/3.

(from Sargent)

Twigs/Buds: Twigs slender; glabrous; green. Terminal bud present; buds 1/8" to 1/4" long, scaly.

Flowers/Fruit: Flowers dioecious, small, borne in small bunches when leaves are opening; white, inconspicuous. Fruit a fleshy drupe maturing in October and persisting into winter; red or yellow, depending on cultivar; 1/4" to 1/2" diameter.

Bark: Thin; smooth; light gray; with many warty bumps.

Wood: Somewhat important; white; hard; heavy; growth rings not very distinct; diffuse-porous; often dyed for use in marquetry and inlays; also used for turnings.

General: Native to the eastern and southeastern U.S., as far west as Texas and Missouri and as far north as Massachusetts. Shade tolerant.

Landscape Use: Attractive, medium-sized broadleaved evergreen that grows fairly slowly. Foliage and fruit, especially on certain cultivars, can be very attractive. Somewhat difficult to transplant. Does not do well in very hot, dry, windy conditions. Will be fuller-crowned when grown in full sun. Zones 5-9. There are many other species of holly, both trees and shrubs, that potentially could be grown in Utah. See Dirr (1990) for a more complete discussion.

ACERACEAE

Maple family. A relatively small family containing only 2 genera and about 117 species. Widely scattered through the Northern Hemisphere, but most common in the Himalayan Mountains and in central China. **Opposite leaf arrangement.**

Maple   Genus *Acer*

This genus contains 115 of the 117 species in Aceraceae. Maples are found throughout the Northern Hemisphere, but are most common in China and the Himalayas. Thirteen maples are native to the U.S. Some maples are fairly important timber trees and maples also are some of the most popular ornamental trees in the world. **Fruit a double samara**.

❖Boxelder ◆ Ash-leaved Maple ◆ Manitoba Maple (*Acer negundo*)

Leaves: Opposite; **once pinnately compound with 3 to 7 leaflets**; deciduous; leaflets quite variable, ovate to lanceolate, coarsely serrate margins or sometimes 3-lobed at base; bright green with yellow to yellow-green fall color; rachis stout, enlarged at the base.

Twigs/Buds: Twigs stout; **green to purple-green**; frequently covered with a blue-white coating. Terminal bud oval, somewhat white and woolly.

Flowers/Fruit: Flowers dioecious; green to yellow; small, inconspicuous; bloom in March or April. Fruit a samara; V-shaped; double-winged; hangs down; ripens in fall.

Bark: Thin; pale gray or light brown; deeply divided by furrows into rounded, interlacing ridges.

Wood: Unimportant; sapwood white; heartwood light brown; often colored by mineral stains; growth rings not very distinct; diffuse-porous; used for cheap furniture, etc.

boxelder (*Acer negundo*)

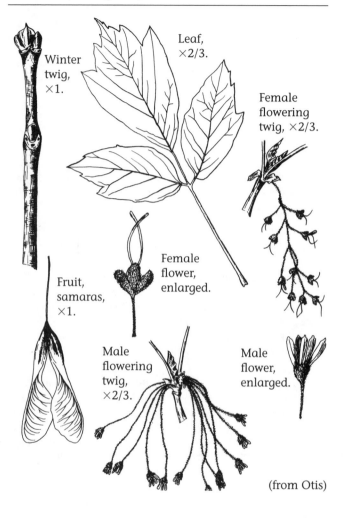

Winter twig, ×1.

Leaf, ×2/3.

Female flowering twig, ×2/3.

Fruit, samaras, ×1.

Female flower, enlarged.

Male flowering twig, ×2/3.

Male flower, enlarged.

(from Otis)

General: Native to much of North America, including Utah. A very tough tree that does best on moist, deep soils, but also will survive on poor soils and dryer sites. Intermediate shade tolerance.

Landscape Use: Very common, but undesirable as an ornamental in all except the worst conditions. Often nearly completely defoliated in early summer by the boxelder leaf roller, but usually puts on new leaves with no problem. Boxelder bugs can be a nuisance where female trees are found (they feed on the fruit). Weak-wooded. Zones 2-9.

❖Canyon Maple ◆ Bigtooth Maple
(Acer grandidentatum)

Leaves: Opposite; simple; 2" to 5" wide and long; deciduous; palmately **3- to 5-lobed; lobe margins entire or sometimes divided into additional small lobes**; bright green and glabrous above, paler with some fine hairs beneath; fall color bright orange-red to red; petiole 1" to 2" long, typically shorter than the leaf blade.

Twigs/Buds: Twigs slender; glabrous; red. Terminal bud 1/16" long; red; pointed.

Flowers/Fruit: Flowers dioecious; yellow; no petals; small, inconspicuous; appearing in spring. Fruit a samara; **U-shaped**, double-winged, wings spread slightly, 1" long; green when mature in fall.

Bark: Gray-brown; shallowly furrowed.

Wood: Somewhat important locally where native; growth rings fairly distinct; diffuse-porous; hard; dense; mainly used for firewood.

General: Native from southern Idaho south to Mexico and east to Texas, including much of Utah in mountainous locations. This is the common maple that gives Logan Canyon and some other northern Utah locations their outstanding fall color. Withstands high soil pH much better than many introduced maples. Intermediate shade tolerance.

Landscape Uses: This is a very good tree that should be used much more in the landscape, especially now that a grafted cultivar is available. It is tolerant of our soil and climatic conditions, and even appears to withstand some drought when planted in the valleys. Fall color is usually very good. Tree shape can be shrubby or tree-like and size can be small to medium. I have seen this planted in Logan both as an individual specimen and as small trees in a dense group and both effects were appealing. Grafted trees planted at Red Butte Garden and Arboretum in Salt Lake City have failed, indicating potential graft compatibility or other problems. Zones 4(3?)-7.

❖Rocky Mountain Maple *(Acer glabrum)*

Leaves: Opposite; simple; 3" to 5" wide and long; deciduous; 3- to 5-lobed or occasionally separated into 3 separate leaflets; **sharply and doubly serrate margin**; dark-green above and paler beneath; glabrous; petiole 1" to 4" long, slender, red; fall color yellow to a muted red.

Twigs/Buds: Twigs slender; glabrous; green to red-brown. Buds 1/8" to 1/4" long, red, glabrous, one pair of scales visible.

canyon maple (*Acer grandidentatum*)

Flowering twig with young leaves, ×1/3.

Fruiting twig, ×1/3.

(from Sargent)

Rocky Mountain maple (*Acer glabrum*)

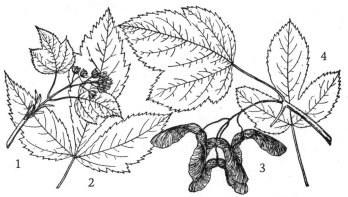

1. Flowering twig with simple, lobed leaves, ×1/2.
2. Compound leaf, ×2/3.
3. Fruiting shoot, ×1/2.
4. Deeply-lobed leaf, ×2/3.

(from Sargent)

Flowers/Fruit: Flowers mostly dioecious (some perfect); yellow-green; no petals; small, inconspicuous; appearing in late spring after leaves. Fruit a samara; **U-shaped, with wings nearly parallel**, 3/4" to 1" long; pink when mature in summer; becoming light brown and wrinkled in fall.

Bark: Thin and fairly smooth; red-brown.

Wood: Unimportant; diffuse-porous; hard; dense.

General: A small tree native from the western Great Plains west to Oregon and Washington and from the Mexican border through most of British Columbia, including mountainous portions of

Utah and the Intermountain West. Prefers moist, protected sites along streams. Shade tolerant.

Landscape Uses: This shrubby tree is rarely planted in cultivated landscapes, maybe because it is not very common in nurseries. Plant in moist protected areas or in the shade of other trees, especially in warm valley sites. Should be fairly tolerant of high soil pH. Zones 4(3?)-7.

Norway Maple *(Acer platanoides)*

Leaves: Opposite; simple; 4" to 7" wide and long; deciduous; typically palmately 5-lobed; lobes sharply pointed; somewhat serrate margin; bright green to dark purple, depending on variety; turning bright yellow or yellow-orange in fall; petiole 2" to 4" long, as long or longer than the leaf blade; **milky sap** is visible when petiole broken or removed from stem (this may disappear late in the summer).

Twigs/Buds: Twigs stout; olive-brown; glabrous; leaf scars meet. Terminal bud 1/4" to 3/8" long, rounded, green-red to red, glabrous; lateral buds smaller.

Flowers/Fruit: Flowers dioecious (some are perfect); yellow-green to yellow and fairly showy; 1/4" to nearly 1/2" diameter; appearing in spring as leaves expand. Fruit a samara; 2 **widespread wings**, 1-1/2" to 2" long; matures in September-October.

Bark: Smooth and gray-brown on young stems; furrowed on older stems.

Wood: Little known in U.S.; presumably similar to sugar maple (see below).

General: Native to Europe from Norway south, though widely planted and occasionally has escaped cultivation in parts of the U.S., including Utah. Intermediate shade tolerance.

Landscape Use: This is a good tree that has become over-planted in parts of Utah. It tolerates a wide range of environmental conditions, though leaves will scorch on very hot, dry sites. Many varieties are available with dark purple to bright green leaf colors. However, there are also green-leaved varieties. Honeydew from aphids can be a nuisance in some years, though the tree is rarely harmed. Its most attractive features are its strong wide crown and its good summer and fall color. Zones 3-8.

Sugar Maple *(Acer saccharum)*

Leaves: Opposite; simple; 3" to 5" wide and long; deciduous; palmately **5-lobed; lobe margins entire or sometimes wavy serrate**, with rounded tips; bright yellow green and glabrous

Norway maple (*Acer platanoides*)

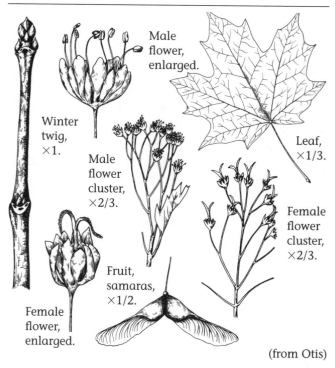

Male flower, enlarged.

Winter twig, ×1.

Male flower cluster, ×2/3.

Leaf, ×1/3.

Female flower cluster, ×2/3.

Fruit, samaras, ×1/2.

Female flower, enlarged.

(from Otis)

sugar maple (*Acer saccharum*)

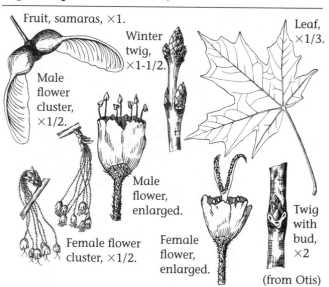

Fruit, samaras, ×1.

Winter twig, ×1-1/2.

Leaf, ×1/3.

Male flower cluster, ×1/2.

Male flower, enlarged.

Female flower cluster, ×1/2.

Female flower, enlarged.

Twig with bud, ×2

(from Otis)

above and below; turning bright red to orange to yellow in the fall; petiole about 2" long, typically shorter than the leaf blade.

Twigs/Buds: Twigs slender; glabrous; red-brown; shiny. Terminal bud 1/4" to 3/8" long, pointed, 4-8 pairs of scales.

Flowers/Fruit: Flowers dioecious (some are perfect); yellow-green and fairly inconspicuous; appearing in spring as leaves expand. Fruit a samara; **U-shaped**, double-winged; matures in fall.

Bark: Gray; deeply furrowed on older trees; with long, irregular plates or ridges; sometimes scaly.

Wood: Important in the eastern U.S.; sapwood white with a red tinge; heartwood light brown; growth rings fairly distinct; diffuse-porous; uses as in silver maple but sugar maple is generally higher quality.

General: Native to most of the northeastern U.S. (east from Iowa and north from Tennessee). Commercially the most important of the maples from a forest products standpoint. Noted for maple syrup made from its sap. Shade tolerant.

black maple (*Acer nigrum*)

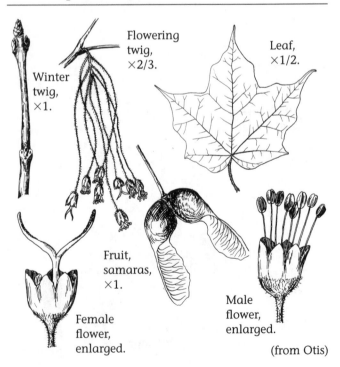

Winter twig, ×1.

Flowering twig, ×2/3.

Leaf, ×1/2.

Fruit, samaras, ×1.

Female flower, enlarged.

Male flower, enlarged.

(from Otis)

Landscape Use: This large tree has a nice crown form and excellent fall color. It can do well in Utah, but hasn't been planted much in recent years. Some large specimens can be found in Logan and elsewhere. Avoid extremely hot, dry sites. Zones 4-8. A similar species (some consider it a variety of sugar maple) that has done well in Salt Lake City is **black maple** (*Acer nigrum*). It differs from sugar maple in having dark green, mostly 3-lobed leaves with drooping tips and hairs beneath; yellow fall color; and darker colored bark. Zones 4-8.

Silver Maple   (*Acer saccharinum*)

Leaves: Opposite; simple; about 4" to 7" wide and long; deciduous; deeply, palmately 5-lobed; coarsely serrate margins; green and glabrous on upper surface; **silver-white beneath**; turn pale yellow in fall; petiole 3" to 5" long.

silver maple (*Acer saccharinum*)

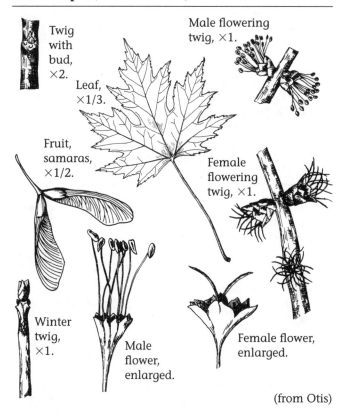

Twig with bud, ×2.

Male flowering twig, ×1.

Leaf, ×1/3.

Fruit, samaras, ×1/2.

Female flowering twig, ×1.

Winter twig, ×1.

Male flower, enlarged.

Female flower, enlarged.

(from Otis)

201

Twigs/Buds: Twigs slender; orange-brown to red; disagreeable odor when bruised. Buds rounded, red to reddish-brown, 1/8" to 1/4" long, clustered.

Flowers/Fruit: Flowers dioecious (some are perfect); red to yellow-green and fairly showy because they appear very early, before the leaves. Fruit a samara; **2 widely spread wings, about 1-1/2" long**; mature in late spring and germinate immediately.

Bark: Smooth and silver-gray on young stems; later breaking into long, thin, scaly plates that curl away from the tree at the ends.

Wood: Moderately important; sapwood white; heartwood light brown; growth rings not very distinct; diffuse-porous; used as a substitute for sugar maple in flooring, furniture, boxes, pallets, crates, and novelties.

General: Native to most of the eastern U.S. on moist, bottomland sites. Intermediate shade tolerance.

Landscape Use: A large and often beautiful tree that grows rapidly, but tends to be brittle and breaks somewhat easily in storms. In the West it also tends towards iron chlorosis because of high soil pH, though the chlorosis must be extreme before it has much effect on the tree. Should be planted only where there's plenty of room and where soil pH isn't very high. Zones 3-9.

Red Maple   *(Acer rubrum)*

Leaves: Opposite; simple; 2" to 6" wide and long; deciduous; **typically palmately 3-lobed** (rarely 5-lobed); coarsely serrate margin; turning scarlet in fall; petiole 2" to 4" long.

Twigs/Buds: Twigs slender; dark red; without a disagreeable odor when crushed. Terminal bud 1/16" to 1/8" long, red to green, not pointed.

Flowers/Fruit: Flowers dioecious (some are perfect); red and fairly showy, appearing very early, well before the leaves. Fruit a samara; **2 slightly spread wings making a V-shape, 1/2" to 1" long**; matures in late spring.

Bark: Smooth and light gray on young stems; eventually breaking into long, scaly plates separated by shallow furrows.

Wood: Moderately important; sapwood white; heartwood light brown; growth rings not very distinct; diffuse-porous; uses similar to silver maple.

General: Native to most of the eastern U.S. Resembles silver maple in some ways, but the smaller, 3-lobed leaf and smaller fruit are distinctive. Intermediate shade tolerance.

Landscape Use: A medium-sized tree occasionally planted in Utah. Doesn't grow as fast as silver maple, but also has weak wood.

red maple (*Acer rubrum*)

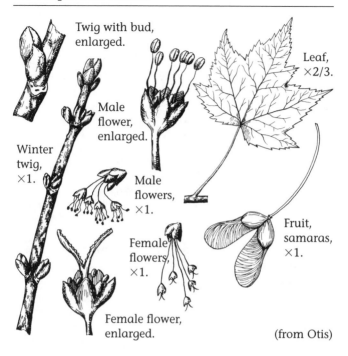

Twig with bud, enlarged.

Leaf, ×2/3.

Male flower, enlarged.

Winter twig, ×1.

Male flowers, ×1.

Female flowers, ×1.

Fruit, samaras, ×1.

Female flower, enlarged.

(from Otis)

Red maple also suffers from chlorosis in high pH soils, though this may be due to manganese deficiency. Has very good fall color, with many cultivars available. Zones 3-9.

Amur Maple ◆ Ginnala Maple (*Acer ginnala*)

Leaves: Opposite; simple; 1-1/2" to 3" long; deciduous; **palmately 3-lobed, middle lobe longer than side lobes**; doubly serrate margin; dark green and lustrous above; light green beneath; turning yellow to red in fall; petiole 1/2" to 1-3/4" long.

Twigs/Buds: Twigs slender; gray-brown; glabrous. Terminal and lateral buds 1/8" long, red-brown, glabrous.

Flowers/Fruit: Flowers dioecious (some are perfect); yellow-white and fairly inconspicuous; appear with the leaves. Fruit a samara; 2 parallel wings, 3/4" to 1" long; matures in fall.

Bark: Smooth and gray-brown with dark streaks like service-berry.

Wood: No information available.

Amur maple *(Acer ginnala)*

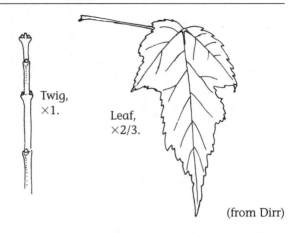

Twig, ×1.

Leaf, ×2/3.

(from Dirr)

General: Native to central and northern China, Manchuria, and Japan. Moderately shade tolerant.

Landscape Use: Many varieties are available commercially that vary from **small shrubs to small trees**. The main problem with this species in Utah is chlorosis on high pH soils, perhaps worse than any other species I've seen. It's use should be limited to areas where soil pH is low (approaching 7). Fall color can be excellent, but is inconsistent. Zones 2-8.

Other Maples
(All have opposite, simple (one is trifoliate), palmately lobed (one is sometimes unlobed), deciduous leaves; small and fairly inconspicuous flowers; and paired samaras with elongated wings)

Hedge Maple   *(Acer campestre)*

Leaves: With 3 to 5 lobes and few rounded teeth; 2" to 4" wide and long; dark green above and pubescent beneath; petiole 4" long, exudes a **milky sap** when broken; yellow fall color.

Twigs/Buds: Twigs with prominent lenticels; older twigs with corky ridges; pith white and solid.

Flowers/Fruit: Fruit a samara; 1" to 1-3/4" long; **wings very wide spread**.

General: Native to Europe, Africa, and western Asia. Prefers well-drained soil, but does well with high soil pH, soil compaction, pollution, and on dry sites. Intolerant to moderately shade tolerant.

Landscape Use: Medium-sized tree widely used as a hedge in Europe, and can stand heavy pruning for that purpose (do not

hedge maple *(Acer campestre)*

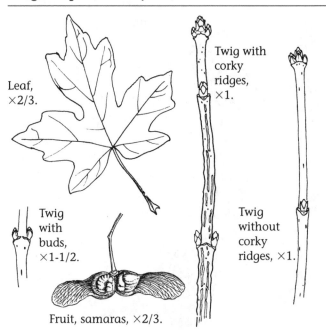

Leaf, ×2/3.

Twig with corky ridges, ×1.

Twig with buds, ×1-1/2.

Twig without corky ridges, ×1.

Fruit, samaras, ×2/3.

(from Dirr, except fruit from Garcke)

heavily prune trees once they have gotten large). Does well in Utah, probably because of its tolerance for dry, alkaline soils. Essentially pest-free. Zones 4-8.

Sycamore Maple *(Acer pseudoplatanus)*

Leaves: Five lobed with many rounded teeth; 3" to 6" wide; dark green above and lighter beneath, with some pubescence on veins; **leathery**; petiole 2" to 4" long; yellow to brown fall color.

Twigs/Buds: Twigs with prominent lenticels; glabrous; brown; slightly four-angled. **Buds remain green throughout the winter**.

Flowers/Fruit: Fruit a samara; 1-1/4" to 2" long; wings angled at about 60 degrees from one another; fall maturing.

Bark: Gray and reddish-brown to orange; scaly, flaking off and exposing orange inner bark.

General: Native to Europe and western Asia. Tolerates a wide variety of soil and environmental conditions, including considerable salt tolerance. Intolerant to moderately shade tolerant.

sycamore maple (*Acer pseudoplatanus*)

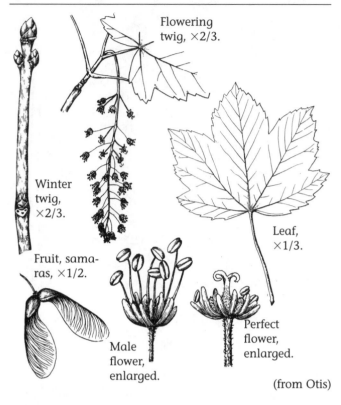

Flowering twig, ×2/3.

Winter twig, ×2/3.

Fruit, samaras, ×1/2.

Leaf, ×1/3.

Male flower, enlarged.

Perfect flower, enlarged.

(from Otis)

Landscape Use: A large tree somewhat similar to Norway maple. Heavily planted in Europe and very adaptable. I have seen it doing well in a park in Utah County. Needs considerable pruning to keep it in good shape. Zones 4-7.

Trident Maple (*Acer buergeranum*)

Leaves: Three lobed with **3 main veins and lobes pointing forward**; few small teeth; 1-1/2" to 3" wide; shiny green and glabrous when mature; petiole 1-1/2" to 3" long; yellow, orange, or red fall color.

Flowers/Fruit: Fruit a samara; **3/4" to 1" long; wings parallel**; fall maturing.

Bark: After a few years becomes gray, orange, brown and scaly; attractive.

General: Native to China. Fairly drought resistant. Shade intolerant.

trident maple *(Acer buergeranum)*

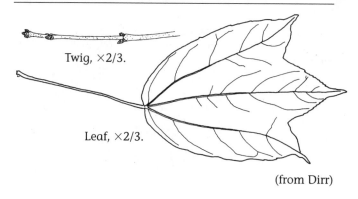

Twig, ×2/3.

Leaf, ×2/3.

(from Dirr)

paperbark maple *(Acer griseum)*

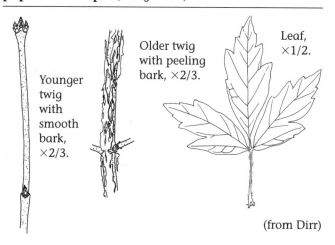

Younger twig with smooth bark, ×2/3.

Older twig with peeling bark, ×2/3.

Leaf, ×1/2.

(from Dirr)

Landscape Use: This small to medium-sized tree is rarely planted in Utah and may be hard to find, but its fall color makes it worth trying. Colors very late in the fall. Zones 5-9.

Paperbark Maple *(Acer griseum)*

Leaves: Compound; **trifoliolate (3 leaflets)**; 3" to 6" long; few coarse teeth; leaflets short-stalked or with no stalk; blue-green and glabrous above, pubescent on veins beneath; petiole 2" to 3" long and pubescent; red fall color.

Flowers/Fruit: Fruit a samara; 1" to 1-1/2" long; pubescent; wings at 60 to 90 degree angle; fall maturing.

Bark: Older twigs and trunk with beautiful **peeling red-brown bark**.

General: Native to China. Fairly drought resistant and tolerates a variety of soil conditions including moderately high pH. Shade intolerant.

Landscape Use: This beautiful small to medium-sized tree is uncommon in Utah and definitely should be planted more often. Its bark is outstanding and fall color can be good. Zones 4-8.

Japanese Maple   *(Acer palmatum)*

Leaves: **Deeply 5- to 9-lobed**; 2" to 5" long; doubly serrate; green to reddish-purple depending on cultivar; yellow, orange, purple, or red fall color.

Flowers/Fruit: Fruit a samara; **1/2" to 3/4" long; wings curved in toward one another**; fall maturing.

General: Native to China, Japan, and Korea. Does not like cold or intense heat. Intermediate shade tolerance.

Landscape Use: Beautiful small tree that has planted a fair amount in Utah, but is limited by cold and heat. Its foliage texture, fall color, and small size make it very desirable. I have seen one doing well on the USU campus in Logan in a sunken area on the southwest side of a building. Best planted where afternoon shade and wind protection are available. Zones 5-8.

Tatarian Maple   *(Acer tataricum)*

Leaves: Similar to Amur maple; **unlobed or slightly 3-lobed**; doubly serrate; 2" to 4" long; bright green and glabrous above, pubescent on veins below; yellow or red fall color.

Flowers/Fruit: Flowers greenish-white; somewhat ornamental. Fruit a samara; **3/4" to 1" long; wings parallel; red for several weeks**; fall maturing.

General: Native to southeastern Europe and western Asia. Drought resistant and fairly adaptable. Shade intolerant.

Landscape Use: A small, shrubby maple rarely planted in Utah but worth trying as a substitute for Amur maple. The red fruit is quite attractive. Zones 3-8.

Purpleblow Maple ◆ Shantung Maple
(Acer truncatum)

Leaves: **Five triangular lobes with drawn-out tips**; no teeth on lobes; 3" to 5" wide; purplish when young; mature leaves dark green and glabrous above, lighter below; 2" to 4" long petiole with **milky sap when broken**; yellow, orange, and red fall color.

Japanese maple (*Acer palmatum*)

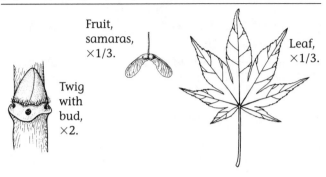

Fruit, samaras, ×1/3.

Twig with bud, ×2.

Leaf, ×1/3.

(from Farrar)

Tatarian maple (*Acer tataricum*)

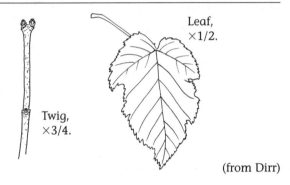

Leaf, ×1/2.

Twig, ×3/4.

(from Dirr)

purpleblow maple (*Acer truncatum*)

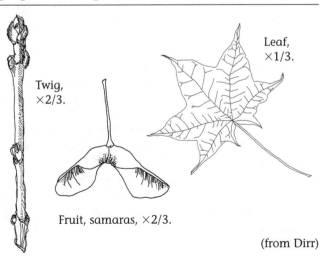

Twig, ×2/3.

Leaf, ×1/3.

Fruit, samaras, ×2/3.

(from Dirr)

209

Flowers/Fruit: Fruit a samara; 1-1/4" to 1-1/2" long; sometimes purple-colored; wings at a 90 degree angle.

General: Native to China. Drought and heat resistant and quite adaptable. Shade intolerant.

Landscape Use: A small to medium sized tree that again is uncommon in Utah. Good fall color. Few pests. Zones 4-8.

HIPPOCASTANACEAE

Buckeye family. Contains 3 genera and about 30 species widely scattered through the forests of North America, Europe, and Asia. Little importance for products. **Opposite, palmately compound leaves**.

Horsechestnut   Genus *Aesculus*

This genus contains about 13 tree and shrub species found in northern temperate forests, with 5 species native to North America growing on a variety of sites in mixed hardwood stands; fairly shade tolerant. None are native to Utah. Several species and hybrids are important ornamentally, but the tree has little economic importance otherwise. The inedible fruit is not a true chestnut (genus *Castanea*), but is a **large capsule containing 1 to 3 seeds.**

Horsechestnut   *(Aesculus hippocastanum)*

Leaves: Opposite; palmately compound; deciduous; **usually 7 leaflets** (occasionally 5), obovate, 5" to 7" long, margins doubly serrate; rusty hairs beneath when young; fall color yellow-brown.

Twigs/Buds: Twigs stout; glabrous; red-brown. Terminal buds over 1" long, brown, covered with waxy gum, shiny.

Flowers/Fruit: Very showy **white to light yellow flowers with red spots, held in large cone-shaped clusters** in May. The fruit is a round capsule; thick; leathery; prickly; yellow-brown; 1" to 2" in diameter; containing **1 to 3 smooth, shiny, brown kernels**.

Bark: Dark gray to brown; platy and peeling on older stems with orange-brown inner-bark.

Wood: Moderately important where native. Creamy-white; diffuse-porous; used for containers, furniture, etc.

General: Native of Asia. Prefers moist, protected sites; generally will leaf scorch on hot, dry sites. Very pH adaptable. Shade tolerant.

horsechestnut (*Aesculus hippocastanum*)

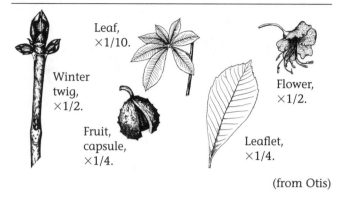

Leaf, ×1/10.

Winter twig, ×1/2.

Fruit, capsule, ×1/4.

Flower, ×1/2.

Leaflet, ×1/4.

(from Otis)

Ohio buckeye (*Aesculus glabra*)

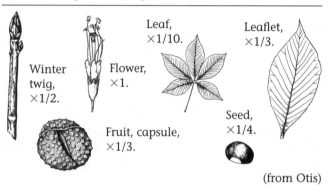

Leaf, ×1/10.

Leaflet, ×1/3.

Winter twig, ×1/2.

Flower, ×1.

Fruit, capsule, ×1/3.

Seed, ×1/4.

(from Otis)

Landscape Use: A popular shade tree around the world that was planted a lot in some parts of Utah many years ago. Flowers are beautiful and the fruit is interesting, but can be a real nuisance, as evidenced along many sidewalks on the USU campus in autumn. Crown shape is wide and spreading and the shade is very intense. It might be interesting to grow this tree in a shady spot. Zones 3-7. **Red horsechestnut** (*Aesculus × carnea*) is a cross between *A. hippocastanum* and *A. pavia* that is slightly smaller than horsechestnut at maturity and has 5 leaflets instead of 7 and less sticky buds. Its most attractive feature is its beautiful red flowers. This hybrid is uncommon in Utah, though it does well in Logan, Salt Lake City, and Provo. Zones 4-7. **Ohio buckeye** (*Aesculus glabra*) is another species very rarely planted in Utah that could do well on moist sites. It differs from horsechestnut in usually having 5 leaflets per leaf without rusty hairs beneath, a fruit that is not as spiny, and

211

California buckeye (*Aesculus californica*)

Flowering
twig with
leaves, ×1/6.

Fruit,
capsules,
×1/6.

(from Sargent)

yellow-green flowers. Zones 3-7. Finally, **California buckeye** (*Aesculus californica*) may be a good choice for a flowering tree in the St. George area. Zones 7-8.

SAPINDACEAE

Soapberry family. Contains 120 genera and more than 1200 species. Most abundant in tropical regions, with only a few species in the temperate zone. **Leaves usually pinnately compound**.

Goldenraintree   Genus *Koelreuteria*

This small genus contains 4 deciduous tree species native to eastern Asia, with several widely planted around the world, mainly for their **beautiful flowers**. One species is commonly planted in Utah.

Goldenraintree   (*Koelreuteria paniculata*)

Leaves: Alternate; once pinnately compound (some leaflets may be deeply lobed enough to appear twice pinnately compound); 6" to 18" long; 7 to 15 ovate to ovate-oblong leaflets, 1" to 4" long; deciduous; **margins with coarse, irregular, rounded teeth; leaflets often lobed near base with lobes reaching nearly to midrib**; glabrous above, glabrous to slightly hairy along veins beneath; yellow to orange fall color.

Twigs/Buds: Twigs stout; glabrous; greenish to light brown. No terminal bud; lateral buds brown with 2 scales, 1/8" to 3/16" long.

Flowers/Fruit: Flowers perfect; bright yellow; 1/2" wide; arranged in 12" to 15" long, loose bunches, appearing from early June to early July; very attractive. Fruit a capsule; papery; 3-valved; 1-1/2" to 2" long; green at first, changing to yellow and then brown; with 3 black, hard, pea-like seeds inside; ripens in August to October.

goldenraintree (*Koelreuteria paniculata*)

Leaf, ×1/8.

Fruit, capsule, ×1/4.

Seeds, ×1/4.

(from USDA 1949)

Bark: Light gray to brown; smooth when young; becoming furrowed and ridged on older portions of trunk.

Wood: No information available.

General: Native to China, Japan, and Korea. Fairly slow growing. Adaptable to many different soil conditions, including high pH. Shade intolerant.

Landscape Use: A good, medium-sized ornamental tree, especially liked for its flowers. I have seen this doing well all along the Wasatch Front, in Price, and elsewhere. In full flower it is truly beautiful. Can be weak-wooded and suffers some branch dieback in winter. Zones 5(4?)-9.

TILIACEAE

Linden family. Contains 41 genera and about 400 species. Most abundant in the Southern Hemisphere, but widely scattered throughout the world.

Linden   Genus *Tilia*

This genus includes mostly large trees found in the northern temperate zone, with 4 to 7 native to North America and none native to the western U.S. They are moderately important for their wood and very important ornamentally, tolerating urban conditions quite well.

American Basswood ◆ American Linden
(Tilia americana)

Leaves: Alternate; simple; **unevenly heart-shaped; 5" to 8" long and almost as wide**; deciduous; coarsely serrate margin; pointed tip; glabrous; dark green above; paler beneath; petiole thin, 1" to 2" long.

213

Twigs/Buds: Twigs usually zigzag; glabrous; green to red-gray. No terminal bud; lateral buds dark red or green, about 1/4" long, rounded, lopsided, usually with two visible scales.

Flowers/Fruit: Flowers perfect; light yellow; 1/3" to 1/2" wide; arranged in bunches of 5 to 10 attached by stalks to a light green, **3" to 4" long, leafy bract**; appearing in late June or early July. Fruit a nut-like drupe; round; 1/3" to 1/2" in diameter; clustered; covered with fine pubescence; the bract drying out and turning light brown when the fruit matures in late summer.

Bark: Smooth and gray-green on young stems; later turning gray-brown, furrowed, with narrow, scaly ridges.

Wood: Important; sapwood white to pale brown; heartwood pale brown; light; soft; growth rings fairly distinct; diffuse-porous; rays not visible without a hand lens; used for novelties, excelsior, containers, carving, etc.

General: Native to most of the northern and eastern U.S. as far west as the eastern edge of the Great Plains. Does best in rich, moist woodlands and along river bottoms, and does well on soils with fairly high pH. Shade tolerant.

American basswood (*Tilia americana*)

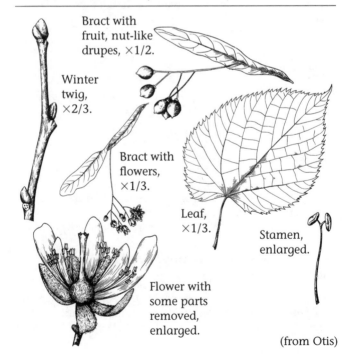

Bract with fruit, nut-like drupes, ×1/2.

Winter twig, ×2/3.

Bract with flowers, ×1/3.

Leaf, ×1/3.

Stamen, enlarged.

Flower with some parts removed, enlarged.

(from Otis)

214

Landscape Use: A popular large shade tree, with nice, fragrant flowers and pleasing foliage. Planted mostly as the cultivar 'Redmond' because of its strongly conical crown form. I prefer the species, which has stronger branch attachment and a nice, wider crown; a number of these old trees can be seen in older parts of Logan and other Utah towns. Free of most serious pests, though aphids can be a nuisance in some years. Zones 2-9. **Littleleaf European linden (*T. cordata*)** is a European native similar in appearance to American linden, but with smaller leaves (up to 3" long), flowers, and fruit. It is a good quality landscape tree that is quite popular throughout Utah and the U.S., though weak branch attachment is a potential problem with some cultivars. Aphids also are a common problem. Mostly planted as cultivars with a strong conical habit and medium size at maturity. **Crimean linden (*Tilia × euchlora*)** is a hybrid of *T. cordata* and *T. dasystyla* with a looser, more graceful habit than littleleaf linden. Zones 3-7.

littleleaf European linden (*Tilia cordata*)

Leaf,
×1/3.

(from USDA 1949)

Crimean linden (*Tilia × euchlora*)

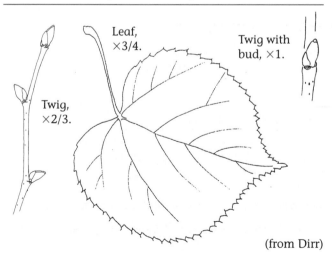

Leaf,
×3/4.

Twig with
bud, ×1.

Twig,
×2/3.

(from Dirr)

Other Lindens

Silver Linden   *(Tilia tomentosa)*

Leaves: Alternate; simple; more evenly heart-shaped; 2" to 5" long and almost as wide; deciduous; coarsely doubly serrate margin; pointed tip; dark green and glabrous to slightly pubescent above; covered with **dense silver-white pubescence beneath**; petiole thin and hairy, 1" to 1-1/2" long; yellow fall color.

Twigs/Buds: Twigs usually zigzag; densely pubescent. No terminal bud; lateral buds partially covered with soft hairs, otherwise dark red-brown or green, about 1/4" long, rounded, usually with two visible scales.

Flowers/Fruit: Flowers perfect; yellow-white; similar to littleleaf European linden, with a bract 1-1/2" to 2-1/2" long. Fruit similar to American linden but hairier and slightly smaller.

Bark: Smooth and light gray for many years; later turning dark gray-brown and furrowed.

Wood: Presumably similar to American linden; little information available.

General: Native to southeastern Europe and western Asia. Like other lindens prefers moist sites with rich soil but is adaptable to poorer soils; more heat and drought tolerant than other lindens. Shade tolerant.

Landscape Use: A good, large shade tree that should be planted more in Utah. Its foliage is very attractive, with contrasting dark green and silver-white. Zones 4-7.

TAMARICACEAE

Tamarisk family. Contains 4 genera and about 100 species of trees and shrubs from Europe to east Asia and India. Leaves are alternate and often small and needle- or scale-like.

Tamarisk   Genus *Tamarix*

This genus contains about 75 species of deciduous trees and shrubs grown for their fine foliage, slender branches, and pinkish flowers, and for their toughness and adaptability.

Tamarisk ◆ Salt-cedar   *(Tamarix ramosissima)*

Leaves: Alternate; simple; **scaly; very small**; deciduous; blue-green; no petiole.

silver linden (*Tilia tomentosa*)

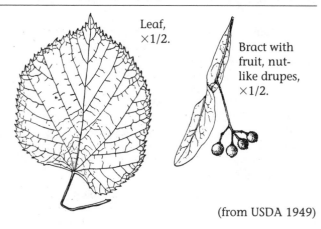

Leaf, ×1/2.

Bract with fruit, nut-like drupes, ×1/2.

(from USDA 1949)

tamarisk (*Tamarix ramosissima*)

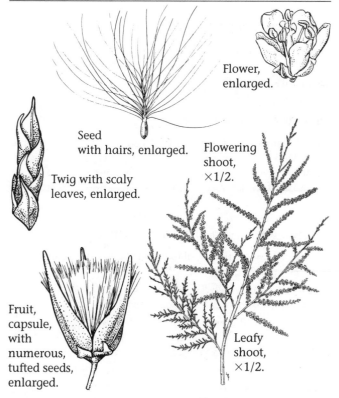

Flower, enlarged.

Seed with hairs, enlarged.

Twig with scaly leaves, enlarged.

Flowering shoot, ×1/2.

Fruit, capsule, with numerous, tufted seeds, enlarged.

Leafy shoot, ×1/2.

(from Benson & Darrow)

217

Twigs/Buds: Twigs slender, spreading, and drooping. Buds small, round.

Flowers/Fruit: Flowers perfect; 5 petals; very small; pink; arranged in large, drooping inflorescences at branch ends; open in May. Fruit a small capsule.

Bark: Gray; smooth.

Wood: No information available.

General: Native to China. Much planted in the past in the western U.S., including Utah, for conservation reasons, but has become a naturalized weed along streams in dry areas where it out-competes most native plants. Very salt and drought tolerant. Shade intolerant.

Landscape Use: This shrubby tree is a pest and should no longer be planted. Other species may also have been planted and are occasionally available in nurseries, including *Tamarix parviflora*. Hardiness ranges from zones 7-10 to zones 2-7, depending on species.

ELAEAGNACEAE

Oleaster family. Contains 3 genera and about 45 species. Found in North America, Europe, and Asia. Most have their **surfaces covered with silver or brown scales**.

Oleaster   Genus *Elaeagnus*

A genus with about 40 species of deciduous or evergreen trees or shrubs with a drupe or olive-like fruit. One species, Russian-olive, has been widely planted in Utah and is naturalized in many areas. These generally are very tough trees and shrubs with attractive foliage, but they can be weedy.

Russian-olive   *(Elaeagnus angustifolia)*

Leaves: Alternate; simple; oblong; 1-1/2" to 3" long; deciduous; entire margin; **silvery; scaly**; petiole short.

Twigs/Buds: Twigs silvery; sometimes with spines. Buds small, round, gray-brown, with 4 exposed, silvery scales.

Flowers/Fruit: Flowers perfect; no petals; 3/8" long; whitish-yellow; fragrant; open in May. Fruit a **drupe; silver-yellow**; 1/4" to 1/2" in diameter; matures in August and September.

Bark: Gray-brown; shallow furrows with narrow plates between.

Wood: Unimportant; little information available; yellow to brown.

Russian-olive (*Elaeagnus angustifolia*)

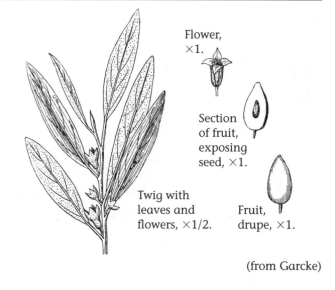

Flower, ×1.

Section of fruit, exposing seed, ×1.

Twig with leaves and flowers, ×1/2.

Fruit, drupe, ×1.

(from Garcke)

General: Native to Asia and southern Europe. Has been planted extensively on the Great Plains and in the West and has become naturalized. Shade intolerant.

Landscape Use: A medium-sized tree attractive for its foliage and interesting, irregular, spreading crown form. Has been strongly affected by a stem canker in the Midwest but not yet in Utah. This tree is very aggressive and weedy and has been declared a noxious weed in Carbon, Duchesne, and Uintah Counties in Utah. It has caused some serious environmental degradation and should not be planted.

LYTHRACEAE

Crapemyrtle or Loosestrife family. A large family of shrubs or small trees with about 22 genera and 450 species that are mostly tropical.

Crapemyrtle   Genus *Lagerstroemia*

A genus of about 30 species of evergreen or deciduous trees and shrubs native to Asia and Australia. Leaves are opposite, simple, and entire; **flowers are perfect and pink, purple, or white, and are arranged in large, showy groups at the ends of branches**.

219

Crapemyrtle *(Lagerstroemia indica)*

Leaves: Opposite, or occasionally alternate or whorled near branch ends; simple; 1" to 3" long; 3/4" to 1-1/2" wide; deciduous; entire; elliptic to oblong; dark green and glabrous on top, glossy; lighter and glabrous beneath, often with hair on midrib; petiole very short or missing; yellow, orange, or red fall color.

Twigs/Buds: Twigs slender; almost square in cross-section on young stems; red-green at first turning brown; glabrous. Buds pointed, with 2 outer scales fringed with small hairs; pressed against twig.

Flowers/Fruit: Flowers perfect; 1" to 1-1/2" wide; **fringed or crinkled petals; showy; white, pink, purple, or red**; in 6" to 8" long clusters at the ends of the branches; appear in July to September. Fruit a 6-part capsule that splits open at maturity releasing winged seeds; 1/2" wide; matures in fall and stays on through winter.

Bark: Gray; smooth; **peels off in thin layers** exposing gray to brown inner bark; very attractive.

Wood: No information available.

General: Shrub to small tree native to China. Shade intolerant.

Landscape Use: Very attractive flowers and bark. My main experience with this shrubby tree was in Alabama, where it was widely planted for its flowers. I found it to be somewhat leggy and awkward when planted as a small street tree, but many cultivars exist with a variety of sizes and growth habits. Would need a warm climate if planted in Utah, but at least one cultivar, 'Hopi' may be hardy to zone 5. Zones 6(5?)-9.

crapemyrtle *(Lagerstroemia indica)*

Leaf,
×1/2.

Flowers,
×1/2.

(from Apgar)

CORNACEAE

Dogwood family. Contains about 10 genera and 100 species. Scattered around the world, but more common in temperate areas in the Northern Hemisphere. Generally unimportant for wood products, but some have great ornamental value. **Opposite, simple leaves.**

Dogwood   Genus *Cornus*

A genus with about 40 species of mostly deciduous trees, shrubs, or herbaceous plants with mostly opposite leaves and fruit a drupe. Of great ornamental value. Only one shrubby dogwood is native to Utah.

Flowering Dogwood   *(Cornus florida)*

Leaves: Opposite; simple; oval; 3" to 6" long; deciduous; **leaf veins parallel margin in an arc**; entire margin; surfaces hairy; bright green above; paler beneath; petiole short; turning scarlet in fall.

flowering dogwood (*Cornus florida*)

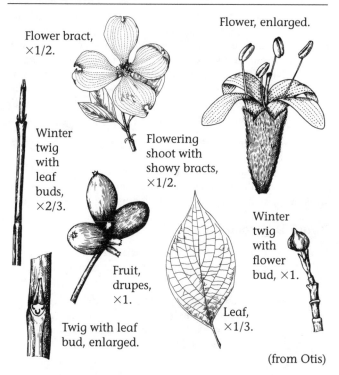

Flower bract, ×1/2.

Flower, enlarged.

Winter twig with leaf buds, ×2/3.

Flowering shoot with showy bracts, ×1/2.

Fruit, drupes, ×1.

Winter twig with flower bud, ×1.

Twig with leaf bud, enlarged.

Leaf, ×1/3.

(from Otis)

221

Twigs/Buds: Twigs slender; purple; more or less covered with a white, waxy coating; red to purple-red fall color. Terminal bud 1/8" long, 2 scales meet in a straight line without overlapping; flower buds look like small lanterns or urns on branch tips.

Flowers/Fruit: Flowers perfect; yellow; inconspicuous; arranged in a 1/2" wide head; surrounded by **4 large showy white or deep pink bracts**, 3" to 4" across; appear in early spring before leaves. Fruit a **drupe; bright red**; about 1/3" long; in compact clusters.

Bark: Thin; dark red-brown; broken into small, square blocks; very distinctive.

Wood: Unimportant; sapwood light pink-brown; heartwood dark brown; hard; heavy; growth rings distinct but not sharply delineated; diffuse-porous; rays visible to naked eye.

General: Native to most of the eastern U.S. A small tree that occurs naturally in the shady understory of other trees. Very shade tolerant.

Landscape Use: A good, small tree widely planted as an ornamental because of its beautiful flowers, good fall color, and ornamental fruit. Sensitive to pollution and not well-adapted to alkaline soils. Worth trying in protected situations, preferably with some shade. Zones 5-9 (many cultivars are of southern origin and will not flower reliably or do well in cold areas; in zones 5 and 6 make sure your tree is from a more northern source). ❖**Red-osier** or **red-stemmed dogwood** (*Cornus sericea*; formerly *C. stolonifera*) is a shrub that is native to Utah's mountains in moist areas near streams, and also makes an excellent landscape plant with its bright red stems in winter. A cultivar, **'Flaviramea'** also is available with bright yellow stems. Zones 2-8.

Other Dogwoods

(All have opposite, simple, entire, ovate to elliptic, deciduous leaves; small inconspicuous flowers arranged in heads, with or without showy bracts; and fruit a small drupe.)

Kousa Dogwood *(Cornus kousa)*

Leaves: 2" to 4" long; 1" to 2" wide; dark green above; paler and **hairy beneath, especially where veins meet**; turning red to purple; petiole short.

Flowers/Fruit: Flowers and white to pink bracts similar to flowering dogwood, but **on 2" long stalks** with bracts more pointed and blooming several weeks later. Fruit a small drupe; pinkish-red to red; **grouped in a raspberry-like, round bundle, 1/2" to 1" in diameter.**

red-osier dogwood (*Cornus sericea*)

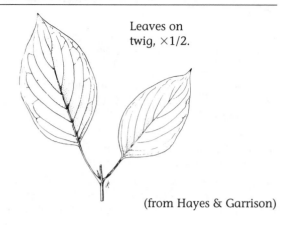

Leaves on twig, ×1/2.

(from Hayes & Garrison)

Kousa Dogwood (*Cornus kousa*)

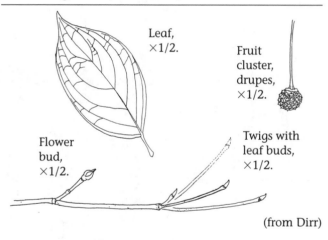

Leaf, ×1/2.

Fruit cluster, drupes, ×1/2.

Flower bud, ×1/2.

Twigs with leaf buds, ×1/2.

(from Dirr)

Bark: Flakes off as it ages, leaving patches of brown, tan, and gray.

General: Native to China, Korea, and Japan. Doesn't like very high soil pH; more drought hardy than flowering dogwood. Intermediate shade tolerance.

Landscape Use: A small tree rarely planted in Utah, but with some promise. More cold-hardy than flowering dogwood. Zones 4-8.

Pagoda Dogwood ◆ Alternate-leaf Dogwood
(Cornus alternifolia)

Leaves: Similar to flowering dogwood, but **alternate (clumped on ends of twigs to where they appear whorled)** and pubescent beneath.

Flowers/Fruit: Flowers perfect; yellowish-white; small, but in 1-1/2" to 2-1/2" bunches. Fruit a drupe; green at first, maturing **blue-black and waxy** in August; 1/2" to 1/3" in diameter.

General: Native to the eastern U.S. and Canada, where it is an understory plant in hardwood forests. Cultural preferences similar to flowering dogwood. Shade tolerant.

Landscape Use: Another small dogwood rarely planted in Utah, but worth using in colder areas. Prefers shady, cool sites. Not as ornamental in some ways as those described above, though the crown shape and horizontal branches give it a nice appearance. Zones 3-7.

pagoda dogwood *(Cornus alternifolia)*

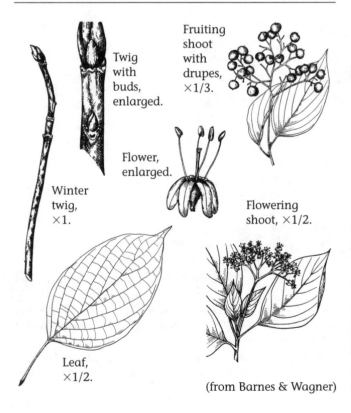

Twig with buds, enlarged.

Fruiting shoot with drupes, ×1/3.

Flower, enlarged.

Winter twig, ×1.

Flowering shoot, ×1/2.

Leaf, ×1/2.

(from Barnes & Wagner)

224

Corneliancherry Dogwood *(Cornus mas)*

Leaves: Similar to flowering dogwood, but pubescent on both sides and somewhat smaller.

Flowers/Fruit: Flowers perfect; yellow; small, but in 3/4" bunches; **appear very early, before leaves**. Fruit a **cherry-red, oblong drupe**; 1/2" in diameter; matures in July; edible and used for jams and jellies.

General: Native to the western Asia and central and southern Europe. Better adapted to high soil pH and poor conditions than most other non-shrub dogwoods. Intermediate shade tolerance.

Landscape Use: A small to medium sized tree rarely planted in Utah. I saw a planting of these growing at an NRCS Plant Materials Center near Manhattan, Kansas. They looked good, were growing well, and had attractive, edible fruit. Zones 4-8.

corneliancherry dogwood *(Cornus mas)*

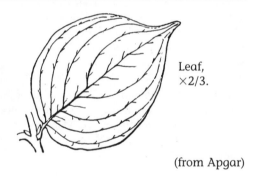

Leaf,
×2/3.

(from Apgar)

OLEACEAE

Olive family. Contains about 30 genera and more than 400 species. Distributed through the temperate and tropical forests of the Northern Hemisphere. Olives and olive oil are produced by one species in this family (*Olea europaea*). Several popular ornamental shrubs and trees are also part of this family, including ash (*Fraxinus*), lilac (*Syringa*), Forsythia (*Forsythia*), and privet (*Ligustrum*).

Ash Genus *Fraxinus*

This genus has about 70 species growing mostly in the Northern Hemisphere, with about 16 species native to North America and 2 native to Utah. Leaves are **compound (simple in one species) and opposite**, and fruit is a samara.

❖Singleleaf Ash • Dwarf Ash   *(Fraxinus anomala)*

Leaves: **Opposite; simple and 1" to 2" long, or sometimes once pinnately compound** with 2-5 smaller leaflets; deciduous; leaves or leaflets ovate or nearly round; glabrous above and dark green, pale below; margin entire or with very fine teeth.

Twigs/Buds: Twigs fairly stout; somewhat 4-winged or ridged and orange when young; round and gray when older. Terminal bud broad-ovoid; 1/8" to 1/4" long; orange-hairy.

Flowers/Fruit: Flowers perfect or dioecious; small and inconspicuous; in small, conical bunches; appear as the leaves emerge. Fruit a **samara; 1/2" long, 1/8" to 1/4" wide**; paddle-shaped in small clusters; often clinging to twigs into or throughout the winter; tip of wing rounded or notched.

Bark: Brown to red-brown; thin; with scaly ridges.

Wood: Unimportant; sapwood light colored and thick; heartwood light brown; growth rings distinct; ring-porous; heavy; hard.

General: A large shrub to small tree native to the canyons of southern Utah and scattered throughout the southwestern U.S., where it is generally found along streams or locations where moisture collects. I have seen it growing out of soil-collecting depressions on red sandstone slopes near St. George. Tolerant of drought, heat, and high soil pH. Shade intolerant.

Landscape Use: I'm not familiar with use of this plant in cultivated landscapes, but it may have some application in warmer parts of Utah where native plants and low water use are important. I have seen it carried in one nursery catalogue out of Oregon. Zones 6-9(10?).

singleleaf ash *(Fraxinus anomala)*

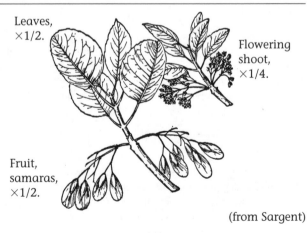

Leaves, ×1/2.

Flowering shoot, ×1/4.

Fruit, samaras, ×1/2.

(from Sargent)

❖Velvet Ash • Modesto Ash *(Fraxinus velutina)*

Leaves: Opposite; once pinnately compound; 3" to 6" long; deciduous; 3-9 leaflets (usually 5); **densely hairy petiole; leaflets thick, narrow elliptic to lanceolate**, 1" to 2" long, glabrous on top and densely hairy below, finely serrate margin above the middle.

Twigs/Buds: Twigs thin; rounded; **hairy-velvety when young**. Terminal bud small, ovoid; 1/8" long; hairy.

Flowers/Fruit: Flowers dioecious; small and inconspicuous, in small, hairy bunches; appearing in spring. Fruit a samara; 3/4" long, 1/4" wide; paddle-shaped in small clusters; matures in fall.

Bark: Gray with some red; thin; furrowed.

Wood: Unimportant; growth rings distinct; ring-porous; presumably heavy; hard.

General: A small to medium-sized tree native to the canyons of extreme southwestern Utah and scattered throughout the southwestern U.S. and northern Mexico. Mostly found growing in canyons near intermittent streams. Tolerant of drought, heat, and high soil pH. Shade intolerant.

Landscape Use: As with singleleaf ash, I have not seen this plant used in cultivated landscapes. 'Modesto Ash' is a cultivar of this species that is more readily available. It makes an interesting and useful plant in a low water use and native plant-focused landscape. Zones 7(6?)-10.

velvet ash *(Fraxinus velutina)*

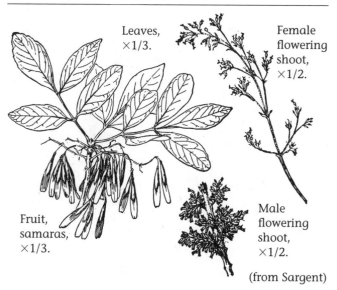

Leaves, ×1/3.

Female flowering shoot, ×1/2.

Fruit, samaras, ×1/3.

Male flowering shoot, ×1/2.

(from Sargent)

227

Green Ash *(Fraxinus pennsylvanica)*

Leaves: Opposite; once pinnately compound; 10" to 12" long; deciduous; 7-9 leaflets; leaflets oblong-lanceolate to elliptic, 4" to 6" long, glabrous above and pubescent below, bright green, finely serrate margin, short-stalked; **turn bright yellow in fall**.

Twigs/Buds: Twigs fairly stout; gray to brown; **leaf scar half-circular, straight or shallowly notched across the upper edge**. Terminal bud rusty brown, conical, hairy; lateral buds smaller.

Flowers/Fruit: Flowers dioecious; small and inconspicuous, arranged in clusters; appear in spring as leaves expand. Fruit a samara; 1" to 2-1/2" long, 1/4" wide; paddle-shaped in dense clusters; often clinging to twigs into or throughout the winter; abruptly narrowed wing along the slender seed cavity.

green ash *(Fraxinus pennsylvanica)*

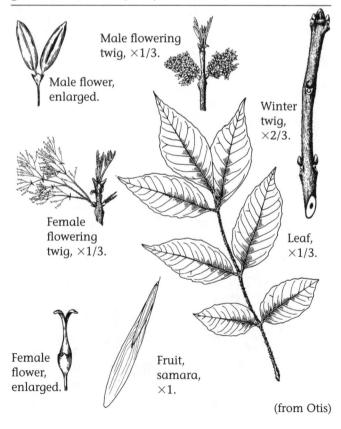

Male flower, enlarged.

Male flowering twig, ×1/3.

Winter twig, ×2/3.

Female flowering twig, ×1/3.

Leaf, ×1/3.

Female flower, enlarged.

Fruit, samara, ×1.

(from Otis)

228

Bark: Ash-gray; sometimes with an orange tinge on younger trees; on older trees furrowed into diamond-shaped areas separated by narrow interlacing ridges; distinctive.

Wood: Important where native; sapwood white; heartwood light brown; growth rings distinct; ring-porous; rays not distinct; used for handles, tools, containers, furniture, lumber, etc.

General: Native from the Great Plains east, including southern Canada. Prefers moist sites, but fairly drought resistant and tolerant of fairly high soil pH. Intermediate shade tolerance.

Landscape Use: A tough, durable, large tree used extensively in Utah in landscapes since pioneer times. Also good for windbreaks. Lilac borers can be an especially severe problem that is difficult to treat effectively, though they may be most likely to affect stressed trees. I have seen many old green ashes that show no signs of borers, while a nearby young, vigorous, 30' tall tree might be riddled with borers. Seedless cultivars are available, but they can set large amounts of seed under stressful conditions. Zones 3-9. **Blue ash** (*Fraxinus quadrangulata*) is a similar tree that can be planted and will do well in Utah. It differs from green ash in having twigs with four corky ridges and sharply serrate leaflets. Zones 4-7.

blue ash (*Fraxinus quadrangulata*)

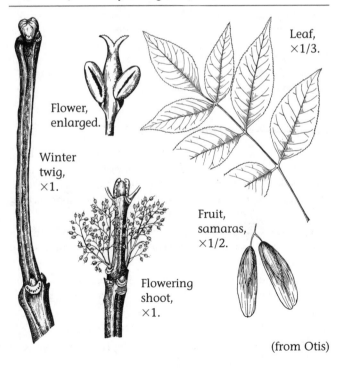

Leaf, ×1/3.

Flower, enlarged.

Winter twig, ×1.

Fruit, samaras, ×1/2.

Flowering shoot, ×1.

(from Otis)

229

White Ash *(Fraxinus americana)*

Leaves: Opposite; once pinnately compound; 8" to 12" long; 5 to 9 (mostly 7) leaflets; deciduous; leaflets ovate to oblong-lanceolate, 3" to 5" long, glabrous on both sides, dark green on top and lighter beneath, margins entire or barely serrate, usually short-stalked; rachis slightly grooved, glabrous; **turn purple to yellow-purple in fall**.

Twigs/Buds: Twigs fairly stout; dark green to gray-green, occasionally purplish; glabrous; **leaf scar U-shaped with deep to shallow notch across top edge**. Terminal bud rusty brown, blunt, covered with 4-6 brown scales, glabrous (generally not hairy); lateral buds smaller, almost triangular.

Flowers/Fruit: Flowers dioecious; small and inconspicuous, arranged in conical clusters; appear in spring before the leaves expand. Fruit a samara; 1" to 2" long; 1/4" wide; paddle-shaped in dense clusters; often clinging to twigs into or throughout the winter.

Bark: Similar to green ash but more deeply furrowed.

Wood: Important where native; like green ash in characteristics and uses.

General: A large tree native to moist sites in most of the eastern U.S. Intermediate shade tolerance.

Landscape Use: Sometimes called by the name of one of its cultivars, 'Autumn Purple' ash, this is a very desirable landscape tree. Some feel that it may be less susceptible to borers than green ash, but I've not seen evidence of this. I have seen several white ashes in Logan, including one about 30" in diameter and 60' tall. Should be planted more as a substitute for green ash to add diversity to our landscapes. Zones 3-9.

European Ash *(Fraxinus excelsior)*

Leaves: Opposite; once pinnately compound; 10" to 12" long; 7 to 11 leaflets; deciduous; leaflets ovate to lanceolate, 2" to 4" long and half as wide, glabrous on both sides but with hair beneath along midrib, dark green on top and light below, **margins serrate**; rachis pubescent or glabrous; yellow to green fall color.

Twigs/Buds: Twigs fairly stout; gray to gray-brown; glabrous when mature; round in cross-section. **Buds black, pubescent**, covered with 4-6 scales.

Flowers/Fruit: Flowers dioecious; small and inconspicuous, arranged in clusters; appear in spring. Fruit a samara; 1" to 1-1/2" long; 1/4" wide; paddle-shaped in dense clusters.

Bark: Tightly ridged, somewhat similar to green ash.

Wood: No information available; presumably similar to green ash.

white ash (*Fraxinus americana*)

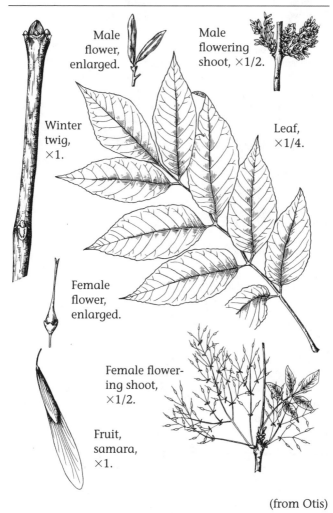

Male flower, enlarged.

Male flowering shoot, ×1/2.

Winter twig, ×1.

Leaf, ×1/4.

Female flower, enlarged.

Female flowering shoot, ×1/2.

Fruit, samara, ×1.

(from Otis)

European ash (*Fraxinus excelsior*)

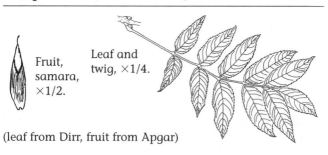

Fruit, samara, ×1/2.

Leaf and twig, ×1/4.

(leaf from Dirr, fruit from Apgar)

231

General: Native throughout much of Europe and in Asia Minor. Does well on high pH soils. Intermediate shade tolerance.

Landscape Use: This medium to large tree is occasionally planted in Utah, but does not do as well as green or white ash. It seems especially susceptible to borers, and is not as cold hardy as many of its relatives. Zones 5-8.

Lilac   Genus *Syringa*

A genus of about 28 species of ornamental shrubs or small trees native to Asia and Europe. The leaves are **simple and opposite**, and flowers are showy. This genus includes the commonly planted shrub lilac, *Syringa vulgaris.*

Japanese Tree Lilac   *(Syringa reticulata)*

Leaves: Opposite; simple; broad ovate to ovate; 2" to 5-1/2" long; deciduous; entire margin; dark green above; gray-green beneath and glabrous to slightly hairy; petiole 1/2" to 1" long; yellow to brown fall color.

Twigs/Buds: Twigs stout; glossy; glabrous; brown. Often with no terminal bud; lateral buds round with 4 sets of scales, brown.

Flowers/Fruit: Flowers perfect; **white; held in 6" to 12" long heads that bloom in June**. Fruit a capsule; curved; 3/4" long; warty; brown.

Bark: **On young and older branches reddish brown to brown with horizontal ridges or lenticels, cherry-like**; gray and scaly on older trunks.

Wood: No information available.

General: Native of Japan. Small to medium-sized tree. Shade intolerant.

Landscape Use: An outstanding small to medium-sized tree known for its beautiful flowers. It has a broad crown, somewhat shrubby in appearance, but easily pruned to a tree form. It also is fairly tough, relatively insect and disease free, and tolerates high pH soils. This tree should be planted more throughout Utah, except in the hottest locations. Zones 3-7(8?).

Fringetree   Genus *Chionanthus*

This is a small genus of 2 to 3 species of deciduous trees or shrubs native to North America and China. The leaves are **simple and opposite**, and the flowers are showy, with the fruit a dark blue drupe.

Japanese tree lilac (*Syringa reticulata*)

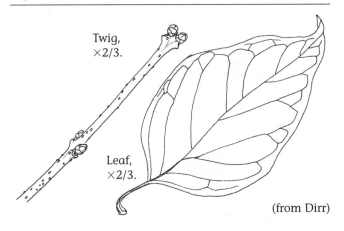

Twig, ×2/3.

Leaf, ×2/3.

(from Dirr)

fringetree (*Chionanthus virginicus*)

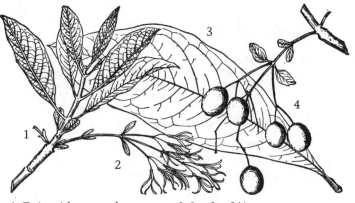

1. Twig with young leaves, ×1/2.
2. Flowers, ×1/2.
3. Leaf, ×3/4.
4. Fruiting shoot, drupes, ×1/2.

(from Sargent)

Fringetree ◆ White Fringetree
(Chionanthus virginicus)

Leaves: Opposite; simple; oval to ovate; 4" to 8" long, 1/2 as wide; deciduous; entire margin; dark green and shiny above; paler beneath with at least some pubescence; petiole 1/2" to 1" long and hairy; fall color yellow to yellow-brown.

233

Twigs/Buds: Twigs stout; more or less hairy; green-brown; somewhat 4-angled. Terminal bud present; ovoid, with 3 sets of ridged scales, green to brown.

Flowers/Fruit: Flowers polygamo-dioecious; showy; **white; with 3/4" to 1-1/4" long petals on male and female flowers that give a soft, fleecy effect; held in 4" to 8" long groups** that bloom in late may to early June. Fruit a **blue-black, ovoid drupe; 1/2" to 3/4" long**; covered with a whitish waxy coating; ripens late summer.

Bark: Thin and smooth on young branches; gray to red-brown; becoming scaly and ridged.

Wood: Unimportant; dense; hard.

General: Native to the southeastern U.S. Adaptable to a wide range of sites. Naturally grows in wet areas and is shade tolerant.

Landscape Use: A large shrub to medium-sized tree with beautiful flowers and good form. This tree is doing well in Salt Lake City, particularly at Red Butte Gardens and Arboretum. Very popular in Europe. Should tolerate high pH soils and heat, but also is cold hardy. Should be planted more often in Utah. Zones 3-9.

BIGNONIACEAE

Trumpet Creeper or Bignonia family. Contains about 100 genera and 750 species of trees, shrubs, and vines. Most of the family is tropical, including some very fine furniture woods.

Catalpa   Genus *Catalpa*

This genus consists of about 10 species of mostly deciduous trees native to North America, eastern Asia, and the West Indies. Leaves are **simple, alternate, and often very large**; flowers are fairly large, perfect, and showy.

Northern Catalpa ◆ Western Catalpa
(Catalpa speciosa)

Leaves: Opposite or whorled in 3's; simple; **heart-shaped; 8" to 12" long, 5" to 8" wide**; deciduous; entire margin; fall color yellow-brown.

Twigs/Buds: Twigs stout; green to purple; circular leaf scars. No terminal bud; buds smaller than leaf scars.

Flowers/Fruit: Flowers perfect; showy; trumpet-like; white with yellow and purple spots; 2-1/2" wide; appear in May to June in 4" to 8" long, upright clusters. Fruit a **capsule; slender; 8" to 20" long**; 1/2" in diameter; hangs on through the winter, splitting down its length to release fringed, winged seeds.

northern catalpa (*Catalpa speciosa*)

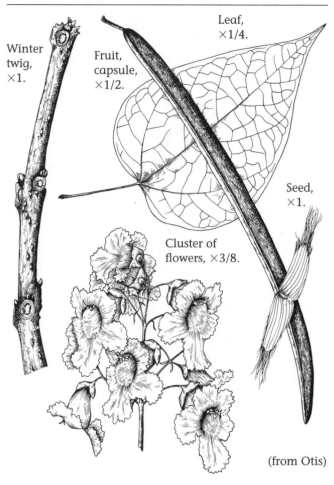

Winter twig, ×1.

Fruit, capsule, ×1/2.

Leaf, ×1/4.

Seed, ×1.

Cluster of flowers, ×3/8.

(from Otis)

Bark: Brown; broken into thick scales.

Wood: Not important; sapwood pale gray; heartwood gray-brown; growth rings distinct; ring-porous; durable; soft; used some for fence posts and railroad ties.

General: Native to a small area in southeastern Missouri, southern Illinois and Indiana, western Tennessee and Kentucky, and northeastern Arkansas. Has escaped cultivation and is naturalized in the Midwest. Shade intolerant.

Landscape Use: A large, but fairly narrow-crowned tree with beautiful white flowers and an interesting, though messy, fruit. The wood is somewhat weak and brittle, branch breakage is common,

235

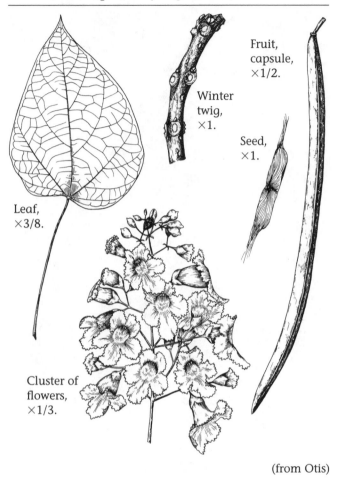

Leaf,
×3/8.

Winter
twig,
×1.

Fruit,
capsule,
×1/2.

Seed,
×1.

Cluster of
flowers,
×1/3.

(from Otis)

and verticillium wilt is a problem. Though catalpa has its draw-backs, I would hate to see it disappear from our landscapes, as it adds a lot with its distinctive crown form, even in winter. It also is very tough and tolerant of wet or dry and high pH soils. Does well throughout most of Utah. Zones 4-9. **Southern catalpa** (*Catalpa bignonioides*) is a similar species with a smaller crown size and smaller leaves, flowers, and fruit. Occasionally planted in Utah; not as cold tolerant as northern catalpa. One grafted dwarf cultivar, 'Nana', looks like a large mushroom and is often called umbrella catalpa. Zones 5-9.

Chilopsis Genus *Chilopsis*

A genus with only one species, which is a Utah native; described below.

❖Desertwillow *(Chilopsis linearis)*

Leaves: Opposite or scattered along stem; simple; **linear or narrowly-lanceolate; 6" to 12" long, 1/2" wide or less**; deciduous; glabrous; sometimes sticky; entire margin.

Twigs/Buds: Twigs slender; glabrous or hairy; light brown. No terminal bud; lateral buds small, with several overlapping scales; rusty-red and hairy.

Flowers/Fruit: Flowers perfect; similar to northern catalpa but smaller with some purple; 3/4" to 1-1/2" wide; appear in May-June in small clusters. **Fruit and seeds similar to northern catalpa, but smaller**; 7" to 12" long and 1/4" wide.

Bark: Brown; scaly.

Wood: No information available.

desertwillow *(Chilopsis linearis)*

1. Flowering shoot, ×1/2.
2. Leaves, ×1/2.
3. Flowers, ×1/2.
4. Fruit, capsule, ×1/2.
5. Seeds, ×1.

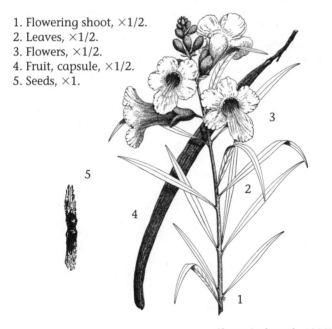

(from Sudworth 1908)

237

General: Native to warm locations along streams in southwestern Utah and throughout the extreme southwestern U.S. Fairly short-lived. Not a true willow. Shade intolerant.

Landscape Use: This small, shrubby tree is rarely used in Utah landscapes, but could be used more as a small, interesting ornamental in warm areas. Will be hard to find in nurseries. I have seen a small one growing in a large pot outdoors next to a greenhouse in Jensen, Utah. Zones 7-10.

CAPRIFOLIACEAE

Honeysuckle family. This is a large family of shrubs or small trees with about 14 genera and 400 species. Most are located in northern, temperate areas. Some very valuable ornamental shrubs and vines are part of this family, including honeysuckles (*Lonicera*), and viburnums (*Viburnum*).

Elder   Genus *Sambucus*

A genus of about 20 species of deciduous trees and shrubs, with 5 native to North America. Leaves are **compound and opposite**; flowers are perfect and small, but in larger, showy clusters. Two species are native to Utah and both are usually shrubby. However, blue elder (*Sambucus cerulea*) also occasionally reaches tree size.

❖Blue Elder   *(Sambucus cerulea)*

Leaves: Opposite; once pinnately compound; 4" to 7" long; deciduous; 5 to 9 leaflets with short stalks, coarsely serrate margins, narrow and ovate to oblong, 1" to 6" long, green and glabrous on top, lighter and glabrous or pubescent beneath.

Twigs/Buds: Twigs stout; somewhat angled or ridged; brownish-red; large, triangular leaf scars that nearly circle stem; pith large and soft. No terminal bud; lateral buds green, scaly.

Flowers/Fruit: Flowers perfect; small; yellow-white; in large, showy, flat-topped clusters at the ends of the branches; appear in June or July. Fruit a berry-like drupe; dark blue; 1/4" diameter; sweet, juicy, and edible; matures in late summer.

Bark: Brown with some red; thin; scaly.

Wood: Not important; soft; weak; heartwood yellow; diffuse-porous.

General: Native to much of the western U.S., including most of Utah. Grows in moist areas along streams in the mountains. Fairly short-lived. Shade intolerant, but likes protected sites.

blue elder *(Sambucus cerulea)*

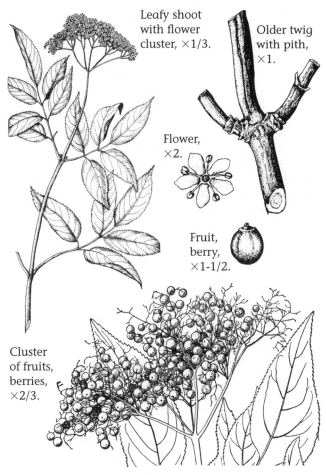

Leafy shoot with flower cluster, ×1/3.

Older twig with pith, ×1.

Flower, ×2.

Fruit, berry, ×1-1/2.

Cluster of fruits, berries, ×2/3.

(from Hayes & Garrison, except cluster of fruits from Sudworth 1908)

Landscape Use: Seldom used, but could be in a native-type landscape. Fruit is collected and used for jellies, jams, pies, and wine. Flowers are quite attractive and open well into the summer. Though generally a shrub or small tree, I have seen a blue elder near the Guinavah-Malibu amphitheater in Logan Canyon that was 20' to 30' high and 8" to 10" in diameter. Zones 4-8. Red elder *(Sambucus racemosa)*, with its red fruit, also is native to higher elevation sites in Utah, but always occurs as a shrub.

LILIACEAE

Lily family. This is the only monocot family mentioned in this book—the rest of the angiosperms listed are all dicots. The lily family includes about 200 genera and 2,000 species of shrubs, trees, and herbs found all over the world. *Asparagus* and *Yucca* are two of the better known genera in this family. As with all monocots, flower parts generally are in threes or sixes.

Yucca   Genus *Yucca*

This is a genus of about 30 species of evergreen plants native to Central and North America. Leaves are **sword-shaped and clustered**; flowers are perfect and large, in large, clusters at the ends of stems. Only one *Yucca* native to Utah can be considered a tree. Welsh *et al.* and some others place this genus in the Agavaceae.

❖Joshua-tree   *(Yucca brevifolia)*

Leaves: Clustered at plant base and along stem; simple; sword-shaped; stiff and pointed; 12" long; evergreen; serrate margins; blue-green.

Twigs: Leaves attached to and covering main stem; lower stems are covered with old dead leaves that curl downward after they die.

Flowers/Fruit: Flowers perfect; large; yellow-white; in showy, clusters on a long stalk at the ends of the stems; appear in April. Fruit a large capsule that hangs down at maturity.

Bark: Dark-brown; platy.

Wood: Little known or used, though formerly used occasionally for paper, packing materials, fuel, and novelties.

General: Native to much of desert southwest, including extreme southwestern Utah under an elevation of 3,500 feet; some can be seen between the lanes of Interstate 15 as you approach St. George. Grows in hot, dry areas and along valley bottoms. Often shrubby, but can reach 20' tall and 24" trunk diameter. Can be quite long-lived. Shade intolerant.

Landscape Use: Rarely used, but obviously is a good native plant for hot dry sites where freezing temperatures are rare. Flowers and foliage are fairly attractive. Supposedly zones 7-10, though I've seen several Joshua-trees doing well at Hill Air Force Base in Davis County.

Joshua-tree *(Yucca brevifolia)*

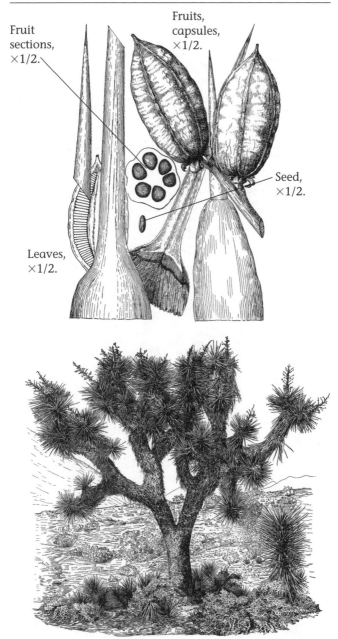

Fruit sections, ×1/2.

Fruits, capsules, ×1/2.

Seed, ×1/2.

Leaves, ×1/2.

Old and young trees, greatly reduced.

(from Sudworth 1908)

TREE SELECTION GUIDE

The table on the next several pages summarizes a great deal of tree selection information for Utah and the surrounding regions. Nearly all trees that are commonly planted are included, plus many that are fairly rare. All native trees are also included, since many of these may make good landscape plants but are rarely planted. The information included in this table is based on the author's knowledge or has been obtained from reliable sources. Little cultural information exists for some species, however.

USING THIS GUIDE

This tree selection guide is divided into broadleaved trees, most of which are deciduous, and coniferous trees, most of which are evergreen. Characteristics mentioned in the table are generally for the species or most commonly planted cultivar, though some species show a wide range in characteristics between cultivars. Cultural characteristics involved with site selection and planting, along with some comments and limitations, are shown on the left. General species characteristics and ornamental features are shown on the right, along with some common cultivars. A detailed description of table information and symbols follows:

- Species are listed alphabetically by Latin name in italics, followed by common name(s).
- (❖) in front of the name indicates a tree native to Utah.
- (†) in front of the name indicates a tree that rarely should be planted, though limited use in specific situations may be justified.
- Tolerance of poor drainage (flooded or compacted soils with low oxygen availability), drought (lack of water),

alkalinity (high soil pH; higher than 6.5 to 7), salt (mainly referring to salt spray or deposition on tops, though this may indicate some tolerance to soil salinity), and shade (lack of sunlight) is indicated by the letters **L**(ow), **M**(edium), or **H**(igh).

♦ Ease of transplanting also is indicated as **L**(ow), **M**(edium), or **H**(igh). Low ease of transplanting indicates plants that must be especially well-cared for during and after the transplanting process. Such trees often do better when their size at transplanting is small.

♦ USDA plant hardiness zones are given to indicate a plant's cold-hardiness. Refer to the section following the selection guides for more details and for a hardiness zone map and table.

♦ Comments and limitations are referred to by number and are defined as:

1. May be insect and/or disease prone, especially when stressed.
2. Weak wood and/or branch structure.
3. Fruit and/or plant parts can be nuisances; use fruitless varieties if possible.
4. Thorns or spines that can be dangerous; use thornless varieties if possible.
5. Sucker (sprout) growth can be a problem.
6. Prefers abundant water, but some of these species may survive on a drier site.
7. Evergreen broadleaf (retains its leaves for more than one year).
8. Deciduous conifer (loses its needles every year).

♦ Growth rate refers to height growth for the first ten years after a tree is planted and is shown as follows: **Low** — <12 inches/year; **Medium** — 12-24 inches/year; **High** — >24 inches/year.

♦ Mature height will vary considerably by cultivar and site and is shown here for the species assuming adequate care: **Low** — <20 feet; **Medium** — 20-40 feet; **High** — >40 feet.

♦ Longevity refers to the average life span of a tree and may be much shorter on harsh sites or where the species is poorly adapted. Longevity is shown as: **Low** — <25 years; **Medium** — 25-50 years; **High** — >50 years.

- Trees that are suitable for planting under or near most powerlines are indicated by a check () in that column. This means that their mature height is under about 25 feet. Be careful to check cultivar heights when buying. If in doubt, contact your Extension Agent or your electricity provider.

- Crown shape varies considerably by cultivar and sometimes by site. The common crown shape for a species is indicated by a letter as follows: **B**road, **C**olumnar, **I**rregular, **L**ayered, **O**val, **P**yramidal, **R**ound, **S**hrubby, **V**ase, **W**eeping. These shapes, except for irregular, are illustrated below.

- The availability of cultivars for a species is indicated in the last column. A few noteworthy cultivars are listed for each species where available, with a note about the cultivar's distinguishing characteristic(s). Some common cultivar names and their meanings are:

'Aurea' or 'Aureum' — golden or yellow leaves during the growing season

'Columnaris' or 'Columnare' — very tight, columnar crown

'Compactum', 'Compacta', or 'Nana' — dwarf or small-crowned

Crown types

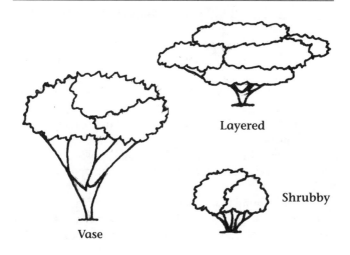

Layered

Shrubby

Vase

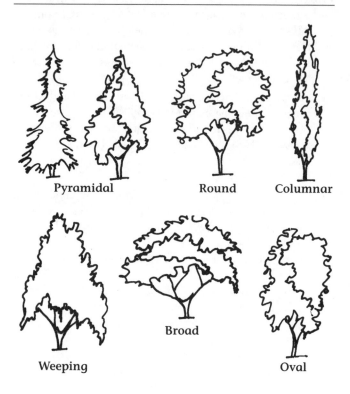

Pyramidal   Round   Columnar

Weeping   Broad   Oval

'Fastigiata' — narrow crown form

'Glauca' — foliage with a whitish or silvery cast, usually due to a white waxy coating

'Globosa' or 'Globosum' — globe-shaped crown

'Laciniata' or 'Laciniatum' — "cut" or deeply lobed leaves

'Pendula' or 'Pendulum' — pendulous branches or weeping crown shape

'Purpurea', 'Atropurpurea', or 'Atropurpureum' — purple leaves in growing season

'Umbraculifera' — umbrella-shaped crown

'Variegata' — variegated leaves showing multiple colors

Keep in mind that this is only a partial listing, and cultivars often exist with much different characteristics from the original species. Even where named cultivars don't exist, it is important to know the seed source or seed collection location for the tree you are planting. Choose species or seed sources from locations as similar as possible to your planting site. A few of the species listed here would not be found at all outside of extreme southern Utah and are not included under the detailed species descriptions earlier in the book.

Finally, remember that cultivars can be interesting and unique, but don't ignore the value of the original species. For example, typical native trees of the species American linden (*Tilia americana*) in many ways are better than any of the cultivars that have been selected.

Cultural Characteristics / **Tree Selection Guide** / **General Species Characteristics**

Tolerant of: Poor Drainage	Drought	Alkalinity	Salt	Shade	Trnsplnt Ease	Hrdiness Zones	Comments	Tree Selection Guide	Growth Rate	Mature Height	Longevity	Power Lines OK	Crown Shape	Flowers	Fruit	Fall Color	Bark	Foliage	Available Cultivars
Conifers (mostly evergreen)																			
L	M	H	H	H	M	1-5		❖*Abies lasiocarpa* — subalpine or alpine fir	L	H	H		P					✔	None available
L	M	M	M	M	M	3-7		❖*Abies concolor* — white or concolor fir	L	H	H		P				✔	✔	'Candicans' (long, blue needles; narrow crown), 'Compacta', 'Violacea' (silver-blue needles)
M	M	H	M	M	M	5-8		*Calocedrus (Libocedrus) decurrens* — incense-cedar	M	H	H		P				✔	✔	'Aureo-Variegata' (yellow-variegated), some columnar forms available
L	M	M	M	M	L	6-9		*Cedrus atlantica* — Atlas cedar	L	H	H		P		✔		✔	✔	'Argentea' (silver-blue), 'Aurea' (yellowish), 'Fastigiata', 'Glauca', 'Glauca Pendula'
M	M	M	M	L	H	7-9		*Cedrus deodara* — Deodar cedar	M	H	H		P		✔		✔	✔	'Kashmir' (cold hardy to -5°F), 'Shalimar' (cold hardy to -15°F; good blue-green color)
L	M	M	M	L	M	5-7		*Cedrus libani* — cedar of Lebanon	L	H	H		P		✔		✔	✔	'Argentea' (silver-blue), var. *brevifolia* (smaller than species), 'Pendula', 'Sargentii' (5' dwarf), var. *stenocoma* (more cold hardy; stiff)

248

					Zone		Species								Cultivars
L	M	M	M	M	4-8		*Chamaecyparis obtusa* — Hinoki falsecypress	L	M	H		P		✓ ✓	'Crippsii' (broad, yellow-green), 'Filicoides' (shrubby; pendulous twigs), 'Gracilis' (dark green, narrow pyramid), 'Nana' (small shrub)
L	H	H	M	M	7-9		*Cupressus arizonica* — Arizona cypress	M	M	H		P		✓	'Gareei' (silver-blue), 'Pyramidalis' (narrow, conical; blue foliage)
L	H	H	M	M	7-9		*Cupressus sempervirens* — Italian cypress	M	H	H		P		✓	'Glauca' (blue-green; columnar), 'Roylei' (bright green; stiff-upright), 'Stricta' (narrow, columnar; green), 'Swane's Gold' (yellow-green; narrow)
L	H	H	L	H	3-9		*Juniperus chinensis* — Chinese juniper	M	M	M	✓	P		✓	Numerous, all forms, sizes, and colors; includes 'Hetzii' (15' tall) and 'Pfitzeriana' (wide shrub)
L	H	H	L	H	4-7		❖*Juniperus osteosperma* — Utah juniper	M	M	H	✓	R		✓	None available
L	H	H	L	H	3-7		❖*Juniperus scopulorum* — Rocky Mountain juniper	M	M	H		P		✓	Numerous; many are blue; 'Pathfinder' (narrow pyramidal), 'Wichita Blue' (tall pyramidal)
L	H	H	L	H	2-9		*Juniperus virginiana* — eastern redcedar	M	M	H		P		✓	Numerous; 'Glauca', 'Globosa', 'Manhattan Blue' (compact pyramidal), 'Pendula'
M	L	M	L	H	2-6	6,8	*Larix decidua* — European larch	H	H	H		P		✓ ✓	'Fastigiata' (very narrow), 'Pendula'
M	L	M	L	H	4-7	6,8	*Larix kaempferi* — Japanese larch	H	H	H		P		✓ ✓	'Blue Rabbit' (narrow pyramidal with blue-green foliage), 'Dervaes' (horizontal branches, drooping branchlets), 'Pendula'

Tolerant of: Poor Drnge	Drought	Alkalinity	Salt	Shade	Transplt Ease	Hrdiness Zones	Comments	Tree Selection Guide	Growth Rate	Mature Height	Longevity	Power Lines OK	Crown Shape	Flowers	Fruit	Fall Color	Bark	Foliage	Available Cultivars
L	M	L	L	M	M	4-8	8	*Metasequoia glyptostroboides* — dawn redwood	H	H			P			✓	✓	✓	'National' (narrow pyramidal), 'Sheridan Spire' (upright)
M	M	M	L	M	M	2-7		*Picea abies* — Norway spruce	M	H			P		✓			✓	Numerous; 'Nidiformis' (called "bird's nest spruce"; tight, spreading, shrubby), 'Pendula' (name for cultivars with weeping branchlets)
L	M	M	M	H	M	2-5		❖ *Picea engelmannii* — Engelmann spruce	L	H			P					✓	None available
L	M	M	M	H	H	2-6		*Picea glauca* — white or Blackhills spruce	L	H			P		✓			✓	'Conica' or 'Dwarf Alberta' (very small, tight, tiny needles; common in Utah), 'Densata' (also called "Blackhills spruce"; tall, narrow; nice form)
L	M	M	M	H	M	4-7		*Picea omorika* — Serbian spruce	L	H			P					✓	'Expansa' (wide shrub), 'Nana' (round or conical; 10' high), 'Pendula' (tall, narrow; branches droop)
L	M	M	M	M	M	2-7		❖ *Picea pungens* — blue or Colorado blue spruce	M	H			P					✓	Numerous; 'Argentea' (silver-white needles), 'Glauca Globosa', 'Glauca Pendula', 'Hoopsii' (dense pyramidal), 'Mission Blue' (very blue)

							Species							Cultivars / Notes
L	H	M	M	L	M	5-7	❖*Pinus aristata* — bristlecone pine	L	M	H	I		✓	None available
L	M	M	M	L	M	4-8	*Pinus bungeana* — lacebark pine	L	H	H	P		✓	None available
L	H	M	M	L	M	2-6	❖*Pinus contorta* — lodgepole pine	M	H	H	P			None available; plant local sources
L	M	M	M	L	M	3-7	*Pinus densiflora* — Japanese red pine	M	H	H	I		✓	'Globosa' (round shrub to 10'-15'), 'Oculis-draconis' (yellow banded leaves), 'Pendula', 'Umbraculifera'
L	H	M	M	L	M	4-8	❖*Pinus edulis* — pinyon, Colorado pinyon	L	M	H	R		✓	None available
L	H	M	M	L	M	4-7	❖*Pinus flexilis* — limber pine	L	M	H	P			'Columnaris', 'Glauca Pendula', 'Nana', 'Pendula', 'Vandewolf's Pyramid' (upright; fast growth; blue)
M	H	H	L	L	M	8-10	*Pinus halepensis* — Aleppo pine	M	M	H	P			None available
L	H	M	M	L	M	5-9	❖*Pinus monophylla* — singleleaf pinyon	L	M	H	✓	R		None available
L	M	M	L	M	M	5-8	*Pinus monticola* — western white pine	M	H	H	P		✓	None available
M	H	H	M	L	H	2-8	*Pinus mugo* — Mugo pine	M	L	M	✓	S		'Compacta' (dense, round, 4' tall), 'Gnom' (15" tall by 3' wide), 'Mops' (3' tall by 3' wide), var. *mugo* (8' tall), var. *pumilio* (prostrate, 10' wide)
L	H	M	H	L	M	4-7	*Pinus nigra* — Austrian pine	M	H	H	P			'Hornibrookiana' (very compact dwarf, 6' wide and 2' high), 'Pyramidalis'

251

Tree Selection Guide

Tree Selection Guide	Growth Rate	Mature Height	Longevity	Power Lines OK	Crown Shape	Flowers	Fruit	Fall Color	Bark	Foliage	Available Cultivars	Poor Drainage	Drought	Alkalinity	Salt	Shade	Transplnt Ease	Hrdiness Zones	Comments
Pinus parviflora — Japanese white pine	L	M	H	P						✓	'Bergman' (wide, rounded shrub), 'Brevifolia' (narrow crown; short needles), 'Glauca'	L	M	M	H	L	M	4-7	
❖ *Pinus ponderosa* — ponderosa pine	M	H	H	P					✓		None available	L	H	M	M	L	M	3-7	
Pinus strobiformis — southwestern white pine	M	M	M	P						✓	None available; plant cold-hardy sources	L	M	M	M	L	M	5-9	
Pinus strobus — eastern white pine	M	H	M	P						✓	'Compacta', 'Contorta' (irregular crown; twisted branches), 'Fastigiata', var. *glauca*, 'Pendula' (weeping crown)	L	M	M	M	L	M	3-8	
Pinus sylvestris — Scotch or Scots pine	M	H	H	P					✓	✓	'Argentea' (silvery leaves), 'Aurea', 'Fastigiata', 'French Blue' (leaves blue-green in winter)	L	H	M	L	L	M	2-8	
Pinus thunbergiana — Japanese black pine	M	M	H	I						✓	'Compacta', 'Globosa', 'Iseli' (gold variegated; small), 'Majestic Beauty' (large tree; dark green)	L	H	M	M	L	M	5-9	
Pinus wallichiana — Himalayan or Bhutan pine	M	H	H	P			✓			✓	'Oculis-draconis' (leaves with cream-colored bands)	L	M	M	M	L	M	5-7	

252

Broadleaves (mostly deciduous)

								Species							Cultivars / Notes
M	L	H	M	L	M	4-6		*Pseudotsuga menziesii* — Douglas-fir	M	H	H	P		✓	'Fastigiata', 'Fletcheri' (6' dwarf), var. *glauca* (blue-green needles), 'Pendula'
M	L	M	H	M	M	6-8		*Sequoiadendron giganteum* — giant sequoia	M	H	H	P		✓	'Pendulum' (main stem curves and twists)
H	M	M	H	L	M	4-9	6,8	*Taxodium distichum* — baldcypress	M	H	H	P		✓✓✓	'Monarch of Illinois' (wide, large crown), 'Pendens' (pyramidal; branchlets droop), 'Shawnee Brave' (narrow crown)
H	M	H	H	L	M	2-8	6	*Thuja occidentalis* — northern white-cedar, eastern arborvitae	M	M	M	P		✓	Numerous; cold hardy include 'Emerald' and 'Nigra' (narrow pyramidal), 'Techny' (broad pyramidal)
H	M	H	H	L	M	6-9	6	*Thuja (Platycladus) orientalis* — Oriental arborvitae	L	M	M	P		✓	Numerous; 'Aurea Nana' (5'; round), 'Baker' (bright green; likes heat), 'Compacta' (small, pyramidal)
H	L	H	H	H	H	5-7	6	*Thuja plicata* — western redcedar	M	H	H	P		✓	'Canadian Gold' (gold leaves), 'Fastigiata', 'Zebrina' (yellow variegated foliage; gets 60' tall)
M	H	M	M	L	H	5-9		*Acer buergeranum* — trident maple	L	M	M	✓	R	✓✓✓	Dwarf and variegated cultivars available
M	H	H	M	M	H	4-8		*Acer campestre* — hedge maple	M	M	M	B		✓	'Compactum' (shrubby), 'Fastigiatum', 'Queen Elizabeth' (small to medium size)
M	H	M	M	M	H	2-8		*Acer ginnala* — Amur or Ginnala maple	M	L	M	✓	R	✓	'Compactum' (shrubby), 'Flame' (shrub to small tree; red fruits; deep red fall color)
M	H	M	M	M	M	4-7		*Acer grandidentatum* — canyon or bigtooth maple	M	M	H	O		✓	'Autumn Glow' (upright tree form; good fall color)

Tree Selection Guide

	Cultural Characteristics — Tolerant of								General Species Characteristics					Orn. Features					Available Cultivars
	Poor Drainage	Drought	Alkalinity	Salt	Shade	Transplnt Ease	Hrdiness Zones	Comments	Growth Rate	Mature Height	Longevity	Power Lines OK	Crown Shape	Flowers	Fruit	Fall Color	Bark	Foliage	
❖*Acer glabrum* — Rocky Mountain maple	M	M	M	M	M	H	2-8		M	L	M	✓	R			✓			None available
Acer griseum — paperbark maple	M	L	M	M	M	L	4-8		L	M	M	✓	O			✓	✓		Some hybrids available
❖†*Acer negundo* — boxelder, ash-leaved or Manitoba maple	H	H	H	H	M	H	2-9	2	H	H	M		O						'Baron' (seedless), 'Sensation' (red fall color), several with variegated foliage
Acer nigrum — black maple	L	H	H	M	M	M	4-8		M	H	H		O			✓			'Greencolumn' (upright, columnar; often called *A. saccharum*)
Acer palmatum — Japanese maple	L	L	M	M	H	M	5-8		L	L	M	✓	R			✓	✓	✓	Numerous; var. *atropurpureum* and 'Bloodgood' (reddish-purple leaves), 'Crimson Queen' (red, deeply lobed leaves), 'Viridis' (green leaves)
Acer platanoides — Norway maple	M	M	H	M	M	H	3-8		M	H	H		R	✓		✓		✓	Numerous; 'Columnare', 'Erectum' (narrow), 'Crimson King' (maroon), 'Emerald Queen' (dark green), 'Schwedleri' (starts purple, turns green)
Acer pseudoplatanus — sycamore maple	M	H	H	M	M	M	4-7		M	H	H		O		✓			✓	'Atropurpureum' (leaves purple underneath), 'Brilliantissimum' (leaves start pink to cream)

						Zones			Scientific / Common Name				Avail.		Cultivars and Remarks
H	L	M	L	M	M	3-9	M		*Acer rubrum* — red maple	M	H	H	O	✓	Numerous; 'Autumn Blaze' (orange-red fall color), 'Autumn Flame' (red fall color, small leaves), 'Columnare', 'Red Sunset' (pyramidal)
H	H	M	H	M	H	3-9	H		†*Acer saccharinum* — silver maple	H	H	H	O	✓	'Blair' (strong branching), 'Laciniatum', 'Silver Queen' (leaves silver beneath), 'Wieri' (drooping branches)
L	M	H	L	H	M	4-8	M		*Acer saccharum* — sugar maple	M	H	H	O	✓	Numerous; 'Bonfire' (good red fall color), 'Globosum', 'Green Mountain' (heat tolerant)
M	H	H	M	M	M	3-8	M		*Acer tataricum* — Tatarian maple	M	M	H✓	R	✓	'Rubrum' (deep red fall color)
M	M	M	M	M	H	4-8	M		*Acer truncatum* — purpleblow or Shantung maple	L	M	M✓	R	✓	'Norwegian Sunset' (upright-oval; heat tolerant), 'Pacific Sunset' (upright-spreading; red in fall)
M	M	M	M	M	M	7-8	M	3	*Aesculus californica* — California buckeye	M	M	H	R	✓✓✓	None available
M	M	M	M	M	M	3-8	M	3	*Aesculus × carnea* — red horsechestnut	M	M	M	R	✓	'Briotii' (flowers deeper red in 10" groups), 'O'Neill' (better red flowers in 10"-12" groups)
M	M	M	M	H	M	3-7	M	3	*Aesculus glabra* — Ohio buckeye	M	M	H	R	✓	var. *nana* (dwarf, shrubby)
M	M	M	H	M	H	3-8	M	3	*Aesculus hippocastanum* — horsechestnut	M	H	H	R	✓	'Baumannii' (double white flowers; no fruit)
H	H	H	H	M	H	4-8	H	2,3,5	†*Ailanthus altissima* — tree-of-heaven, ailanthus	H	H	M	V	✓	'Erythrocarpa' (red fruit), 'Metro' (male, no fruit; tight crown), 'Pendulifolia' (long leaves hang down)

Tree Selection Guide

Tree Selection Guide	Poor Drnage	Drought	Alkalinity	Salt	Shade	Trnsplnt Ease	Hrdiness Zones	Comments	Growth Rate	Mature Height	Longevity	Power Lines OK	Crown Shape	Flowers	Fruit	Fall Color	Bark	Foliage	Available Cultivars
Albizia julibrissin — mimosa, silk-tree, albizia	L	H	M	M	L	H	6-9	1,3	H	M	M		B	✓				✓	'E.H. Wilson' and 'Rosea' (hardy to -15°F)
Alnus glutinosa — European or common alder	H	M	M	L	M	H	3-7	6	H	M	M		O		✓				'Aurea', 'Laciniata', 'Fastigiata' (narrow like Lombardy poplar)
❖*Alnus tenuifolia* — thinleaf or mountain alder	H	M	H	L	M	H	1-7	6	M	M	M		O						None available
❖*Amelanchier alnifolia* — Saskatoon, western serviceberry	L	H	M	M	M	M	2-7		L	L	M	✓	S	✓		✓			'Regent' (compact, shrubby), 'Success' (heavy fruit)
Amelanchier arborea — downy serviceberry	L	M	M	M	H	M	4-9		L	L	M	✓	I	✓		✓			'Autumn Sunset' (good orange fall color), 'Springtime' (good flowers and fall color; 12' tall)
❖*Amelanchier utahensis* — Utah serviceberry	L	M	M	M	M	M	4-8		L	L	M	✓	S	✓		✓			None available
Betula nigra — river birch	H	L	L	L	M	M	4-9	6	H	H	M		O				✓		'Heritage' (attractive bark; superior selection)
❖*Betula occidentalis* — water or river birch	H	L	M	M	H	M	3-7	6	L	L	M	✓	S			✓	✓		None available
Betula papyrifera — paper birch	L	L	M	M	M	M	2-7	1,6	M	M	L		P			✓	✓		None available

					Name						✓	✓	✓	Cultivars
1,6	L L M M M	H	2-7	L L M M M	*Betula pendula* — European white birch	M H M	P			✓				'Dalecarlica' (cut leaves; weeping form), 'Fastigiata', 'Purpurea'
	M M M L M	M	4-8	M M M L M	*Carpinus betulus* — European hornbeam	L M M	R		✓	✓				'Asplenifolia' (deeply toothed leaves), 'Columnaris', 'Fastigiata' (20'-30' wide), 'Globosa', 'Pendula', 'Purpurea', 'Variegata'
	M M M L H	M	3-9	M M M L H	*Carpinus caroliniana* — American hornbeam, musclewood	L M M	R		✓	✓	✓			'Pyramidalis' (similar to species)
3	M M M M L	M	4-9	M M M M L	*Castanea mollissima* — Chinese chestnut	M L M	R		✓	✓	✓			Some hybrids available
2,3	M M H M M	H	5-9	M M H M M	*Catalpa bignonioides* — southern catalpa	M M M	R		✓	✓				'Aurea', 'Nana' (see below)
2	M M H M M	H	5-9	L L M ✓	*Catalpa bignonioides* 'Nana' — umbrella catalpa	L L M	R		✓	✓				'Nana' (sterile, grafted dwarf)
2,3	M H H M M	H	4-9	H H M	†*Catalpa speciosa* — northern or western catalpa	H H M	O		✓	✓				None available
	H H M M H	H	2-9	H H H	*Celtis occidentalis* — hackberry, common hackberry	H H H	V		✓	✓	✓			'Chicagoland' (single leader), 'Prairie Pride' (very good form), 'Windy City' (good form)
	M M H M M	H	5-9	M M H	❖*Celtis reticulata* — netleaf hackberry	M M H	V		✓	✓	✓			None available
6	M L M M M	L	4-8	M L M	*Cercidiphyllum japonicum* — katsuratree	M L M	O		✓	✓	✓			'Pendula' (graceful, weeping, blue-green mound)

Tree Selection Guide

Tree Selection Guide	Poor Drnage	Drought	Alkalinity	Salt	Shade	Trnsplnt Ease	Hrdiness Zones	Comments	Growth Rate	Mature Height	Longevity	Power Lines OK	Crown Shape	Flowers	Fruit	Fall Color	Bark	Foliage	Available Cultivars
Cercis canadensis — eastern redbud, Judas-tree	L	H	H	L	H	M	3-9		M	L	H	✓	B	✓		✓	✓	✓	var. *alba* (white flowers), 'Forest Pansy' (purple leaves), 'Silver Cloud' (white variegated leaves)
❖*Cercis occidentalis* — California or western redbud	L	H	H	H	H	M	7-9		M	L	H	✓	B	✓			✓	✓	None known
❖*Cercocarpus ledifolius* — curlleaf mountain-mahogany	M	H	H	M	L	M	3-8	7	M	L	H	✓	I	✓				✓	None available
❖*Chilopsis linearis* — desertwillow	M	M	H	M	L	M	8-10	3	M	M	L		I	✓	✓				None available
Chionanthus virginicus — fringetree, white fringetree	H	M	H	M	H	M	3-9		L	M	M		S	✓	✓				'Floyd' (upright habit; mostly male, little fruit)
Cladrastis lutea — yellowwood	M	M	H	M	M	M	4-8		M	H	M		R	✓		✓	✓	✓	'Rosea' (pink flowers)
Cornus alternifolia — pagoda or alternate-leaf dogwood	L	L	M	M	M	L	3-7		M	L	M	✓	L	✓	✓		✓		'Argentea' (leaves with white variegations; shrubby)
Cornus florida — flowering dogwood	L	L	M	M	H	L	5-9		L	L	M	✓	L	✓	✓	✓	✓		Numerous; 'Cherokee Chief' (red flowers), 'Cloud 9' (cold-hardy), var. *rubra* (pink-red flowers), 'World's Fair' (cold hardy; drought resistant)

258

Species						Zone							Cultivars
Cornus kousa — Kousa dogwood	L	L	M	M	M	3-7	L L M	✓	L	✓ ✓ ✓ ✓			Numerous; var. *chinensis* (larger flowers and tree size), 'Dwarf Pink' (small tree; pink flowers), 'Fanfare' (upright form; very cold-hardy)
Cornus mas — corneliancherry dogwood	M	M	H	L	M	4-8	L L M	✓	R	✓ ✓			'Alba' (white fruit), 'Flava' (yellow fruit), 'Golden Glory' (heavy flowering), 'Nana', 'Variegata'
❖*Cornus sericea* — red-osier or red-stemmed dogwood	H	M	H	L	M	2-8	M L M	✓	S	✓			'Cardinal' (bright red stems), 'Flaviramea' (yellow stems), 'Isanti' (bright red stems; compact), 'Kelseyi' (compact)
Corylus americana — American hazelnut	M	M	H	L	M	4-9	M L M	✓	S	✓ ✓ ✓ ✓			None known
Corylus colurna — Turkish filbert, Turkish hazel	M	M	H	L	L	4-7	M M H		P	✓ ✓ ✓ ✓			None available
Corylus cornuta — beaked hazelnut	M	M	H	L	L	4-8	M L M	✓	S	✓ ✓ ✓ ✓			None available
Cotinus coggygria — common smoketree, smokebush	L	H	H	M	M	4-9	M L M	✓	S	✓ ✓ ✓ ✓			'Flame' (good orange-red fall color), 'Royal Purple' (dark purple mature leaves), 'Pendulus'
Cotinus obovatus — American smoketree, chittamwood	L	H	H	M	M	3-8	M M M		O	✓ ✓ ✓ ✓			'Grace' (red leaves; pink flowers), 'Red Leaf'
❖*Cocvania mexicana* — cliffrose, quininebush	L	H	H	M	L	5-9 7	L L M	✓	S	✓ ✓			None available
Crataegus crusgalli — cockspur hawthorn	M	H	H	M	L	3-8 4	M L M	✓	B	✓ ✓ ✓ ✓			var. *inermis* (thornless), 'Hooks' (fewer thorns)

259

Tree Selection Guide

Tree Selection Guide	Poor Drainage	Drought	Alkalinity	Salt	Shade	Transplnt Ease	Hrdiness Zones	Comments	Growth Rate	Mature Height	Longevity	Power Lines OK	Crown Shape	Flowers	Fruit	Fall Color	Bark	Foliage	Available Cultivars
Crataegus × *lavallei* — Lavalle hawthorn	M	H	H	M	L	M	4-8	4	M	L	M	✓	I	✓	✓	✓			Hybrid of *C. stipulacea* and *C. crusgalli*
Crataegus laevigata — English hawthorn	M	M	M	M	L	M	4-8	4	M	L	M	✓	R	✓	✓				'Crimson Cloud' (blight resistant), 'Paul's Scarlet' (red, doubled flowers; very showy)
Crataegus phaenopyrum — Washington hawthorn	M	H	H	M	L	M	3-8	4	M	L	M	✓	B	✓	✓	✓			'Clark' (heavy fruiting), 'Fastigiata', 'Vaughn' (hybrid with *C. crusgalli*; heavy fruiting)
Crataegus viridis — green hawthorn	M	H	H	M	L	M	4-8	4	M	L	M	✓	B	✓	✓	✓			'Winter King' (vase-shaped; red fruit attractive in winter; excellent tree)
†*Elaeagnus angustifolia* — Russian-olive	L	H	H	H	L	M	2-7		H	M	M	✓	R		✓			✓	'Red King' (rust red fruits)
Eriobotrya japonica — loquat	M	H	H	M	M	H	8-10	3,7	M	L	M	✓	I	✓	✓			✓	'Golden Nugget' (large; abundant fruit), 'Variegata' (white variegations)
Fagus grandifolia — American beech	L	L	M	L	H	M	3-9		L	H	H		O			✓	✓	✓	None available
Fagus sylvatica — European beech	L	L	M	L	H	M	4-7		L	M	H		O			✓	✓	✓	'Asplenifolia' (cut leaves), 'Pendula', 'Purpurea Tricolor' (purple variegated leaves)

Cultural Characteristics — Tolerant of: Poor Drainage, Drought, Alkalinity, Salt, Shade

General Species Characteristics — Orn. Features: Flowers, Fruit, Fall Color, Bark, Foliage

Scientific name — common name	(left attributes)						Zone	Note	✓	(right attributes)				✓	Cultivars and comments
Fraxinus americana — white ash	M	M	H	H	M	M	3-9			M	H	H	O	✓	'Autumn Applause' (tight, oval crown), 'Autumn Purple' (seedless), 'Rosehill' (seedless)
❖ *Fraxinus anomala* — singleleaf or dwarf ash	M	H	H	H	L	M	6-9			L	L	M	✓ I		None available
† *Fraxinus excelsior* — European ash	M	M	H	H	M	M	3-9	1		M	H	H	R		'Aurea', 'Globosa' (30' tall), 'Pendula', 'Rancho' (30' tall; yellow fall color)
Fraxinus pennsylvanica — green ash	H	H	H	H	M	H	3-9	1	✓	H	H	H	O	✓	'Marshall's Seedless', 'Patmore' (seedless), 'Summit' (upright, pyramidal)
Fraxinus quadrangulata — blue ash	M	H	M	M	M	M	4-7			M	H	H	R		'True Blue' (very good for high pH soils, leaves stay dark green)
❖ *Fraxinus velutina* — velvet or Modesto ash	M	H	M	M	M	M	7-9			M	M	M	R		'Modesto' (glabrous leaves)
Ginkgo biloba — ginkgo, maidenhair tree	M	H	H	M	L	M	3-9	3	✓	M	H	H	O	✓	All males; 'Autumn Gold' (good fall color), 'Fastigiata', 'Pendula', 'Santa Cruz' (spreading)
Gleditsia triacanthos — honeylocust	H	H	H	H	L	H	3-9	3,4	✓	H	H	M	R	✓	All thornless; 'Imperial' (few pods), 'Moraine' (fruitless; very good tree), 'Shademaster' (dark green; few pods), 'Skyline' (good fall color)
Gymnocladus dioicus — Kentucky coffeetree	M	M	H	H	M	M	3-8	3	✓	M	H	H	R	✓ ✓	'Variegata' (white variegations on green leaves)
Ilex opaca — American holly	M	M	M	M	L		5-9	7		L	M	M	I	✓	'Amy' (large leaves; abundant fruit), 'Goldie' (yellow fruit), 'Wyetta' (pyramidal)
Juglans cinerea — butternut	M	M	H	M	L		3-7			M	H	M	R		None available

Tree Selection Guide

Species	Poor Drnage	Drought	Alkalinity	Salt	Shade	Tnsplnt Ease	Hrdiness Zones	Comments	Growth Rate	Mature Height	Longevity	Power Lines OK	Crown Shape	Flowers	Fruit	Fall Color	Bark	Foliage	Available Cultivars
Juglans major — Arizona walnut	M	H	H	M	L	L	7-9		L	M	H		O					✔	None available
Juglans nigra — black walnut	M	M	M	M	L	L	4-9	3	M	H	H		O			✔		✔	'Laciniata' (dissected leaflets)
Juglans regia — English or Persian walnut	M	M	H	M	L	L	4-8	3	M	H	H		R					✔	'Carpathian' (very cold hardy), 'Hansen' (good fruit production), 'Laciniata', 'Pendula'
Koelreuteria paniculata — goldenraintree	M	H	H	H	L	M	5-9	2	M	M	M		O	✔	✔				'Fastigiata', 'September' (flowers late summer; not as cold-hardy as others)
Laburnum × watereri — goldenchain tree, Waterer laburnum	M	M	M	H	M	L	5-7		M	L	M	✔	O	✔					'Alford's Weeping', 'Aureum' (golden-yellow leaves), 'Pendulum', 'Vossii' (dense crown; 2' long inflorescences)
Lagerstroemia indica — crapemyrtle	L	M	H	H	M	H	7-9	5	M	L	M	✔	S	✔		✔	✔		Numerous; 'Acoma' (white flowers; semi-dwarf), 'Hopi' (pink flowers; semi-dwarf), 'Yuma' (lavender flowers; taller; upright)
Liquidambar styraciflua — sweetgum, American sweetgum	H	M	L	M	L	M	5-9	3	H	H	H		P			✔			'Burgundy' (deep red fall color), 'Festival' (narrower crown; yellow to pink fall color), 'Rotundiloba' (fruitless; rounded leaf lobes)

	Zone	Ref	Species — common name		Code	✓	Cultivars / notes
M M M L M	4-9		*Liriodendron tulipifera* — yellow-poplar, tuliptree, tulip-poplar	H H H	O	✓	'Compactum' (medium size), 'Fastigiatum' (20' wide), 'Tortuosum' (curled leaves and stems)
M H H L	4-9	3,4	*Maclura pomifera* — Osage-orange	M M H	R	✓ ✓	var. *inermis* (thornless)
L L M M	3-8		*Magnolia acuminata* — cucumbertree, cucumber magnolia	M H H	O	✓	'Golden Glow' and 'Yellow Bird' (good yellow flowers); 'Variegata' (yellow leaf blotches)
M M M M	6-9	7	*Magnolia grandiflora* — southern magnolia	M H H	P	✓ ✓	Numerous; 'Bracken's Brown Beauty' (good, dense crown), 'Majestic Beauty' (large leaves)
L L M M	3-8		*Magnolia kobus* — Kobus magnolia	L M H	O	✓	var. *borealis* (large, pyramidal crown), 'Wada's Memory' (hybrid; large flowers; fast growing)
L L M M	3-8		*Magnolia × loebneri* — Loebner magnolia	L M M	O	✓	'Ballerina' (many petals; fragrant), 'Merrill' (medium height; heavy flowering), 'Spring Snow' (superior cultivar; medium height)
L L M M	4-9		*Magnolia × soulangiana* — saucer magnolia	M M H	R	✓	'Brozzonii' (large white flowers open late), 'Lennei' (dark purple-pink petals; shrubby), 'San Jose' (large, pink-purple flowers; fast grower)
L L M M	4-9		*Magnolia stellata* — star magnolia	L L M	✓ R	✓	'Centennial' (doubled flowers, pinkish), 'Dawn' (pink stripe on petal), 'Royal Star' (superior)
M M H M L	3-9	3,5	*Malus pumila* — apple	M M M	V	✓	Many choices available

Cultural Characteristics / Tree Selection Guide / General Species Characteristics

Tree Selection Guide	Poor Drnage	Drought	Alkalinity	Salt	Shade	Tnsplnt Base	Hrdiness Zones	Comments	Growth Rate	Mature Height	Longevity	Power Lines OK	Crown Shape	Flowers	Fruit	Fall Color	Bark	Foliage	Available Cultivars
Malus spp. — crabapple	M	M	H	H	L	H	3-9	3,5	M	L	M		R	✓	✓				See crabapple selection table below
†*Melia azedarach* — Chinaberry	M	H	H	H	M	H	8-10	1,2,3,5	H	M	M	✓	R	✓	✓			✓	'Umbraculiformis' (domed shape; multi-stemmed; called "Texas Umbrellatree")
Morus alba — white mulberry	H	H	H	H	L	H	4-9	3	H	H	M		R					✓	'Hampton' (fruitless; wide crown), 'Mapleleaf' (large, maple-like leaves; fruitless), 'Pendula' (weeping, twisted; fruiting), 'Pyramidalis'
Morus rubra — red mulberry	H	H	H	H	L	H	5-9	3	H	H	M		R			✓		✓	None available
❖*Ostrya knowltonii* — Knowlton hophornbeam	L	H	H	M	H	M	6-9		L	M	H		I					✓	None available
Ostrya virginiana — eastern hophornbeam, ironwood	L	M	H	H	H	M	3-9		L	M	H		I		✓			✓	None available
Phellodendron amurense — Amur corktree	M	H	H	M	L	M	3-8		M	M	H		R		✓	✓	✓		'Macho' (fruitless; good branching habit), 'Shademaster' (fruitless)
Pistacia chinensis — Chinese pistache	M	H	H	H	L	H	6-9		M	M	H		R			✓			'Keith Davey' (male; no fruit)
Pistacia vera — pistachio	M	H	H	L	L	H	4-9		L	L	H	✓	R		✓	✓			Unknown
Platanus × *acerifolia* — London planetree	M	H	M	M	M	H	4-9	3	H	H	H		R		✓		✓		'Bloodgood', 'Columbia', and 'Liberty' (all anthracnose resistant)

264

					Zone		Species				O/C		Cultivars / Notes
H	H	H	M	M	H	4-9	3	*Platanus occidentalis* — American sycamore or planetree	H H H	O	✓	'Howard' (uncommon; new foliage yellow)
M	M	H	L	H	3-9	2,5,6	*Populus alba* — white poplar	H H H	O	✓	'Pyramidalis', 'Richardii' (upper leaf surfaces white)
H	M	H	L	H	3-9	2,6	❖*Populus angustifolia* — narrowleaf cottonwood	H H H	O	✓	None available; naturally forms hybrids, such as lanceleaf cottonwood, *P.* × *acuminata*
M	M	H	L	H	2-5	2,6	❖*Populus balsamifera* — balsam poplar	H H M	O		Some hybrids
M	M	H	L	H	3-9	2,6	†*Populus* × *canadensis* — Carolina poplar	H H M	O		'Eugenei' (columnar), 'Noreaster' (some canker resistance), 'Robusta' (small oval)
H	M	M	L	H	2-8	1,2,6	†*Populus candicans* — balm-of-Gilead	H H M	O		'Aurora' (leaves variegated when young)
H	M	H	L	H	2-9	2,6	*Populus deltoides* — eastern cottonwood	H H H	O	✓	'Platte', 'Noreaster' (both canker resistant), 'Siouxland' (canker susceptible), many hybrids
H	M	H	L	H	5-9	2,6	❖*Populus fremontii* — Fremont cottonwood	H H H	O	✓	None available
M	M	H	L	H	3-9	1,6	†*Populus nigra* 'Italica' — Lombardy poplar	H H L	C	✓	'Italica' (typical narrow crown), 'Theves' (wider)
M	M	M	L	H	3-7	1,5	❖†*Populus tremuloides* — quaking or trembling aspen	M H M	O	✓	None available
H	M	H	L	H	3-8	2,6	❖*Populus tricbocarpa* — black cottonwood	H H H	O	✓	None available

Tolerant of: Poor Drng	Drought	Alkalinity	Salt	Shade	Transplt Ease	Hrdins Zones	Comments	Tree Selection Guide	Growth Rate	Mature Height	Longevity	Power Lines OK	Crown Shape	Flowers	Fruit	Fall Color	Bark	Foliage	Available Cultivars
L	H	H	H	L	M	7-10	3,4	❖*Prosopis juliflora* — honey mesquite	L	M	H		B	✓	✓				None available
L	M	M	H	L	M	4-9	3,5	*Prunus armeniaca* — apricot	M	M	M		V	✓	✓				'Manchurian' (20' tall; round crown; pink flowers), many others available
L	M	M	M	L	M	3-8	3	*Prunus avium* — sweet cherry, mazzard	M	M	M		V	✓					'Plena' (double white flowers)
L	M	M	M	L	M	5-8	2,3	*Prunus cerasifera* — purpleleaf, cherry, or Myrobalan plum	M	L	L	✓	R	✓			✓	✓	'Newport' (dark purple leaves; more cold hardy), 'Thundercloud' (less cold hardy; pink flowers)
L	M	M	M	M	M	3-9	3	*Prunus cerasus* — sour cherry	M	M	M		V	✓			✓		var. *umbraculifera* (compact; round habit), var. *persiciflora* (pink flowers), many others
L	M	M	M	L	M	4-9	3	*Prunus domestica* — common plum	M	L	L		R	✓					Numerous
L	M	M	M	M	M	3-6	1,3	*Prunus padus* — European birdcherry, May Day tree	M	M	M		I	✓			✓		'Albertii' (30' pyramidal), var. *commutata* (1/2" flowers), 'Summer Glow' (purple leaves)

266

L	M	M	M	L	M	5-9	1,3	*Prunus persica* — peach	M	M	M	R	✓	✓	Numerous; 'Alba Plena' (double white flowers), 'Early Double Red, Pink, or White' (early blooming), 'Royal Red Leaf' (red-purple leaves)
L	M	M	M	L	M	4-7	3	*Prunus sargentii* — Sargent cherry	M	M	M	V	✓	✓	'Columnaris', 'Rancho' (very narrow crown), also many hybrids
L	M	M	M	L	M	5-9		*Prunus serrulata* — Japanese flowering or Oriental cherry	M	M	M ✓	V	✓	✓	'Amanogawa' (narrow upright form), 'Kwanzan' (double flowers; often grafted at 4'-6')
L	M	M	M	L	M	4-9		*Prunus subhirtella* — Higan cherry	M	M	M	B	✓		var. *pendula*, var. *autumnalis* (double flowers), 'Yae-shidare-higan' (weeping; double flowers)
L	M	M	M	L	M	2-9	3	❖*Prunus virginiana* — common chokecherry	M	M ✓	L	S	✓		'Schubert' or 'Canada Red' (pyramidal form; red-green foliage)
L	M	M	M	L	M	5-8		*Prunus × yedoensis* — Yoshino cherry	M	M	M	V	✓		'Afterglow' (pink flowers; 25'x25'), 'Ivensii' (white flowers; weeping)
L	M	M	M	H	H	3-9		❖*Ptelea angustifolia* — common or western hoptree, wafer-ash	L	L	M ✓	S	✓ ✓	✓ ✓	None available
M	H	H	M	L	L	5-9	2	*Pyrus calleryana* — Callery pear	M	M	M	P	✓		'Aristocrat' (better branch attachment), 'Bradford' (poor branch attachment), 'Chanticleer' (narrower crown, more cold hardy), 'Redspire' (pyramidal)
M	H	H	M	L	L	4-9	1,3	*Pyrus communis* — common pear	M	M	M	R	✓		Rarely planted as an ornamental
M	H	H	M	L	L	3-7	3	*Pyrus ussuriensis* — Ussurian pear	M	H	M	R	✓		None available

Tree Selection Guide

Species	Poor Drng	Drought	Alkalinity	Salt	Shade	Tnsplnt Ease	Hrdlnss Zones	Comments	Growth Rate	Mature Height	Longevity	Power Lines OK	Crown Shape	Flowers	Fruit	Fall Color	Bark	Foliage	Available Cultivars
Quercus acutissima — sawtooth oak	M	H	L	L	M	M	5-9	3	M	H	H		R			✔		✔	'Gobbler' (abundant acorns)
Quercus alba — white oak	L	M	L	H	M	M	3-9	3	M	H	H		R			✔		✔	None available
Quercus bicolor — swamp white oak	H	H	M	M	M	M	3-8	3	M	H	H		R			✔		✔	None available
Quercus cerris — turkey oak	M	H	H	M	M	M	5-7	3	M	H	H		R		✔	✔	✔	✔	'Argenteo-variegata' (white blotches on leaf edges)
❖*Quercus gambelii* — Gambel, scrub, or Rocky Mountain white oak	M	H	H	M	L	L	4-8	3,5	L	L	M	✔	S						None readily available
Quercus imbricaria — shingle or laurel oak	M	H	M	M	M	M	4-8	3	M	H	H		O			✔		✔	None available
Quercus macrocarpa — bur or mossycup oak	M	H	H	H	M	M	2-8	3	M	H	H		B	✔	✔			✔	None available
Quercus muehlenbergii — chinkapin oak	M	H	H	M	M	M	4-7	3	M	H	H		O			✔		✔	None available
†*Quercus palustris* — pin oak	H	M	L	L	M	H	4-8	3	H	H	H		P			✔		✔	'Crownright' (upright habit), 'Sovereign' (lower branches do not sweep down)

Cultural Characteristics — Tolerant of: Poor Drainage, Drought, Alkalinity, Salt, Shade

General Species Characteristics — Orn. Features: Flowers, Fruit, Fall Color, Bark, Foliage

					Zone	Region	Species				Form			Cultivars
M	M	H	M	M	4-8	3	*Quercus robur* — English oak	M	H	H	R		✓	'Atropurpurea', 'Fastigiata' (upright, narrow), 'Pendula', 'Westminster Globe' (large, round)
L	M	M	M	M	4-8	3	*Quercus rubra* — northern red oak	M	H	H	O	✓	✓	'Aurea' (new leaves yellow, becoming green)
M	H	M	M	M	5-9	3	*Quercus shumardii* — Shumard oak	M	H	M	P		✓	None available
M	H	M	M	L	7-9	3,7	❖*Quercus turbinella* — shrub live oak	L	L	M ✓	S		✓	None available
M	H	M	M	L	7-9	3,7	❖*Quercus undulata* wavyleaf oak	L	L	M	S	✓	✓	None available
M	H	L	M	M	3-8	4	*Robinia* × *ambigua* — Idaho flowering locust	M	M	M	O	✓	✓	'Idaho' (pink flowers; tough)
M	H	L	M	M	6-9	4	❖*Robinia neomexicana* — New Mexico locust	M	M	M	O		✓	None available
M	H	L	M	M	3-9	1,4,5	*Robinia pseudoacacia* — black locust	M	M	M	O	✓	✓	'Purple Robe' (medium height; dark pink flowers), 'Pyramidalis' (no spines on twigs)
H	L	H	H	M	2-8	2,6	❖*Salix amygdaloides* — peachleaf willow	H	M	M	O			None known
H	L	H	H	M	5-8	2,6	†*Salix babylonica* — weeping willow	H	H	M	W			'Crispa' (spiral leaves)
H	L	H	H	M	4-9	2,6	*Salix fragilis* — crack willow	H	H	M	O			Unknown
H	L	H	H	M	4-9	1,2,6	†*Salix matsudana* — Hankow willow ('Globe Navajo', etc.)	H	M	L	R			'Golden Curls' (hybrid; twisting, golden stems, 'Navajo' (round crown; troublesome), 'Pendula'
H	L	H	H	L	4-9	2,6	*Salix nigra* — black willow	H	H	M	O			None known

Tree Selection Guide

Species	Poor Drainage	Drought	Alkalinity	Salt	Shade	Transplt Ease	Hrdinss Zones	Comments	Growth Rate	Mature Height	Longevity	Power Lines OK	Crown Shape	Flowers	Fruit	Fall Color	Bark	Foliage	Available Cultivars
❖*Sambucus cerulea* — blue elder	H	M	M	M	L	M	5-9	6	M	M	L		R	✓					None available
Sophora japonica — Japanese pagodatree, scholar-tree	M	M	H	M	M	M	4-8	3	M	M	H		R	✓			✓		'Columnaris', 'Fastigiata', 'Pendula', 'Regent' (fast growth), 'Variegata'
Sorbus alnifolia — Korean mountain-ash	L	L	M	M	L	M	3-7		M	M	M		O	✓	✓	✓			'Redbird' (persistent red fruit), some upright forms
Sorbus americana — American mountain-ash	L	L	M	M	L	M	2-7	1	M	M	L		O	✓	✓	✓			None available
†*Sorbus aucuparia* — European mountain-ash or rowan	L	M	M	M	L	M	3-7	1	M	M	L		O	✓	✓	✓			Numerous; 'Asplenifolia' (deeply divided leaves), 'Cardinal Royal' (fast growth, upright)
❖*Sorbus scopulina* — Greene mountain-ash	L	M	H	M	L	M	2-6	1	L	L	L	✓	S	✓	✓	✓			None available
Syringa reticulata — Japanese tree lilac	M	M	H	H	L	M	3-7		M	L	H	✓	O	✓			✓		'Chantilly Lace' (leaf edges yellow), 'Ivory Silk' (flowers young, heavy), 'Regent' (vigorous; upright), 'Summer Snow' (heavy flowering)
†*Tamarix ramosissima* — tamarisk, salt-cedar	H	H	H	H	L	M	5-8		M	L	M		S	✓					None available

								Species							Cultivars / Remarks
M	M	H	L	M	H	2-9	5	*Tilia americana* — American basswood, American linden	M	H	H	O		✓	'Fastigiata', 'Lincoln' (slender-upright), 'Redmond' (dense pyramidal crown)
M	M	H	L	M	H	3-7	2	*Tilia cordata* — littleleaf European linden	M	M	M	P		✓ ✓	'Chancellor' (fastigiate when young, later pyramidal), 'Greenspire' (tough; common; upright), 'Prestige' (fast growing; strong form)
M	M	H	L	M	H	3-7	5	*Tilia × euchlora* — Crimean linden	M	H	H	O		✓	'Laurelhurst' (broad, pyramidal crown)
M	M	H	M	M	H	4-7	5	*Tilia tomentosa* — silver linden	M	H	M	P		✓ ✓	'Fastigiata' ('Erecta'), 'Green Mountain' (rapid growing; tough), 'Sterling' (wide, pyramidal)
H	H	H	M	M	M	2-9	1	†*Ulmus americana* — American or white elm	H	H	L	V		✓	Some claimed to be disease resistant; not proven long-term — 'Liberty', 'Washington'
M	H	H	M	M	M	4-9		*Ulmus parvifolia* — lacebark or Chinese elm	M	H	H	O		✓ ✓	'Emerald Isle' (broad crown; good bark), 'Emerald Vase' (upright-spreading crown)
H	H	H	H	M	H	3-9	1,2	†*Ulmus pumila* — Siberian elm	H	H	H	O		✓ ✓	'Chinkota' (very cold-hardy), 'Pendula'
M	H	H	L	M	M	6-9	7	❖*Yucca brevifolia* — Joshua-tree	L	L	M	I	✓		None available
L	H	H	M	M	M	5-8		*Zelkova serrata* — Japanese zelkova	H	H	M	V		✓ ✓	'Autumn Glow' (purple fall color), 'Green Vase' (vase-shaped; orange fall color; fast growth), 'Variegata', 'Village Green' (good growth rate)
M	H	H	H	M	M	6-9	4,5	*Zizyphus jujuba* — Chinese date	M	M	M	O		✓	'Lang' (fruits young), 'Li' (2" fruits)

271

CRABAPPLE SELECTION GUIDE

The following table includes flower, fruit, crown shape, size, and other characteristics for several good crabapple species or cultivars. These trees have done well nationally and in a test being conducted at Utah State University. Most have good aesthetics (flowers, foliage, and fruit), good disease resistance in our dry climate, a medium to small crown, and fruit that is small and persistent so it is ornamental after the leaves drop and creates less mess. It is not a complete list of good crabapples, so check with a knowledgeable nursery professional for additional choices. Michael Dirr's "Manual of Woody Landscape Plants" also has a good, fairly complete listing of crabapples.

Common crabapples to avoid include 'Candied Apple' (poor aesthetics), 'Dolgo' (large crown, large fruit), 'Hopa' (large crown, abundant fruit, disease-prone), 'Ralph Shay' (poor aesthetics), 'Selkirk' (poor aesthetics), 'Velvet Pillar' (disease-prone), and *Malus yunnanensis* var. *veitchii* (overall poor performance). 'Bechtel' or 'Klehm's Improved' crabapple is commonly planted in Utah and has beautiful, doubled pink flowers and a nice crown shape. However, it has proven susceptible to fireblight and has large fruit that can be a nuisance.

The table below contains a species or cultivar name, flowering characteristics, fruit characteristics, and comments. Fruits noted as persistent remain on the tree well after leaves fall and tend to be fed on by birds, causing less mess than fruits that drop quickly. The comment column includes crown shape and size, leaf color if other than green, and a quality rating. National ratings were determined by the National Crabapple Evaluation Program and integrate disease and aesthetic aspects. Trees are rated 0 (best) to 4 (worst), with the top crabapple being *Malus sieboldii* var. *zumi* 'Calocarpa,' with a rating of 1.04. Utah spring (flowers) and fall (fruit and fall color) ratings are included where available, and were done as part of the national program. Several species or cultivars also are included that were listed as favorites by Michael Dirr in his *Manual of Woody Landscape Plants*.

Species/Cultivar Name	Flowers	Fruit	Comments/Rating (0-Best, 4-Worst)
'Adams'	Deep pink buds; pink flowers	Red; 5/8"; persistent	Rounded crown; 20' tall by 20' wide; Utah spring rating 1.2
'Bob White'	Pink buds; white flowers	Yellow; 1/2" to 5/8"; persistent	Dense-rounded crown; 20' tall by 20' wide; Utah fall rating 1.2
'Centurion'	Rose-red flowers	Bright-red; 5/8"; persistent	Red-purple foliage; narrow-upright crown; 20' tall by 15' wide; Utah spring rating 0.8
'David'	Light pink buds; white flowers	Bright-red; 3/8" to 1/2"; persistent	Compact-rounded crown; 12' tall by 12' wide; national rating 1.41
'Donald Wyman'	Red/pink buds; white flowers	Glossy red; 3/8"; persistent	Large-spreading crown; 20' tall by 24' wide; national rating 1.13
'Indian Magic'	Red buds; deep pink flowers	Bright-red to orange; 1/2"; persistent	Rounded-spreading crown; 15' tall by 15' wide; national rating 1.41
'Indian Summer'	Rose-red flowers	Bright red; 5/8"; persistent	Bronze-green foliage; rounded crown; 18' tall by 20' wide; Utah spring rating 1.1
Malus × atrosanguinea Carmine Crabapple	Crimson buds; rose-pink flowers	Dark-red; 3/8"; persistent	Dense-mounded, shrubby; 20' tall by 20' wide; Dirr selection
Malus floribunda Japanese Flowering Crabapple	Pinkish-red buds; pink to white flowers	Yellow-red; 3/8"	Wide-rounded crown; 18' tall by 25' wide; Utah spring rating 1.2; Dirr selection
Malus halliana var. parkmanii	Rose-red buds; light pink flowers; double	Dull-red; 1/4"	Dense-upright crown; 18' tall by 18' wide; Dirr selection
Malus hupehensis Tea Crabapple	Deep pink buds; pink-white flowers; fragrant	Greenish-yellow to red; 3/8"	Open-spreading crown; 16' tall by 25' wide; Dirr selection

274

Cultivar	Buds/flowers	Fruit	Habit
Malus sargentii Sargent Crabapple	Red buds; white flowers; fragrant	Bright-red; 1/4"; persistent	Dense-spreading crown; 8' tall by 12' wide; Dirr selection
Malus sieboldii var. *zumi* 'Calocarpa'	Red buds; white to light pink flowers	Bright red; 1/2"; persistent	Fireblight a problem; rounded-spreading crown; 25' tall by 25' wide; national rating 1.04
'Mary Potter'	Pink buds; white flowers	Red; 3/8"; persistent	Horizontal, low-spreading crown; 10' tall by 15' wide; Utah fall rating 1.2
'Molten Lava'	Dark red buds; white flowers	Red-orange; 3/8"; persistent	Wide-weeping crown; 15' tall; national rating 1.17
'Prairifire'	Red buds; bright pinkish-red flowers	Dark-red; 3/8" to 1/2"; persistent	Reddish-green foliage; upright-spreading crown; 20' tall by 20' wide; Utah fall rating 1.0
'Professor Sprenger'	Pink buds; white flowers	Orange-red; 1/2" to 5/8"; persistent	Upright-spreading crown; 20' tall by 20' wide; national rating 1.13
'Profusion'	Red buds; purplish-red to pink flowers	Deep-red; 1/2"; persistent	Upright-spreading crown; 20' tall by 20' wide; Utah fall rating 0.7
'Radiant'	Red buds; pink flowers	Bright-red, colors early; 1/2"; persistent	Disease prone in humid areas; broad crown; 25' tall by 20' wide; Utah spring rating 1.0
'Red Jewel'	Pure white flowers	Bright red; 1/2"; persistent	Upright-pyramidal crown; 15' tall by 12' wide; national rating 1.41
'Robinson'	Red buds; deep pink flowers	Dark-red; 3/8"; persistent	Reddish-green foliage; upright-spreading crown; 25' tall by 25' wide; Utah fall rating 1.0
'Sentinel'	Red buds; white to light pink flowers	Bright-red; 1/2"; persistent	Narrow-upright crown; 20' tall by 12' wide; national rating 1.41
'Snowdrift'	Pink buds; white flowers	Orange; 3/8" or less; persistent	Rounded crown; 20' tall by 20' wide; national rating 1.41
'Sugartyme'	Light pink buds; white flowers	Red; 1/2"; persistent	Upright-spreading crown; 15' tall by 20' wide; national rating 1.37

Species/Cultivar Name	Flowers	Fruit	Comments/Rating (0-Best, 4-Worst)
'White Angel'	Pink buds; white flowers	Glossy-red; 5/8"; abundant	Rounded upright-spreading crown; 20' tall by 20' wide; Dirr selection
'White Cascade'	Deep pink buds; abundant white flowers	Yellow; 3/8"	Weeping crown; 15' tall by 15' wide; Utah spring rating 0.9

USDA PLANT HARDINESS ZONES
FOR THE INTERMOUNTAIN STATES

USDA hardiness zones are used in most of the U.S. to indicate a plant's degree of cold hardiness, though they also give some indication of heat tolerance. The contiguous United States and southern Canada have been divided by the USDA into eleven zones numbered one through eleven that correspond to a 10°F range in average annual minimum temperatures. These zones area then subdivided into 5°F sub-zones lettered "a" and "b", with "a" being cooler and "b" warmer, though these sub-zones are not used here. The average annual minimum temperature is calculated by averaging the minimum temperatures reached each year at a particular location over the years of interest. Annual average minimum temperatures for each zone are as follows:

Zone 1 — below -50°F   Zone 7 — 0 to 10°F
Zone 2 — -50 to -40°F   Zone 8 — 10 to 20°F
Zone 3 — -40 to -30°F   Zone 9 — 20 to 30°F
Zone 4 — -30 to -20°F   Zone 10 — 30 to 40°F
Zone 5 — -20 to -10°F   Zone 11 — 40°F and above
Zone 6 — -10 to 0°F

Utah's hardiness zones range from zone 3 in eastern Rich County and eastern Summit County, to zones 5 and 6 in the Salt Lake City area and most of the rest of the state at lower elevations, to zone 7 in southern Utah and even zone 8 in the Glen Canyon and St. George areas. Species should be planted outside their recommended zone ranges only on a trial basis. A map of hardiness zones for the western U.S. excluding Alaska and Hawaii is included below.

The map is not very detailed and does not accurately show hardiness zones in much of the West due to elevation and microclimate variations. The table below includes

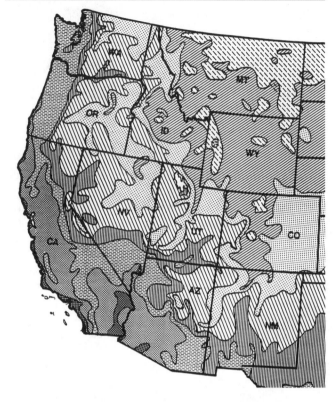

RANGE OF AVERAGE ANNUAL MINIMUM
TEMPERATURES FOR EACH ZONE

ZONE 1	BELOW -50°F	
ZONE 2	-50° TO -40°	
ZONE 3	-40° TO -30°	
ZONE 4	-30° TO -20°	
ZONE 5	-20° TO -10°	
ZONE 6	-10° TO 0°	
ZONE 7	0° TO 10°	
ZONE 8	10° TO 20°	
ZONE 9	20° TO 30°	
ZONE 10	30° TO 40°	
ZONE 11	ABOVE 40°	

hardiness zones using the USDA temperature ranges but calculated with local weather data gathered from 1961 to 1990. A hardiness zone is included for most weather stations in Utah and for several stations in each of the surrounding states. Calculations were done by the Utah Climate Center at Utah State University. To find your zone find a station near you that is similar in elevation and other factors. A station designation like "Klagetoh 12 WNW" indicates that the station is located 12 miles west-northwest of Klagetoh, Arizona.

Though this table gives more detailed coverage, these zones should be used with caution. Slight differences between weather station conditions and your site could mean large differences in the hardiness zone value. Also, these are means rather than absolute minimums, so if your area occasionally gets much colder than the mean temperature in the table then you might consider going with a lower hardiness zone. Overall the average zones in this table tend to be higher than those from the official USDA map in some of the colder locations. Cache County in Utah, for example, shows as mostly zone 4 on the map but the figures below for Cache County range from zone 2 to zone 6. When in doubt, or if you are worried about losing a plant, use a more conservative zone value (lower zone number).

Calculated Average and Minimum USDA Hardiness Zones for 1961–1990 by State, County, and Weather Station

State	County	Weather Station	Elev. (feet)	Avg. Annual Min. & Absolute Min. Temperatures (°F)		Avg. & Min. Hardiness Zones	Years of Data
Arizona	Apache	Canyon De Chelly	5610	–4	–24	Zones 6, 4	20
Arizona	Apache	Ganado	6340	–10	–26	Zones 5, 4	23
Arizona	Apache	Klagetoh 12 WNW	6500	–1	–20	Zones 6, 4	30
Arizona	Apache	Lukachukai	6520	–6	–20	Zones 6, 4	26
Arizona	Apache	Sanders	5850	–9	–23	Zones 6, 4	25
Arizona	Apache	Sanders 11 ESE	6250	–13	–35	Zones 5, 3	25
Arizona	Apache	Teec Nos Pos	5290	–2	–17	Zones 6, 5	25
Arizona	Apache	Window Rock 4 SW	6900	–12	–29	Zones 5, 4	30
Arizona	Coconino	Cameron 1 NNE	4160	4	–7	Zones 7, 6	27
Arizona	Coconino	Flagstaff Airport	7000	–13	–23	Zones 5, 4	30
Arizona	Coconino	Fort Valley	7350	–19	–37	Zones 5, 3	30
Arizona	Coconino	Lee's Ferry	3210	16	6	Zones 8, 7	28
Arizona	Coconino	Leupp	4700	–6	–18	Zones 6, 5	21
Arizona	Coconino	Page	4270	10	–11	Zones 7, 5	29
Arizona	Coconino	Phantom Ranch	2570	25	12	Zones 9, 8	21
Arizona	Coconino	Sunset Crater Natl. Monu.	6980	–15	–28	Zones 5, 4	21
Arizona	Coconino	Supai	3200	13	–4	Zones 8, 6	26
Arizona	Coconino	Wahweap	3730	12	–2	Zones 8, 6	29
Arizona	Coconino	Williams	6750	–1	–14	Zones 6, 5	30

State	County	Location				Zones	
Arizona	Coconino	Wupatki Natl. Monu.	4910	5	−18	Zones 7, 5	30
Arizona	Mohave	Beaver Dam	1880	16	4	Zones 8, 7	24
Arizona	Mohave	Colorado City	5010	2	−9	Zones 7, 6	25
Arizona	Mohave	Kingman	3540	16	4	Zones 8, 7	23
Arizona	Mohave	Pierce Ferry 17 SSW	3860	12	3	Zones 8, 7	21
Arizona	Mohave	Pipe Springs Natl. Monu.	4920	0	−13	Zones 6, 5	26
Arizona	Mohave	Truxton Canyon	3820	10	0	Zones 8, 6	20
Arizona	Mohave	Tuweep	4780	12	0	Zones 8, 6	23
Arizona	Mohave	Willow Beach	760	27	21	Zones 9, 9	23
Arizona	Navajo	Betatakin	7290	−1	−14	Zones 6, 5	30
Arizona	Navajo	Keams Canyon	6210	−6	−23	Zones 6, 4	28
Arizona	Navajo	Winslow Airport	4890	−2	−15	Zones 6, 5	30
Arizona	Yavapai	Seligman	5250	0	−12	Zones 7, 5	30
Colorado	Delta	Cedaredge	6240	−7	−24	Zones 6, 4	30
Colorado	Delta	Delta	4930	−8	−27	Zones 6, 4	28
Colorado	Delta	Paonia 1 SW	5580	−10	−31	Zones 6, 3	30
Colorado	Dolores	Northdale	6680	−20	−33	Zones 4, 3	30
Colorado	Dolores	Rico	8780	−21	−36	Zones 4, 3	30
Colorado	Garfield	Altenbern	5690	−15	−32	Zones 5, 3	30
Colorado	Garfield	Rifle	5320	−17	−38	Zones 5, 3	29
Colorado	Hinsdale	Lake City	8670	−26	−38	Zones 4, 3	30
Colorado	La Plata	Durango	6600	−11	−30	Zones 5, 3	30
Colorado	La Plata	Fort Lewis	7600	−16	−35	Zones 5, 3	30

State	County	Weather Station	Elev. (feet)	Avg. Annual Min. & Absolute Min. Temperatures (°F)		Avg. & Min. Hardiness Zones	Years of Data
Colorado	La Plata	Ignacio 1 N	6460	-15	-34	Zones 5, 3	28
Colorado	La Plata	Vallecito Dam	7650	-19	-35	Zones 5, 3	30
Colorado	Mesa	Collbran	5980	-13	-27	Zones 5, 4	25
Colorado	Mesa	Colorado Natl. Monu.	5780	-1	-18	Zones 6, 5	30
Colorado	Mesa	Fruita 1 W	4480	-11	-36	Zones 5, 3	28
Colorado	Mesa	Gateway 1 SE	4550	-4	-28	Zones 6, 4	30
Colorado	Mesa	Grand Junction 6 ESE	4760	-3	-21	Zones 6, 4	27
Colorado	Mesa	Palisade	4800	0	-20	Zones 6, 4	29
Colorado	Mesa	Grand Junction Airport	4840	-5	-23	Zones 6, 4	30
Colorado	Moffat	Browns Park Refuge	5350	-22	-41	Zones 4, 2	24
Colorado	Moffat	Dinosaur Natl. Monu.	5920	-15	-29	Zones 5, 4	25
Colorado	Moffat	Maybell	5910	-36	-61	Zones 3, 1	24
Colorado	Montezuma	Cortez	6210	-12	-27	Zones 5, 4	29
Colorado	Montezuma	Mesa Verde Natl. Park	7110	-2	-20	Zones 6, 4	30
Colorado	Montezuma	Yellow Jacket 2 W	6860	-10	-26	Zones 6, 4	28
Colorado	Montrose	Cimarron	6900	-27	-43	Zones 4, 2	30
Colorado	Montrose	Montrose	5790	-7	-23	Zones 6, 4	30
Colorado	Montrose	Uravan	5010	-5	-23	Zones 6, 4	30
Colorado	Ouray	Ouray	7840	-8	-22	Zones 6, 4	30
Colorado	Rio Blanco	Little Hills	6140	-28	-48	Zones 4, 2	30

Colorado	Rio Blanco	Rangely 1 E	5290	-23	-33	Zones 4, 3	29
Colorado	San Juan	Silverton	9270	-28	-39	Zones 4, 3	27
Colorado	San Miguel	Norwood	7020	-17	-31	Zones 5, 3	30
Colorado	San Miguel	Telluride	8800	-19	-32	Zones 5, 3	30
Idaho	Ada	Boise Lucky Peak Dam	2840	-2	-17	Zones 6, 5	23
Idaho	Ada	Boise Airport	2840	-4	-25	Zones 6, 4	30
Idaho	Ada	Kuna 2 NNE	2680	-7	-26	Zones 6, 4	29
Idaho	Ada	Swan Falls Power House	2320	1	-21	Zones 7, 4	30
Idaho	Bear Lake	Lifton Pumping Stn.	5930	-24	-41	Zones 4, 2	30
Idaho	Bear Lake	Montpelier Ranger Stn.	5960	-21	-34	Zones 4, 3	27
Idaho	Bingham	Aberdeen Experiment Stn.	4410	-19	-38	Zones 5, 3	30
Idaho	Bingham	Blackfoot 2 SSW	4490	-16	-35	Zones 5, 3	30
Idaho	Bingham	Fort Hall Indian Agency	4460	-17	-33	Zones 5, 3	30
Idaho	Blaine	Hailey 3 NNW	5420	-17	-28	Zones 5, 4	21
Idaho	Blaine	Picabo	4880	-21	-37	Zones 4, 3	30
Idaho	Bonneville	Idaho Falls 2 ESE	4770	-17	-34	Zones 5, 3	30
Idaho	Bonneville	Idaho Falls 16 SE	5850	-29	-51	Zones 4, 1	30
Idaho	Bonneville	Idaho Falls Airport	4730	-20	-38	Zones 5, 3	30
Idaho	Bonneville	Palisades	5390	-19	-32	Zones 5, 3	29
Idaho	Bonneville	Swan Valley 2 E	5360	-27	-43	Zones 4, 2	30
Idaho	Butte	Arco 3 SW	5330	-25	-45	Zones 4, 2	30
Idaho	Butte	Craters of the Moon Natl. Mon.	5900	-16	-37	Zones 5, 3	30
Idaho	Butte	Idaho Falls 46 W	4940	-28	-47	Zones 4, 2	30

State	County	Weather Station	Elev. (feet)	Avg. Annual Min. & Absolute Min. Temperatures (°F)		Avg. & Min. Hardiness Zones	Years of Data
Idaho	Camas	Fairfield Ranger Stn.	5070	−25	−42	Zones 4, 2	29
Idaho	Camas	Hill City 1 W	5000	−28	−42	Zones 4, 2	30
Idaho	Canyon	Deer Flat Dam	2510	−4	−22	Zones 6, 4	30
Idaho	Caribou	Grace	5550	−23	−40	Zones 4, 2	30
Idaho	Cassia	Burley Airport	4160	−11	−30	Zones 5, 3	30
Idaho	Cassia	Malta 2 E	4540	−15	−29	Zones 5, 4	25
Idaho	Cassia	Oakley	4600	−9	−24	Zones 6, 4	30
Idaho	Elmore	Anderson Dam	3880	−4	−21	Zones 6, 4	25
Idaho	Elmore	Arrowrock Dam	3280	−3	−19	Zones 6, 5	30
Idaho	Elmore	Glenns Ferry	2510	−4	−23	Zones 6, 4	29
Idaho	Elmore	Mountain Home	3190	−5	−25	Zones 6, 4	30
Idaho	Gooding	Bliss 4 NW	3280	−6	−22	Zones 6, 4	30
Idaho	Jerome	Hazelton	4060	−9	−27	Zones 6, 4	30
Idaho	Jerome	Jerome	3740	−8	−24	Zones 6, 4	30
Idaho	Lincoln	Richfield	4310	−17	−36	Zones 5, 3	30
Idaho	Lincoln	Shoshone 1 WNW	3950	−11	−27	Zones 5, 4	30
Idaho	Minidoka	Minidoka Dam	4210	−13	−41	Zones 5, 2	29
Idaho	Minidoka	Paul 1 ENE	4210	−9	−28	Zones 6, 4	30
Idaho	Oneida	Malad	4580	−11	−25	Zones 5, 4	22
Idaho	Oneida	Malad City	4470	−18	−35	Zones 5, 3	29

State	County	Station	Elevation			Zones	
Idaho	Owyhee	Bruneau	2530	-5	-32	Zones 6, 3	28
Idaho	Owyhee	Grand View 2 W	2400	-7	-26	Zones 6, 4	30
Idaho	Owyhee	Reynolds	3930	-7	-24	Zones 6, 4	29
Idaho	Owyhee	Three Creek	5460	-19	-37	Zones 5, 3	25
Idaho	Power	American Falls 1 SW	4320	-12	-31	Zones 5, 3	30
Idaho	Power	Arbon 2 NW	5170	-18	-37	Zones 5, 3	28
Idaho	Power	Pocatello Airport	4450	-16	-33	Zones 5, 3	30
Idaho	Twin Falls	Castleford 2 N	3820	-8	-26	Zones 6, 4	27
Idaho	Twin Falls	Hollister	4530	-8	-26	Zones 6, 4	24
Idaho	Twin Falls	Twin Falls WSO	3960	-6	-23	Zones 6, 4	27
Nevada	Clark	Boulder City	2520	22	4	Zones 9, 7	29
Nevada	Clark	Desert Game Range	2920	13	0	Zones 8, 6	30
Nevada	Clark	Logandale	1410	18	7	Zones 8, 7	23
Nevada	Clark	Searchlight	3540	18	8	Zones 8, 7	30
Nevada	Clark	Sunrise Manor Las Vegas	1820	13	0	Zones 8, 6	27
Nevada	Clark	Las Vegas Airport	2160	19	8	Zones 8, 7	30
Nevada	Elko	Arthur 4 NW	6300	-12	-26	Zones 5, 4	27
Nevada	Elko	Clover Valley	5750	-13	-33	Zones 5, 3	25
Nevada	Elko	Contact	5360	-16	-38	Zones 5, 3	28
Nevada	Elko	Deeth 2 SW	5340	-24	-42	Zones 4, 2	29
Nevada	Elko	Elko Airport	5050	-14	-33	Zones 5, 3	30
Nevada	Elko	Gibbs Ranch	6000	-22	-38	Zones 4, 3	27
Nevada	Elko	Metropolis	5800	-5	-25	Zones 6, 4	23

State	County	Weather Station	Elev. (feet)	Avg. Annual Min. & Absolute Min. Temperatures (°F)		Avg. & Min. Hardiness Zones	Years of Data
Nevada	Elko	Montello 1 SE	4900	-18	-32	Zones 5, 3	26
Nevada	Elko	Mountain City Ranger Stn.	5640	-26	-48	Zones 4, 2	30
Nevada	Elko	Owyhee	5400	-12	-25	Zones 5, 4	22
Nevada	Elko	Ruby Lake	6010	-16	-29	Zones 5, 4	26
Nevada	Elko	Wells	5650	-19	-36	Zones 5, 3	30
Nevada	Eureka	Eureka	6540	-8	-21	Zones 6, 4	26
Nevada	Eureka	Rand Ranch Palisade	5050	-23	-39	Zones 4, 3	22
Nevada	Lincoln	Caliente	4400	-2	-19	Zones 6, 5	30
Nevada	Lincoln	Key Pittman Wildlife Mgt. Area	3950	10	0	Zones 7, 6	20
Nevada	Lincoln	Lake Valley Steward	6350	-2	-13	Zones 6, 5	20
Nevada	Lincoln	Pahranagat Wildlife Refuge	3400	11	-1	Zones 8, 6	24
Nevada	Lincoln	Pioche	6180	2	-11	Zones 7, 5	29
Nevada	Nye	Duckwater	5610	-5	-19	Zones 6, 5	23
Nevada	Nye	Pahrump	2670	11	-2	Zones 8, 6	27
Nevada	Nye	Sunnyside	5300	-7	-20	Zones 6, 4	25
Nevada	White Pine	Ely	6250	-17	-30	Zones 5, 3	30
Nevada	White Pine	Lehman Caves Natl. Monu.	6830	-5	-20	Zones 6, 4	27
Nevada	White Pine	Lund	5570	-7	-18	Zones 6, 5	30
Nevada	White Pine	McGill	6300	-9	-23	Zones 6, 4	30
Nevada	White Pine	Ruth	6840	-21	-34	Zones 4, 3	23

State	County	Location	Elevation			Zones	
New Mexico	Cibola	El Morro Natl. Monu.	7230	-15	-38	Zones 5, 3	30
New Mexico	San Juan	Aztec Ruins Natl. Monu.	5640	-9	-23	Zones 6, 4	30
New Mexico	San Juan	Bloomfield 3 SE	5800	-4	-20	Zones 6, 4	30
New Mexico	San Juan	Chaco Canyon Natl. Monu.	6180	-17	-38	Zones 5, 3	30
New Mexico	San Juan	Fruitland 2 E	5150	-3	-17	Zones 6, 5	29
Utah	Beaver	Beaver	5940	-11	-21	Zones 5, 4	29
Utah	Beaver	Milford	5010	-16	-35	Zones 5, 3	30
Utah	Beaver	Wah Wah Ranch	4880	-14	-30	Zones 5, 3	30
Utah	Box Elder	Bear River Refuge	4210	-7	-21	Zones 6, 4	21
Utah	Box Elder	Corinne	4220	-10	-23	Zones 5, 4	28
Utah	Box Elder	Grouse Creek	5320	-13	-26	Zones 5, 4	21
Utah	Box Elder	Park Valley	5440	-6	-21	Zones 6, 4	25
Utah	Box Elder	Snowville	4560	-15	-27	Zones 5, 4	29
Utah	Box Elder	Thiokol Plant 78	4600	-16	-29	Zones 5, 4	28
Utah	Cache	Hardware Ranch	5560	-25	-43	Zones 4, 2	22
Utah	Cache	Logan 5 SW Exp. Farm	4490	-25	-44	Zones 4, 2	21
Utah	Cache	Logan Radio KVNU	4500	-17	-30	Zones 5, 3	30
Utah	Cache	Logan USU Exp. Stn.	4610	-14	-27	Zones 5, 4	23
Utah	Cache	Logan Utah State Univ.	4790	-9	-21	Zones 6, 4	30
Utah	Cache	Richmond	4680	-15	-28	Zones 5, 4	30
Utah	Carbon	Hiawatha	7280	-6	-16	Zones 6, 5	28
Utah	Carbon	Price Warehouses	5700	-6	-15	Zones 6, 5	21
Utah	Carbon	Scofield Dam	7630	-31	-45	Zones 3, 2	30

State	County	Weather Station	Elev. (feet)	Avg. Annual Min. & Absolute Min. Temperatures (°F)		Avg. & Min. Hardiness Zones	Years of Data
Utah	Carbon	Sunnyside	6790	−6	−17	Zones 6, 5	22
Utah	Daggett	Allen's Ranch	5490	−16	−35	Zones 5, 3	28
Utah	Daggett	Flaming Gorge	6270	−20	−38	Zones 5, 3	30
Utah	Davis	Farmington USU Field Stn.	4340	−2	−14	Zones 6, 5	26
Utah	Duchesne	Altamont	6370	−16	−32	Zones 5, 3	28
Utah	Duchesne	Duchesne	5520	−19	−38	Zones 5, 3	23
Utah	Duchesne	Hanna	6740	−18	−27	Zones 5, 4	23
Utah	Duchesne	Myton	5080	−21	−39	Zones 4, 3	27
Utah	Duchesne	Neola	5950	−16	−27	Zones 5, 4	29
Utah	Duchesne	Nutters Ranch	5790	−14	−25	Zones 5, 4	22
Utah	Emery	Castle Dale	5620	−12	−28	Zones 5, 4	30
Utah	Emery	Ferron	5940	−7	−21	Zones 6, 4	29
Utah	Emery	Green River Aviation	4070	−11	−25	Zones 5, 4	29
Utah	Garfield	Boulder	6700	−4	−17	Zones 6, 5	30
Utah	Garfield	Bryce Canyon Airport	7590	−21	−32	Zones 4, 3	20
Utah	Garfield	Bryce Canyon Natl. Pk. Hd.	7910	−15	−26	Zones 5, 4	30
Utah	Garfield	Escalante	5810	−5	−17	Zones 6, 5	30
Utah	Garfield	Panguitch	6610	−18	−31	Zones 5, 3	30
Utah	Garfield	Tropic	6280	−4	−18	Zones 6, 5	29
Utah	Grand	Dewey	4120	−8	−25	Zones 6, 4	23

Utah	Grand	Moab	4020	1	−18	Zones 7, 5	30
Utah	Grand	Thompson	5100	−4	−23	Zones 6, 4	26
Utah	Iron	Blowhard Mountain Radar	10700	−12	−23	Zones 5, 4	25
Utah	Iron	Cedar City Airport	5610	−8	−24	Zones 6, 4	30
Utah	Iron	Cedar City Steam Plant	6000	−3	−17	Zones 6, 5	21
Utah	Iron	Enterprise Beryl Junction	5150	−16	−34	Zones 5, 3	30
Utah	Iron	Modena	5460	−13	−29	Zones 5, 4	29
Utah	Iron	Parowan Power Plant	6000	−10	−22	Zones 5, 4	30
Utah	Juab	Callao	4330	−8	−24	Zones 6, 4	28
Utah	Juab	Fish Springs Refuge	4340	−6	−19	Zones 6, 5	30
Utah	Juab	Levan	5300	−11	−22	Zones 5, 4	30
Utah	Juab	Nephi	5130	−9	−21	Zones 6, 4	30
Utah	Juab	Partoun	4780	−14	−29	Zones 5, 4	29
Utah	Kane	Alton	7040	−8	−24	Zones 6, 4	30
Utah	Kane	Bullfrog Basin	3820	11	0	Zones 8, 6	24
Utah	Kane	Kanab	4950	2	−10	Zones 7, 5	30
Utah	Kane	Orderville	5460	−7	−25	Zones 6, 4	30
Utah	Millard	Black Rock	4900	−16	−37	Zones 5, 3	30
Utah	Millard	Clear Lake Refuge	4600	−12	−27	Zones 5, 4	21
Utah	Millard	Delta	4620	−12	−30	Zones 5, 3	28
Utah	Millard	Deseret	4590	−13	−29	Zones 5, 4	30
Utah	Millard	Desert Experimental Range	5250	−14	−28	Zones 5, 4	24
Utah	Millard	Eskdale	4980	−12	−31	Zones 5, 3	24

State	County	Weather Station	Elev. (feet)	Avg. Annual Min. & Absolute Min. Temperatures (°F)		Avg. & Min. Hardiness Zones	Years of Data
Utah	Millard	Fillmore	5120	−7	−21	Zones 6, 4	30
Utah	Millard	Garrison	5260	−9	−26	Zones 6, 4	30
Utah	Millard	Kanosh	5000	−5	−20	Zones 6, 4	28
Utah	Millard	Oak City	5070	−5	−23	Zones 6, 4	30
Utah	Millard	Scipio	5300	−20	−38	Zones 4, 3	30
Utah	Morgan	Morgan	5060	−19	−33	Zones 5, 3	30
Utah	Piute	Circleville	6070	−12	−31	Zones 5, 3	28
Utah	Piute	Marysvale	5910	−12	−35	Zones 5, 3	25
Utah	Rich	Laketown	5980	−18	−37	Zones 5, 3	30
Utah	Rich	Woodruff	6320	−33	−46	Zones 3, 2	30
Utah	Salt Lake	Alta	8730	−12	−26	Zones 5, 4	27
Utah	Salt Lake	Cottonwood Weir	4960	1	−15	Zones 7, 5	30
Utah	Salt Lake	Garfield	4330	4	−11	Zones 7, 5	29
Utah	Salt Lake	Holladay	4410	0	−9	Zones 6, 6	21
Utah	Salt Lake	Mountain Dell Dam	5420	−13	−30	Zones 5, 3	30
Utah	Salt Lake	Salt Lake City Airport	4220	−4	−18	Zones 6, 5	30
Utah	Salt Lake	Saltair Salt Plant	4210	0	−17	Zones 7, 5	21
Utah	Salt Lake	Silver Lake Brighton	8740	−20	−34	Zones 4, 3	30
Utah	Salt Lake	University of Utah	4800	4	−11	Zones 7, 5	24
Utah	San Juan	Aneth Plant	4620	1	−14	Zones 7, 5	24

State	County	Place	Elevation			Zones	
Utah	San Juan	Blanding	6040	-3	-20	Zones 6, 4	29
Utah	San Juan	Bluff	4320	-4	-22	Zones 6, 4	30
Utah	San Juan	Canyonlands, the Neck	5930	2	-13	Zones 7, 5	25
Utah	San Juan	Canyonlands, the Needle	5040	-6	-16	Zones 6, 5	25
Utah	San Juan	Cedar Point	6760	-6	-20	Zones 6, 4	28
Utah	San Juan	Hovenweep Natl. Monu.	5240	-10	-24	Zones 6, 4	30
Utah	San Juan	Mexican Hat	4130	1	-17	Zones 7, 5	28
Utah	San Juan	Monticello	6820	-10	-22	Zones 6, 4	30
Utah	San Juan	Monument Valley Mission	5300	7	-11	Zones 7, 5	26
Utah	San Juan	Natural Bridges Natl. Monu.	6500	-2	-14	Zones 6, 5	25
Utah	Sanpete	Ephraim Sorensens Field	5670	-13	-34	Zones 5, 3	30
Utah	Sanpete	Gunnison	5150	-13	-28	Zones 5, 4	28
Utah	Sanpete	Manti	5740	-10	-24	Zones 5, 4	30
Utah	Sanpete	Moroni	5560	-15	-26	Zones 5, 4	30
Utah	Sevier	Koosharem	6930	-17	-32	Zones 5, 3	30
Utah	Sevier	Richfield Radio KSVC	5300	-13	-33	Zones 5, 3	30
Utah	Sevier	Salina	5130	-13	-32	Zones 5, 3	30
Utah	Summit	Coalville	5550	-19	-33	Zones 5, 3	28
Utah	Summit	Echo Dam	5470	-21	-34	Zones 4, 3	30
Utah	Summit	Kamas 3 NW	6480	-16	-31	Zones 5, 3	26
Utah	Summit	Wanship Dam	5940	-20	-37	Zones 4, 3	30
Utah	Tooele	Dugway	4340	-8	-29	Zones 6, 4	29
Utah	Tooele	Gold Hill	5250	-2	-15	Zones 6, 5	21

State	County	Weather Station	Elev. (feet)	Avg. Annual Min. & Absolute Min. Temperatures (°F)		Avg. & Min. Hardiness Zones	Years of Data
Utah	Tooele	Ibapah	5280	-17	-31	Zones 5, 3	30
Utah	Tooele	Tooele	5070	-1	-16	Zones 6, 5	30
Utah	Tooele	Vernon	5490	-14	-26	Zones 5, 4	25
Utah	Tooele	Wendover Airport	4240	0	-18	Zones 7, 5	30
Utah	Uintah	Bonanza	5450	-14	-32	Zones 5, 3	20
Utah	Uintah	Dinosaur Natl. Monu. Quarry	4770	-19	-40	Zones 5, 2	30
Utah	Uintah	Fort Duchesne	5050	-21	-39	Zones 4, 3	30
Utah	Uintah	Jensen	4750	-22	-40	Zones 4, 2	30
Utah	Uintah	Ouray 4 NE	4670	-25	-43	Zones 4, 2	28
Utah	Uintah	Roosevelt Radio	5010	-20	-47	Zones 4, 2	29
Utah	Uintah	Vernal Airport	5260	-17	-38	Zones 5, 3	30
Utah	Utah	Birdseye	5720	-24	-37	Zones 4, 3	22
Utah	Utah	Elberta	4680	-9	-29	Zones 6, 4	30
Utah	Utah	Fairfield	4880	-19	-36	Zones 5, 3	28
Utah	Utah	Geneva Steel	4550	-4	-16	Zones 6, 5	22
Utah	Utah	Pleasant Grove	4760	-3	-17	Zones 6, 5	30
Utah	Utah	Santaquin Chlorinator	5160	-7	-22	Zones 6, 4	30
Utah	Utah	Spanish Fork Powerhouse	4720	-4	-20	Zones 6, 4	30
Utah	Utah	Timpanogos Cave	5640	-3	-14	Zones 6, 5	30
Utah	Utah	Utah Lake Lehi	4500	-8	-28	Zones 6, 4	30

State	County	Location					
Utah	Wasatch	Deer Creek Dam	5270	-18	-39	Zones 5, 3	30
Utah	Wasatch	Heber	5630	-20	-36	Zones 5, 3	30
Utah	Wasatch	Snake Creek Powerhouse	6010	-18	-34	Zones 5, 3	30
Utah	Washington	La Verkin	3220	9	-2	Zones 7, 6	30
Utah	Washington	New Harmony	5290	-3	-20	Zones 6, 4	30
Utah	Washington	St. George	2769	12	1	Zones 8, 7	30
Utah	Washington	Veyo Powerhouse	4600	6	-10	Zones 7, 5	30
Utah	Washington	Zion National Park	4050	7	-5	Zones 7, 6	30
Utah	Wayne	Capitol Reef National Park	5500	2	-9	Zones 7, 6	24
Utah	Wayne	Hanksville	4310	-12	-33	Zones 5, 3	30
Utah	Wayne	Loa	7080	-18	-35	Zones 5, 3	30
Utah	Weber	Bear River Bay	4210	0	-9	Zones 7, 6	21
Utah	Weber	Ogden Pioneer Powerhouse	4350	-1	-13	Zones 6, 5	30
Utah	Weber	Ogden Sugar Factory	4280	-6	-18	Zones 6, 5	30
Utah	Weber	Pine View Dam	4940	-22	-39	Zones 4, 3	30
Utah	Weber	Riverdale	4400	-4	-18	Zones 6, 5	29
Wyoming	Carbon	Muddy Gap	6240	-22	-40	Zones 4, 2	27
Wyoming	Fremont	Boysen Dam	4640	-21	-39	Zones 4, 3	30
Wyoming	Fremont	Burris	6120	-26	-45	Zones 4, 2	27
Wyoming	Fremont	Diversion Dam	5580	-28	-44	Zones 4, 2	30
Wyoming	Fremont	Dubois	6960	-25	-49	Zones 4, 2	24
Wyoming	Fremont	Lander Airport	5560	-22	-37	Zones 4, 3	30
Wyoming	Fremont	Pavillion	5440	-25	-40	Zones 4, 2	26

State	County	Weather Station	Elev. (feet)	Avg. Annual Min. & Absolute Min. Temperatures (°F)		Avg. & Min. Hardiness Zones	Years of Data
Wyoming	Fremont	Riverton Bureau of Recl.	4950	−31	−46	Zones 3, 2	29
Wyoming	Lincoln	Afton	6210	−29	−46	Zones 4, 2	30
Wyoming	Lincoln	Border 3 N	6110	−32	−45	Zones 3, 2	30
Wyoming	Lincoln	Fontenelle	6480	−35	−46	Zones 3, 2	26
Wyoming	Lincoln	Kemmerer Water Trt. Plant	6930	−24	−39	Zones 4, 3	28
Wyoming	Lincoln	La Barge	6600	−32	−52	Zones 3, 1	24
Wyoming	Lincoln	Sage 4 NNW	6210	−36	−51	Zones 3, 1	26
Wyoming	Sublette	Bondurant	6620	−42	−52	Zones 2, 1	29
Wyoming	Sublette	Merna	7700	−25	−35	Zones 4, 3	25
Wyoming	Sublette	Pinedale	7180	−32	−49	Zones 3, 2	28
Wyoming	Sweetwater	Bitter Creek 4 NE	6720	−30	−46	Zones 3, 2	25
Wyoming	Sweetwater	Farson	6590	−37	−52	Zones 3, 1	26
Wyoming	Sweetwater	Green River	6090	−28	−42	Zones 4, 2	29
Wyoming	Sweetwater	Rock Springs Airport	6740	−18	−37	Zones 5, 3	28
Wyoming	Sweetwater	Wamsutter	6800	−26	−40	Zones 4, 2	25
Wyoming	Teton	Jackson	6230	−33	−50	Zones 3, 1	30
Wyoming	Uinta	Church Buttes Gas Plant	7080	−17	−35	Zones 5, 3	29
Wyoming	Uinta	Evanston 1 E	6810	−21	−35	Zones 4, 3	29
Wyoming	Uinta	Mountain View	6800	−21	−33	Zones 4, 3	23

TREE IDENTIFICATION KEYS

A *dichotomous key*, or two-branched key, can help you quickly identify trees in the field. The dichotomous key here includes 172 of the species described in this manual. To use a dichotomous key, first go to the line with the lowest letter or number, in this case 1. There will always be two lines with the same letter or number indented the same amount, though sometimes those lines are separated by a number of spaces. Read the descriptions on those two lines and decide which best fits your tree. Then go to the next number below the description you chose. Again, you will have to choose between two descriptions with the same number. At each step you only need to make one or two fairly simple decisions. Keep doing this until you reach the name of your tree. Then look at the species description for that tree and see if it matches.

An example will help you learn how to use the key. Let's say you have a large tree with simple, opposite, broad, sharply-toothed, palmately-lobed leaves, a winged fruit that matures in spring, and twigs with a strong smell when crushed. First go to the overall key or "Key to Keys" and you will see that you want Key 2 for simple, opposite, broad leaves. In Key 2 the first choice (1) is "leaves palmately lobed; fruit a double samara" versus "leaves not lobed". Your leaves are lobed and your fruit is a samara so you go with the first choice. Now you go directly below your choice to number 2 — "leaves with sharply and often doubly toothed margins and sharp-angled sinuses" or "lobes of leaves entire or with a few blunt teeth and more rounded sinuses". Again you take the first choice. You now go on to 3, "fruits maturing in fall" versus "fruits maturing in late spring". Your samaras mature in spring, so you take the second choice and go on to 5. Under 5 you notice that only one choice mentions a strong smell for crushed twigs so you know that your tree is a silver maple.

These keys include most trees you will encounter in Utah, but not all, so you may be fooled into thinking you have something you do not. It is also easy to make a mistake if you make the wrong decision or if the sample you have is not typical of the species overall. Just remember to check your identification against the species descriptions and with other references. The key works best in summer with leaves on, but may work fine in other seasons if you can find old leaves and fruit on the ground, and if you use leaf scars as signs of leaf arrangement. Leaf sizes in the key refer to leaf blade length without the petiole, unless specified otherwise. Some species appear more than once in the key because their characteristics vary. White poplar (*Populus alba*), for example, can have both lobed and unlobed leaves.

Keep in mind that no two trees are exactly the same, and if you look hard enough you will find exceptions to almost every feature used in this key. If number of needles per fascicle is an important keying characteristic, count the number of needles in several fascicles. Leaves receiving full sun, though harder to reach on large trees, are better indicators of leaf size and shape than shade leaves. Fruits often abort and fail to fully develop, giving them a much different size and appearance than fully-developed fruits. In general, characteristics that involve the tree's reproductive parts — flowers and fruits — are much more stable and predictable than characteristics of vegetative parts like leaves, stems, and roots.

Some good references to check for in a bookstore or library are listed below:

Dirr, Michael A. 1990. *Manual of Woody Landscape Plants: Their Identification, Characteristics, Culture, Propagation and Uses.* Champaign, IL: Stipes Publishing Co.

Elias, T.S. 1980. *The Complete Guide to North American Trees.* NY: Von Nostrand Reinhold Co.

Farrar, John Laird. 1995. *Trees of the Northern United States and Canada.* Ames, IA: Iowa State University Press.

Harlow, William H. 1941. *Fruit Key and Twig Key to Trees and Shrubs.* NY: Dover Publ., Inc.

Little, Elbert L. 1979. *Checklist of United States Trees (Native and Naturalized).* USDA Forest Service Ag. Hdbk. 541.

Preston, Richard J. 1989. *North American Trees.* Ames, IA: Iowa State University Press.

Preston, Richard J., and Valerie G. Wright. 1982. *Identification of Southeastern Trees in Winter.* Raleigh, NC: North Carolina Ag. Extension Service.

Rehder, Alfred. 1986. *Manual of Cultivated Trees and Shrubs.* Portland, OR: Dioscorides Press.

Welsh, S.L., N.D. Atwood, S. Goodrich, and L.C. Higgins. 1987. *A Utah Flora.* Great Basin Naturalist Memoirs No. 9. Provo, UT: Brigham Young University.

KEY TO TREES of UTAH and the INTERMOUNTAIN WEST

(usually assumes leaves are present — native trees are indicated by a ❖ symbol after the name)

Key to Keys

1. Leaves long and sword shaped, with parallel veins, attached to and covering the stem; flowers large and yellow-white, flower parts in 3's. . . . . **Joshua-tree**❖ (*Yucca brevifolia*) p. 240

1. Leaves and flowers not as above.

   2. Leaves needle-like, scale-like, or awl-shaped; usually evergreen. . . . . **Key 1** p. 298

   2. Leaves broad and thin; usually deciduous (live leaves not persistent over winter).

      3. Leaves opposite or whorled (attached in 3's or more) on twig.

         4. Leaves simple . . . . **Key 2** p. 303

         4. Leaves compound . . . . **Key 3** p. 306

      3. Leaves alternate on twig.

         5. Leaves simple . . . . **Key 4** p. 307

         5. Leaves compound . . . . **Key 5** p. 322

Key 1. Plants with needle-like, scale-like, or awl-shaped leaves.

(Includes all of the gymnosperms except ginkgo, plus one angiosperm)

1. Leaves needle-like; fruit a dry cone when mature.

   2. Needles occur in clusters of 2-5 (occur singly in one species), with a sheath enclosing the cluster's base; evergreen (**pines**).

      3. Needles occur singly, less than 2" long; cones 1" to 2" long with a few thick scales; large, edible, wingless seeds; small tree native to extreme northwest Utah and the pinyon juniper woodlands of south and central Utah; rarely planted . . . . . .

         . . . . **singleleaf pinyon**❖ (*Pinus monophylla*) p. 38

3. Needles occur in clusters of 2-5.

    4. Needles usually in clusters of 5 (**soft** or **white pines**).

        5. Needles 3" to 5" long, flexible, slender; introduced. . . . . **eastern white pine** (*Pinus strobus*) p. 42

        5. Needles 3" long or less, fairly stiff; usually encountered as native trees.

            6. Needles 1-1/2" to 3" long; cones 3" to 8" long with non-pointed scales; young branches are very flexible . . **limber pine**❖ (*Pinus flexilis*) . . . . p. 34

            6. Needles 1" to 1-1/2" long; cones 3" to 3-1/2" long with scales tipped with a long bristle; white resin dots usually present on leaves . . . . **bristlecone pine**❖ (*Pinus aristata*) p. 36

    4. Needles usually occur in clusters of 2 and/or 3 (**hard pines or pinyon pines**).

        7. Needles 2 and 3 in a cluster, 5" to 10" long; cone scales armed with spines; cinnamon-colored buds; native to southern and central Utah and sometimes planted. . . . . **ponderosa pine**❖ (*Pinus ponderosa*) p 38

        7. Needles mostly 2 in a cluster, usually 6" long or less.

            8. Needles 4" to 6" long, with buds silvery white and 1/2" to 3/4" long; the most widely planted long-needled pine in Utah. **Austrian pine** (*Pinus nigra*) p. 40

            8. Needles mostly less than 4" long, with buds brown to yellow-brown and 1/2" long or less.

                9. Needles strongly twisted, blue-green to yellow-green; buds red-brown; bark on upper trunk of older trees orange-red; only found in planted situations (not native) . . **Scotch pine** (*Pinus sylvestris*) p. 42

                9. Needles not strongly twisted, dark green or yellow-green; upper bark not orange.

                    10. Small shrub to shrubby tree; commonly planted non-native. . . . **Mugo pine** (*Pinus mugo*) p. 44

                    10. Native trees that are rarely planted; more upright and tree-like.

                        11. Cone scales armed with a sharp spine; seeds small and winged; crown upright and can get quite tall; found in mountains at fairly high elevations; cones often remain closed and attached to the tree for many years . . . . **lodgepole pine**❖ (*Pinus contorta*) p. 40

11. Cone scales not armed with a spine; seeds large and wingless; crown fairly short and often as wide as tall; found at lower elevations . . . . **pinyon**❖ (*Pinus edulis*) p. 36

2. Needles occur singly, or in clusters of many (10 to 40) on spur shoots on older twigs, without a sheath at their base; deciduous or evergreen.

12. Needles deciduous; will not have many years worth of live needles attached to older growth; not native.

13. Needles 3/4" to 1-1/2" long, not two-ranked, attached to new growth individually and in rosettes of 30 to 40 needles on spur shoots on older branches; cones upright with 40 to 50 thin scales (**larches**).

14. Needles 3/4" to 1-1/4" long, deep green, turning yellow in fall; cones 1" to 1-1/2" long and 3/4" to 1" wide, tips of scales not curved back giving cone a rosette appearance . . . . **European larch** (*Larix decidua*) p. 48

14. Needles 1" to 1-1/2" long, deep green with whitish bands below, turning golden-yellow in fall; cones 1" to 1-1/2" long and equally as wide, tips of scales curved back giving cone a rosette appearance . . . . **Japanese larch** (*Larix kaempferi*) p. 48

13. Needles mostly 3/4" long or shorter, though some may be up to 1-1/4" long on major shoots; most attached to small twigs in a flattened, 2-ranked, feather-like arrangement, these twigs fall off with the needles in autumn; cones round with fewer hard scales and not upright on the branch.

15. Needles 1/2" to 3/4" long, alternate arrangement on twigs; cones up to 1-1/3" diameter with 9 to 15, 4-sided scales that break away at maturity. . . . . **baldcypress** (*Taxodium distichum*) p. 60

15. Needles 1/2" to 3/4" long except up to 1-1/4" long on major shoots, opposite arrangement on twigs; cones up to 1" diameter with 20 to 30 triangular scales . . . . **dawn redwood** (*Metasequoia glyptostroboides*) p. 63

12. Needles evergreen; will have many years worth of needles attached to young and old twigs or to spur shoots.

16. Needles on older growth in clusters of 30-40 on short lateral spur shoots; cones upright on branch with deciduous scales (like true firs); fairly rare exotic tree in Utah . . . . **Atlas cedar** (*Cedrus atlantica*) p. 48

16. Needles on older branches not on spur shoots; cones upright or pendulous (hang down).

17. Needles 4-sided, square or diamond-shaped in cross-section (generally easy to roll between fingers), tips fairly sharply pointed, held to the twig on peg-like projections that persist after the needle falls; cones papery and hang down (**spruces**).

18. Cones 4" to 8" long; needles with slight odor when crushed, somewhat flattened in cross-section and difficult to roll between fingers; twigs may droop up to several feet on older trees with some cultivars . . . . **Norway spruce** (*Picea abies*) p. 54

18. Cones 1" to 4" long; needles with pungent odor when crushed.

19. Needles 1/3" to 3/4" long; young twigs without hairs; cone scales squarish or rounded and entire at the margins (cones absent in one dwarf cultivar, 'Dwarf Alberta Spruce', with very small needles, slow growth, and a dwarf form; commonly planted in Utah) . . . . **white spruce** (*Picea glauca*) p. 54

19. Needles 1" long; cone scales have toothed margins; young twigs with or without hairs.

20. Cones 1" to 2-1/2" long; needle tips somewhat blunt; young twigs with minute hairs; found at high elevations throughout Utah; rarely planted . **Engelmann spruce**❖ (*Picea engelmannii*) p. 51

20. Cones 2-1/2" to 4-1/2" long; needle tips sharp and bristled; needles variable in color from bluish to greenish; young twigs without hairs; commonly planted in Utah; native to mountain sites from Uintas south near streams . . . . **blue spruce**❖ (*Picea pungens*) p. 52

17. Needles flat in cross-section (hard to roll between fingers), tips rounded or occasionally pointed, may or may not have persistent bumps where needles attach that roughen small twigs; winter bud scales not rolled back on the margins; cones erect on upper branches or hang down, not papery.

21. Needles bases narrow and appear stalked; 3/4" to 1-1/4" long; small branches roughened by small bumps where needles were attached; cones 3" to 4" long, hang down, 3-pointed, fork-like bract sticking out of each scale (resembles mouses's legs and tail); buds pointed. . . **Douglas-fir**❖ (*Pseudotsuga menziesii*) p. 56

301

21. Needles not stalked, leaving a conspicuous round scar where attached to the twig; small branches glabrous and fairly smooth; cones upright on upper branches with deciduous scales; buds rounded (**true firs**).
  22. Needles 2" to 3" long, silver-blue; crown wide. . . . . **white fir❖** (*Abies concolor*) p. 58
  22. Needles less than 2" long, darker blue-green; crown narrow. . . **subalpine fir❖** (*Abies lasiocarpa*) p. 58

1. Leaves scale-like or awl-shaped, often of 2 kinds on the same tree; fruit berry-like and fleshy or a woody cone.
  23. Leaves 1/16" to 1/8" long, scale-like, deciduous; small, pink flowers in showy clusters; fruit a small capsule containing many small seeds . . . . tamarisk (*Tamarix ramosissima*) p. 216
  23. Leaves scale-like or awl-shaped, evergreen; flowers not showy; fruit berry-like or a woody cone.
    24. Fruit berry-like; leaves usually scale-like and awl-shaped on the same tree (**junipers**).
      25. Mature fruit red-brown with a whitish waxy coating, 1/4" to 3/4" diameter; foliage light yellow-green; twigs thick and stiff and arranged in all planes along branches; native and rarely planted . Utah juniper❖ (*Juniperus osteosperma*) p. 72
      25. Mature fruit dark purple to blue-black with a whitish waxy coating, 1/4" to 1/3" diameter; foliage green to blue-green; twigs more flexible and tending to be arranged in two planes along branches; native or planted.
        26. Leaves green to blue-green, not arranged in overlapping pairs; fruit matures in two seasons; habit typically spreading; native and commonly planted . . . . Rocky Mountain juniper❖ (*Juniperus scopulorum*) p. 70
        26. Leaves dark green to purple-green, arranged in overlapping pairs; fruit matures in one season; habit typically more upright; not native but fairly commonly planted . . . . . eastern redcedar (*Juniperus virginiana*) p. 72
    24. Fruit a woody or leathery cone.
      27. Cones round with shield-shaped scales, 2 to 20 seeds per scale.
        28. Cones woody, 1" diameter, 6 to 8 scales; leaves scale-like and awl-shaped on same plant; branchlets 4-angled; crown narrow, columnar; only planted in warm areas like Washington County . . . . Italian cypress (*Cupressus sempervirens*) p. 64

28. Cones leathery, 1/3" to 1/2" diameter, 8 to 10 scales; leaves scale-like; branchlets flattened; crown not as above; planted in warm and cold areas . . . . **Hinoki Falsecypress** (*Chamaecyparis obtusa*) p. 66

27. Cones elongated, 2 or more seeds per scale, or may not be present for many years.

29. Cone 1-3/4" to 3-1/2" long, with 25 to 40 wrinkled, shield-shaped scales; leaves arranged alternately (spirally); fairly common in the Salt Lake City area . . . . **giant sequoia** (*Sequoiadendron giganteum*) p. 61

29. Cone 1-1/2" long or less, with 10 or less non-shield-shaped scales; leaves arranged 2 or 4 at a node.

30. Cone 3/4" to 1-1/2" long, 6 woody to leathery scales (only 5 obvious), 2 becoming long at maturity resemble a duck's bill as they open, third central scale also is elongated; leaves arranged in 4's (4 at each node) . . . . **Incense-cedar** (*Calocedrus decurrens*) p. 67

30. Cones 1/3" to 1" long with 6 to 10 woody to leathery scales that are not elongated as above; leaves arranged in pairs (2 at each node) (**arborvitaes** or **white-cedars**).

31. Foliage and twigs arranged mostly in horizontally flattened or drooping sprays; cone 1/3" to 1/2" long . . . . **northern white-cedar** (*Thuja occidentalis*) p. 68

31. Foliage and twigs arranged mostly in vertically flattened sprays; cone 1/3" to 1" long; foliage often bright yellow in winter . . . . **Oriental arborvitae** (*Thuja orientalis*) p. 70

Key 2. Plants with opposite or whorled, simple (not compound), broad leaves.

1. Leaves palmately lobed; fruit a double samara (**maples**).

2. Leaves with sharply and often doubly toothed margins and sharp-angled sinuses (**soft maples**).

3. Fruits maturing in fall.

4. Leaves with middle lobe much longer than side lobes; introduced . . . . **Amur maple** (*Acer ginnala*) p. 203

303

4. Leaves with middle lobe equal to, or only slightly longer than, side lobes, rarely lobed so deeply the leaf is compound; small tree native to moist canyon sites. . . . . **Rocky Mountain maple**❖ (*Acer glabrum*) p. 196

3. Fruits maturing in late spring.
   5. Leaves 4" across or less, mostly 3-lobed; samara about 3/4" long and V-shaped; twigs without strong smell when bruised; not native to Utah . . . . **red maple** (*Acer rubrum*) p. 202
   5. Leaves 6" to 7" across, mostly 5-lobed, often yellow due to iron chlorosis; samara about 1-1/2" long, with wings widely spread; twigs with strong smell when bruised; not native to Utah . . . **silver maple** (*Acer saccharinum*) p. 201

2. Lobes of leaves entire or with a few blunt teeth and more rounded sinuses (**hard maples**).
   6. Petioles red, as long or longer than the leaf blade, sap from broken petioles milky (may not show if weather very dry); wings of samaras widely spreading; leaves 5 to 7 lobed; buds rounded . . . . . . **Norway maple** (*Acer platanoides*) p. 198
   6. Petioles green, typically shorter than the leaf blade, sap from broken petioles not milky; wings of samaras spreading at right angles or less; leaves 3 to 5 lobed; buds sharp-pointed.
      7. Buds red, terminal bud 1/16" long; leaves slightly hairy beneath; native to Utah canyons; known for its red-orange fall color . . . . **canyon maple**❖ (*Acer grandidentatum*) p. 196
      7. Buds brown, terminal bud 1/4" to 3/8" long; leaves glabrous beneath; non-native, but occasionally planted. . . . . . **sugar maple** (*Acer saccharum*) p. 198

1. Leaves not lobed.
   8. Leaf margins with distinctive round teeth; fruit a 1/2" to 3/4" long pod in groups of 2 to 4, splits to release small winged seeds; leaves blue-green, opposite or sub-opposite, cordate . . . . **Katsuratree** (*Cercidiphyllum japonicum*) p. 135
   8. Leaf margins entire or occasionally with a few small teeth in one species; fruit not as above.
      9. Fruit a 1/2" to 3/4" diameter, blue-black drupe; flowers white, with long, narrow petals, in large, showy bunches with a fringed or fleecy appearance . . . . **fringetree** (*Chionanthus virginicus*) p. 233

9. Fruit not a blue-black drupe; flowers not as above.
   10. Leaf blades 6" to 12" long; fruit a 7" to 20" long capsule; flowers trumpet-like.
      11. Leaf blades 8" to 12" long, 5" to 8" wide, heart-shaped, opposite or in whorls of 3; fruit a slender capsule 8" to 20" long; large tree; not native . . . . **northern catalpa** (*Catalpa speciosa*) p. 234
      11. Leaf blades 6" to 12" long, 1/2" wide, opposite or scattered along twig; fruit a slender capsule 7" to 12" long; shrubby tree; native and rarely planted . . . . **desertwillow**❖ (*Chilopsis linearis*) p. 237
   10. Leaf blades 6" long or less, not heart shaped or very narrow; fruit not a long capsule; flowers not trumpet-like.
      12. Leaves mostly less than 3" long.
         13. Leaves with 1/2" to 1" long petiole, margins occasionally slightly toothed, leaves rarely compound with 2 to 5 leaflets; flowers not showy; small tree native to fairly dry, warm canyon sites in southern and eastern Utah . . . . **singleleaf ash**❖ (*Fraxinus anomala*) p. 226
         13. Leaves nearly sessile (no petiole); flowers in large, showy bunches; not native, planted only in warmest areas of the state like Washington County . . . . **crapemyrtle** (*Lagerstroemia indica*) p. 220
      12. Leaves mostly greater than 3" long.
         14. Twigs bright red (occasionally yellow); flowers small, white, in small bunches; fruit a white drupe; shrubby . . . . **red-osier dogwood**❖ (*Cornus sericea*) p. 222
         14. Twigs not bright red or yellow; flowers large and showy or in large bunches; fruit not as above; small trees.
            15. Twigs slender, terminal bud present; flower buds look like small lanterns or urns on branch tips; fruit a bright red drupe; showy white or pink flowers that appear in early spring before leaves; rarely planted in Utah, though other dogwoods can be found . . . . **flowering dogwood** (*Cornus florida*) p. 221
            15. Twigs stout, often no terminal bud; flower buds not as above; fruit a 3/4" long, curved, brown capsule; flowers showy, white, in 6" to 12" long groups, appear in June; bark cherry-like, red-brown, with horizontal lenticels . . . . **Japanese tree lilac** (*Syringa reticulata*) p. 232

305

Key 3. Plants with opposite, compound leaves.

1. Leaves palmately compound; fruit a spiny capsule with hard, shiny, nut-like seeds (**horsechestnuts** or **buckeyes**).
   2. Leaves mostly with 7 leaflets; winter buds coated with resin . . . . **horsechestnut** (*Aesculus hippocastanum*) p. 210
   2. Leaves mostly with 5 leaflets; winter buds not coated with resin . . . . **Ohio buckeye** (*Aesculus glabra*) p. 211
1. Leaves pinnately compound; fruit a drupe, berry, or samara.
   3. Fruit a fleshy drupe; no terminal bud present.
      4. Fruit a 1/4" diameter dark blue drupe; leaflets toothed; lateral buds not hidden by base of petiole; flowers in showy bunches; shrub or small tree native to cool, moist canyon sites in Utah and rarely planted. . . **blue elder❖** (*Sambucus cerulea*) p. 238
      4. Fruit a 1/2" diameter black drupe (on female trees); leaflets entire; lateral buds hidden by base of petiole when leaves are attached . . . . **Amur corktree** (*Phellodendron amurense*) p. 186
   3. Fruit a samara; terminal bud present.
      5. Leaflets mostly 3 to 5; fruit a double (2-winged) samara . . . . **boxelder❖** (*Acer negundo*) p. 194
      5. Leaflets mostly 5 to 11, fruit a samara (one wing) (**ashes**).
         6. Dense hairs cover lower leaf surfaces, petiole, young twigs, buds, and flowers; 3 to 9 (usually 5) thick leaflets; native to warm canyons of extreme southwestern Utah . . . . **velvet ash❖** (*Fraxinus velutina*) p. 227
         6. Dense hairs not covering all surfaces as above, though pubescence may occur on some parts; leaflets not thick; not native.
            7. Twigs with four corky ridges making them square in cross-section; inner bark turns blue when exposed to air; inner bark turns blue when exposed to air; uncommon . . . . **blue ash** (*Fraxinus quadrangulata*) p. 229
            7. Twigs without four corky ridges; inner bark does not turn blue when exposed to air.
               8. Buds black, pubescent; leaflets sessile (no stalk), sharply toothed . **European ash** (*Fraxinus excelsior*) p. 230
               8. Buds dark brown and more or less pubescent; leaflets sessile or stalked, with fine teeth or entire.

306

9.   Leaves dark green above and glossy; leaflets nearly entire with distinct stalks; twigs glabrous and whitish below; upper edge of leaf scars deeply notched under lateral bud; purple-yellow fall leaf color; fairly uncommon . . . . **white ash** (*Fraxinus americana*) p. 230

9.   Leaves bright green above and below; leaflets sharply serrate above the middle, with very short or no stalks; upper edge of leaf scars curved or straight-across under lateral bud; twigs dull and sometimes pubescent; yellow fall leaf color; common . . . . **green ash** (*Fraxinus pennsylvanica*) p. 228

Key 4. Plants with alternate, simple leaves.
(Sometimes some leaves are clustered on short spurs)

1.   Leaves fan-shaped with parallel-branched veins running to margin, mostly on short, spur-like branches, usually 2 blunt lobes on outer end of leaf . . . . **ginkgo** (*Ginkgo biloba*) p. 32

1.   Leaves not as above.

    2.   Leaves evergreen, with some remaining green on the tree through winter and into the next growing season.

       3.   Leaves 5" to 10" long, densely reddish-hairy underneath; flowers white, fragrant, 6" to 10" diameter; fruit a 3" to 4" long aggregate with red seeds; uncommon . . . . **southern magnolia** (*Magnolia grandiflora*) p. 138

       3.   Leaves less than 5" long, not reddish-hairy underneath; flowers and fruit not as above.

          4.   Leaf margins entire, curled under; fruit a small, dry achene with a 2" to 3" long twisted, hairy plume; shrubby tree native to mountain sites . . . . **curlleaf mountain-mahogany**❖ (*Cercocarpus ledifolius*) p. 164

          4.   Leaf margins lobed or toothed.

             5.   Leaves 1/2" long or less, margins lobed; fruit a small, dry achene with a 2" long white, hairy plume; shrubby . . . . **cliffrose**❖ (*Cowania mexicana*) p. 163

             5.   Leaves 1/2" long or more, margins with sharp, spiny teeth; fruit not as above.

307

6.   Leaves 2" to 4" long; fruit a red or yellow, fleshy drupe; small to medium-sized tree; not native, but sometimes planted . . . . **American holly** (*Ilex opaca*) p. 192

6.   Leaves 1/2" to 1-1/4" long; fruit a small acorn; shrubby trees native to warm southern Utah canyons; rarely planted.

    7.   Leaves with wavy margins . . . . **wavyleaf oak**❖ (*Quercus undulata*) p. 112

    7.   Leaves without wavy margins . . . . **shrub live oak**❖ (*Quercus turbinella*) p. 112

2.   Leaves deciduous.

    8.   Leaves densely white-hairy underneath, lobed or unlobed with rounded teeth; fruit a small capsule that releases cottony seeds; bark whitish on young branches, dark and blocky on old trunks . . . . **white poplar** (*Populus alba*) p. 88

    8.   Leaves not densely white-hairy underneath, lobed or unlobed.

        9.   Leaves lobed.

          10.   Leaves distinctly palmately lobed and veined.

            11.   Leaves distinctly star-shaped, 5-7 lobed, evenly and finely toothed; fruit a spherical head of capsules with a long stalk; twigs often with corky ridges. . . . . **sweetgum** (*Liquidambar styraciflua*) p. 142

            11.   Leaves not distinctly star-shaped, 3-5 lobed, unevenly and coarsely toothed; fruit a ball-shaped aggregate of hairy achenes, hanging on a long stalk; twigs without corky ridges; bark branches and upper trunk rough, smooth or peeling off in large plates all on the same tree; base of petiole surrounding bud and stipules or their scars surrounding the twig (**planetrees**).

               12.   Fruits occur singly on stalks; smooth upper bark gray-white; terminal leaf lobe about as long as wide; planted fairly often in Utah . . . . **American sycamore** (*Platanus occidentalis*) p. 143

               12.   Fruits occur two or three on a stalk; smooth bark greenish; fairly common; terminal leaf lobe longer than wide; planted extensively in Utah. . . . . . . **London planetree** (*Platanus × acerifolia*) p. 143

          10.   Leaves pinnately lobed or at least not distinctly palmately lobed.

13. No terminal buds; leaves with 3 main veins from near the base, with 1 to several lobes (some not lobed); multiple fruit of small, fleshy drupes (**mulberries**).

14. Fruit red to dark purple; leaves usually rough above, fairly hairy below, especially along veins; twigs reddish-brown . . . . **red mulberry** (*Morus rubra*) p. 131

14. Fruit white to pink to violet; leaves glabrous and shiny above; nearly glabrous below; twigs light yellow-brown . . . . **white mulberry** (*Morus alba*) p. 132

13. Terminal buds present; leaves with 1 large main vein (midrib), lobed in various ways; fruit not as above.

15. Leaves 4 lobed, wide and flat across base and tip; flower tulip-shaped, yellow petals with orange interior; terminal bud 1/2" long with 2 scales, resembles a duck's bill. . . . . **yellow-poplar** (*Liriodendron tulipifera*) p. 140

15. Leaves pinnately lobed but not shaped as above, not flat across the tip; buds not as above.

16. Flowers showy; buds not clustered at twig ends; fruit a pome (apple-like); thorny or thornless (some have small lobes or no lobes on some leaves); leaves evenly and fairly finely toothed.

17. Leaves shallowly lobed, usually above middle (many cultivars not lobed); fruit a small apple, fleshy and moist when mature; not thorny, though twigs may be stubby and spine-like; winter buds typically hairy, sharp-pointed, brownish . . . . . . **crabapple** (*Malus* spp.) p. 154

17. Leaves shallowly or deeply lobed; fruit a small pome, not moist when mature; usually thorny, but may not have thorns depending on cultivar; winter buds typically hairless and blunt, reddish (**hawthorns**).

18. Leaves with fairly deep, distinct lobes.

19. Flowers pink to red, though often white in some cultivars; fruit 1/4" to 1/2" long, orange-red, dull; petiole 1/4" to 3/4" long; often not thorny; older trunks often split into longitudinal segments. . . **English hawthorn** (*Crataegus laevigata*) p. 168

19. Flowers white; fruit 1/4" long, bright-red, shiny; petiole 1" long; usually thorny; trunk not as above . . . . . **Washington hawthorn** (*Crataegus phaenopyrum*) p. 166

18. Leaves shallowly and irregularly lobed, mostly above the middle; thorns sometimes not present.

20. Fruit red at first, maturing black, 1/2" to 3/4" diameter; petiole 1/2" long; thorny; shrubby native tree, rarely planted . . **black hawthorn**❖ (*Crataegus douglasii*) p. 165

20. Fruit bright red at maturity, 1/4" to 1/3" diameter; petiole 1/2" to 1-1/2" long; sometimes thornless; introduced . . . . **green hawthorn** (*Crataegus viridis*) p. 170

16. Flowers not showy; buds clustered at branch tip; fruit an acorn; no thorns present; leaf lobes entire or coarsely toothed (**oaks**).

21. Lobes of leaves blunt or rounded, not bristle tipped; acorn matures in 1 season, inner shell surface of acorn nut not hairy (**white oaks**).

22. Ear-lobe-like leaf base; 1" to 3" acorn stalk. . . . . . **English oak** (*Quercus robur*) p. 117

22. Leaf base not as above; acorn with no stalk or a very short stalk.

23. Shrubby oak native to foothills throughout most of Utah; leaves usually fairly small, petiole 1/2" long . . . . **Gambel oak**❖ (*Quercus gambelii*) p. 111

23. Large tree-sized oaks, introduced; leaves 5" to 10" long; petiole 1" long.

24. Leaves with lower surface hairy, usually deeply lobed below middle, sometimes with coarse rounded teeth above; edge of acorn cap bristly; twig bark often in corky ridges . . . . **bur oak** (*Quercus macrocarpa*) p. 113

24. Leaves with lower surface glabrous, entire length deeply lobed; edge of acorn cap warty; twig bark not in corky ridges . . . . **white oak** (*Quercus alba*) p. 114

21. Lobes of leaves sharp, bristle tipped; acorn maturing the second season, inner surface of nut shell hairy (**red oaks**).

    25. Leaves 7 to 11 lobed, openings between lobes extend half way or less to midrib, glabrous except for tufts where veins join on beneath, top dull to glossy dark green; acorns 3/4" to 1-1/4" long . . . . **northern red oak** (*Quercus rubra*) p. 116

    25. Leaves 5 to 9 lobed, openings between lobes extend more than half way to midrib; acorns 1/2" long, striped. . . . . **pin oak** (*Quercus palustris*) p. 120

9. Leaves not lobed.

   26. Leaf margins entire (not toothed).

     27. Leaves and young twigs covered with silver and brown scales; thorns often present; fruit drupe-like, yellowish, coated with silvery scales . . . . **Russian-olive** (*Elaeagnus angustifolia*) p. 218

     27. Leaves and twigs not covered with silvery scales.

      28. Leaves broadly heart-shaped, with 3 to 7 large veins radiating from the base; flowers small, usually pink, and pea-like; fruit a legume; small tree (**redbuds**).

       29. Leaves 2" to 3" wide, tip not pointed; small, shrubby tree native to southern Utah's canyons, seldom planted. . . . . **California redbud**❖ (*Cercis occidentalis*) p. 174

       29.Leaves 3" to 5" wide, tip pointed; small introduced tree . . . **eastern redbud** (*Cercis canadensis*) p. 173

      28. Leaves not heart-shaped; flowers not pea-like; fruit not a legume.

       30. Twigs, fruit, and leaves with milky sap; spines or thorns often present on twigs; fruit large, round, green, rough-textured; planted for windbreaks in Utah in the past . . . . **Osage-orange** (*Maclura pomifera*) p. 132

       30. Twigs, fruit, and leaves without milky sap: spines or thorns not present on twigs; fruit not as above.

        31. Buds clustered at branch tip; fruit an acorn; uncommon . **shingle oak** (*Quercus imbricaria*) p. 122

31. Buds not clustered at branch tip; fruit not an acorn.

    32. Fruit a small orange-red to yellow drupe; bark with distinct corky ridges; some leaves may have a few teeth; small tree native to much of Utah . . . . **netleaf hackberry**❖ (*Celtis reticulata*) p. 128

    32. Fruit and bark not as above.

        33. Flowers very small, in a large inflorescence that matures with a smoky look from many hairy pink or purple stalks; twigs with orange-brown, solid pith; buds very small, 1/16" long, with several overlapping scales . . . **common smoketree** (*Cotinus coggyria*) p. 191

        33. Flowers not as above; pith not orange-brown; buds large, 1/3" long or longer.

            34. No stipule scars circling twig; leaves 2" to 4" long; buds pointed (lance-shaped) and not hairy, with several overlapping scales; flowers small, inconspicuous; fruit a triangular nut, 2 to 3 enclosed in a spiny bur; bark smooth and even on older trees; leaves sometimes have a few small, rounded teeth. . . . . **European beech** (*Fagus sylvatica*) p. 107

            34. Stipule scars form a line circling twig at each bud; leaves mostly larger than 3"; flowers medium to large and often showy; terminal buds large and silky, with one scale covering the entire bud, tip rounded; fruit an aggregate of follicles (**magnolias**).

                35. Blooms late-May to June, yellow-green, 2" to 3" wide, non-showy; leaves 6" to 10" long. . . . . **cucumbertree** (*Magnolia acuminata*) p. 137

                35. Blooms in spring before the leaves, are white, pink, or purple, greater than 3" wide, showy; leaves 6" long or less.

36. Flowers 5" to 10" wide, pink or purple with some white; leaves oval, pointed, 3" to 6" long, half as wide . . . . saucer magnolia (*Magnolia* × *soulangiana*) p. 135

36. Flowers generally 5" wide or less, more commonly white than pink or purple.

    37. Flowers with 12 or more petals, usually white; leaves oval, not pointed, 2" to 4" long, half as wide; small tree or shrub . . . . star magnolia (*Magnolia stellata*) p. 136

    37. Flowers with 6 to 9 petals, white; leaves oval, pointed, 3" to 6" long, half as wide; large tree . . . Kobus magnolia (*Magnolia kobus*) p. 138

26. Leaf margins not entire (with sharp or rounded teeth).

    38. Petioles distinctly flattened in cross-section; leaves generally as wide or wider than they are long; fruit a capsule releasing cottony seeds (some do not bear fruit) (poplars).

        39. Columnar tree with upright branches and very narrow crown; commonly planted in Utah, especially in the past . . . . Lombardy poplar (*Populus nigra* var. *italica*) p. 88

        39. Crown not very narrow.

            40. Leaves nearly round to egg-shaped; buds not resinous; common native tree in Utah's mountains and widely planted . . . . quaking aspen❖ (*Populus tremuloides*) p. 80

            40. Leaves deltoid (triangular), kidney-shaped, or rhombic (diamond shaped); buds resinous.

                41. Leaves rhombic to rhombic-ovate, longer than they are wide, 2" to 6" long, tip long and drawn-out, base wedge-shaped or rounded, coarsely toothed . . . . Carolina poplar (*Populus* × *canadensis*) p. 90

                41. Leaves deltoid to kidney-shaped.

42. Leaves deltoid, with glands or bumps where the petiole and blade meet, tip long and drawn-out; planted occasionally in Utah . . . . **eastern cottonwood** (*Populus deltoides*) p. 86

42. Leaves more kidney-shaped, without glands where petiole and blade meet, tip short; native to canyons of southern and eastern Utah. . . . . **Fremont cottonwood**❖ (*Populus fremontii*) p. 82

38. Petioles not flattened in cross-section.

43. Sap milky; multiple fruit of small, fleshy drupes (blackberry-shaped); may have a few to many lobed leaves (**mulberries**).

44. Fruit red to dark purple; leaves usually rough above, fairly hairy below, especially along veins; twigs reddish-brown . . . . **red mulberry** (*Morus rubra*) p. 131

44. Fruit white to pink to violet; leaves glabrous and shiny above, nearly glabrous below; twigs light yellow-brown. . . . . **white mulberry** (*Morus alba*) p. 132

43. Sap not milky; fruit a fairly large (1/2" diameter or greater) nut in a warty or leafy cup or cap, or in a bur.

45. Fruit a rounded nut.

46. Buds with 2 to 3 visible scales, no terminal bud; fruit 2 to 3 large nuts in a 2" to 2-1/2" diameter spiny bur . . . . **Chinese chestnut** (*Castanea mollissima*) p. 109

46. Buds with many scales; fruit a single nut in a warty or leafy cup or cap.

47. No terminal bud, buds not clustered at twig tip; fruit a nut enclosed by a leaf cup; often shrubby . . . . **Turkish filbert** (*Corylus colurna*) p. 105

47. Terminal bud present and clustered with other buds at twig tip; fruit a nut in a cup or cap (an acorn), medium to large trees (**oaks**).

48. Acorn with a 1" to 4" stalk; leaves with rounded teeth or sometimes shallowly lobed; bark peeling into papery scales on older twigs. . . . . . . **swamp white oak** (*Quercus bicolor*) p. 118

48. Acorn with a short stalk; leaves with sharp, angled teeth; bark on older twigs not as above
. . . . **chinkapin oak** (*Quercus muehlenbergii*) p. 118

45. Fruit not a large nut in a cup, cap, or bur.
49. Leaves with 3 to 5 nearly equal main veins from near the base.
50. Leaves twice as long as wide, taper pointed, with uneven bases; pith usually chambered; bark of trunk with corky ridges; fruit a purple drupe. . . . . **hackberry** (*Celtis occidentalis*) p. 129
50. Leaves about as wide as long, heart-shaped; pith not chambered; bark without corky ridges; fruit several small nuts attached to a wing-like leaf (**lindens**).
51. Leaves 5" to 8" long; flower bracts 3" to 4" long . . . . **American basswood** (*Tilia americana*) p. 213
51. Leaves less than 5" long; flower bracts less than 3" long.
52. Lower leaf surfaces and petioles not covered with white hairs
. . . . **littleleaf European linden** (*Tilia cordata*) p. 215
52. Lower leaf surfaces and petioles covered with white hairs . . . . **silver linden** (*Tilia tomentosa*) p. 216

49. Leaves with 1 main vein (midrib) from the base.
53. Fruit a samara with a thin wing surrounding the seed; leaves strongly 2-ranked (in a flattened arrangement) (**elms**).
54. Mature leaves 4" to 6" long, coarsely doubly serrate, base uneven; fruit matures in spring
. . . . **American elm** (*Ulmus americana*) (also may include hybrids) p. 124
54. Mature leaves less than 3" long, singly serrate or nearly so, base nearly even.

315

55. Fruit matures in spring; bark on trunk not distinctive, gray with shallow furrows and long, flat ridges; commonly planted, and naturalized tree . . . . **Siberian elm** (*Ulmus pumila*) p. 126

55. Fruit matures in fall; bark on trunk very distinctive, gray-green with orange and brown, lacy; only occasionally planted in Utah . . . . . . **lacebark elm** (*Ulmus parvifolia*) p. 126

53. Fruit not a samara.

56. Fruit a small capsule arranged in elongated bunches, capsules full of small, hairy seeds (female trees only).

57. Buds 1/4" long or less, each covered by a single hood-like scale, no terminal bud; leaves generally long and narrow (**willows**).

58. Leaves broadly lanceolate, blade gradually tapers to base and tip; native small tree along streams . . . . **peachleaf willow**❖ (*Salix amygdaloides*) p. 76

58. Leaves narrowly lanceolate; not native, but may be naturalized; typically large trees at maturity.

59. Strongly rounded, globe-shaped crown with bright green leaves; widely planted in Utah . . **globe Navajo willow** (*Salix matsudana* var. 'Navajo') p. 78

59. Crown not strongly globe-shaped.

60. Weeping habit with long flexible branches; capsule with no stalk . . . . . . **weeping willow** (*Salix babylonica*) p. 78

60. Upright habit, capsule stalked.

61. Stamens 3 to 12 per flower; mid-sized tree; branchlets dark brown and not brittle. . . . . **black willow** (*Salix nigra*) p. 76

61. Stamens 2 per flower; large tree; branchlets light brown and brittle
     . . . . **crack willow** (*Salix fragilis*) p. 78

57. Terminal buds present and usually much longer than 1/4", each bud covered by several scales; leaves wide or narrow, with petioles not distinctly flattened (**poplars**).

     62. Leaves narrow (1" wide or less), 2" to 4" long, lanceolate to ovate-lanceolate; petiole short (less than 1/3 length of blade); buds 1/4" to 3/4" long, resinous; native along streams in Utah . . . . **narrowleaf cottonwood❖** (*Populus angustifolia*) p. 80

     62. Leaves wider, 3" to 6" long, ovate to ovate-lanceolate; petiole longer (at least 1/2 length of blade); buds 3/4" to 1" long, very resinous, aromatic; northern Utah only.

           63. Capsule glabrous, 2-valved . . . . **balsam poplar❖** (*Populus balsamifera*) p. 85

           63. Capsule hairy, 3-valved . . . . **black cottonwood❖** (*Populus trichocarpa*) p. 84

56. Fruit a drupe, pome, or small nutlet; terminal bud absent.

     64. Fruit a small nutlet held in small strobiles (cones); terminal bud present.

           65. Fruit a small winged nutlet held in a cone-like woody strobile that persist into the next growing season; buds stalked with 2 to 3 visible scales (**alders**).

                 66. Leaves with 8 to 15 pairs of veins, coarsely doubly toothed to shallowly lobed; twigs with orange lenticels; shrubby tree native to moist canyon sites in Utah and rarely planted . . . . **thinleaf alder❖** (*Alnus tenuifolia*) p. 100

                 66. Leaves with 5 to 6 pairs of veins, rounded at the tips; twigs with gray to white lenticels; introduced; can get quite large . . . .
                      . . . . **European alder** (*Alnus glutinosa*) p. 100

           65. Fruit a wingless nutlet held in papery or flexible strobiles; buds not stalked and with many visible scales.

67. Fruit a small nutlet enclosed in a small, inflated sac, several grouped together in a cone-like, papery, loose strobile with the appearance of hops; branches without short spurs; bark platy . . . .
Knowlton hophornbeam❖ (*Ostrya knowltonii*) p. 100

67. Fruit a winged nutlet held in cone-like, flexible strobiles; branches with short spurs; bark on younger trees smooth or peeling off in rolls (**birches**).

68. Bark of trunk white; strobiles hang down . . . .
European white birch (*Betula pendula*) p. 96

68. Bark of trunk bronze to brown to salmon-pink (not white), papery or smooth; strobiles erect or pendent.

69. Bark reddish-brown, smooth, doesn't peel; strobiles usually pendent, mature in fall; native, occasionally planted . . . .
water birch❖ (*Betula occidentalis*) p. 96

69. Bark brown to salmon-pink, peeling on older branches and trunk; strobiles erect, mature in late spring; not native . . . .
river birch (*Betula nigra*) p. 98

64. Fruit a pome or drupe; terminal bud present or absent.

70. Fruit a small (1/4" or less diameter), green to brown, firm drupe elongated by two small ridges; twigs zig-zag, terminal bud absent; leaves with wavy margins . . . . . .
Japanese zelkova (*Zelkova serrata*) p. 130

70. Fruit a pome or drupe not elongated by ridges as above; terminal bud present.

71. Fruit a pome (apple-like with several seeds).

72. Twigs with sharp thorns (thornless cultivars exist) (**hawthorns**).

318

73. Mature fruit 3/8" to 1/2" diameter; thorns abundant (except on thornless cultivar) . . **cockspur hawthorn** (*Crataegus crusgalli*) p. 166

73. Mature fruit 5/8" to 3/4" diameter; thorns sparse
. . . . **Lavalle hawthorn** (*Crataegus × lavallei*) p. 168

72. Twigs without sharp thorns.

74. Pome generally elongated (**pears**).

75. Fruit small and sparse; small to medium-sized ornamental trees
. . . . **Callery pear** (*Pyrus calleryana*) p. 156

75. Fruit large and fairly abundant; not very ornamental . . . . .
. . . . **common pear** (*Pyrus communis*) p. 157

74. Pome more or less round.

76. Fruit up to several inches diameter, red, yellow, or green; buds ovoid to round; lower leaf surfaces, buds, and young twigs often woolly; flower petals round . **apple** or **crabapple** (*Malus* species)

76. Fruit small (less than 1/2" diameter), dark red to purple; buds taper to a point; flower petals narrow, strap-like
(**serviceberries**).

77. Flowers in 2" to 4" long clusters; leaves 2" to 4" long, oblong; introduced and not common . . . .
. . . . . **downy serviceberry** (*Amelanchier arborea*) p. 162

77. Flowers in 1" long clusters; leaves 1" to 2" long; native to canyon and foothill sites.

321

89. Teeth on leaves often tipped with a small bristle; leaves 2" to 5" long, glabrous beneath . . . . Japanese flowering cherry (*Prunus serrulata*) p. 150

89. Teeth on leaves pointed but not tipped with a small bristle; leaves 3" to 5" long, glabrous beneath . . . . Sargent cherry (*Prunus sargentii*) p. 150

Key 5. Plants with alternate, compound leaves.

1. Leaves twice or three-times pinnately compound (some leaves on a tree may be once compound).

2. Fruit a 3/8" to 5/8" diameter fleshy, yellow drupe; found only in warm locations in southern Utah . . . . Chinaberry (*Melia azedarach*) p. 189

2. Fruit a legume.

3. Leaflets mostly less than 1/2" long; pink showy flowers; fruit a thin pod; commonly planted only in warmer parts of Utah . . . . mimosa (*Albizia julibrissin*) p. 172

3. Leaflets mostly more than 1/2" long; flowers not very showy; fruit a thick legume (pod).

4. Legume yellow; a pair of 1/2" to 2" spines where each leaf is attached; only found in extreme southwestern Utah . . . . honey mesquite❖ (*Prosopis juliflora*) p. 170

4. Legume brown; no spines on twigs; planted more or less commonly throughout Utah.

5. Leaflets 2" to 3" long, margins entire; fruit a 4" to 6" long, brown legume, 1-1/2" to 2" wide, with few large, hard seeds; no thorns; fairly uncommon . . . . Kentucky coffeetree (*Gymnocladus dioicus*) p. 177

322

1. Leaves once compound.
 6. Fruit a legume; leaflet margins entire **(legumes)**.
  7. Leaves with three leaflets; lateral buds exposed; flowers bright yellow and held in 6" to 10" long, showy clusters that hang down; fruit a 1" to 2" long legume . . . . **goldenchain tree** (*Laburnum × watereri*) p. 181
  7. Leaves with many leaflets; lateral buds hidden by base of petiole; flowers white to pink; fruit over 2" long.
   8. Spines not present on twigs; leaflet apex angled.
    9. Leaflets 1" to 2" long; fruit a 3" to 8" long legume; young twigs green; buds blackish, wooly; flowers white; bark furrowed and ridged on older trunks . . . . **Japanese pagodatree** (*Sophora japonica*) p. 180
    9. Leaflets 2" to 4" long; fruit a 2" to 4" long legume; young twigs red-brown; buds brownish, hairy; flowers white; bark smooth and gray on older trunks . . . . **yellowwood** (*Cladrastis lutea*) p. 179
   8. Spines usually present on twigs, paired at nodes; leaflet base and apex rounded, though tip may be bristled or slightly notched.
    10. Fruit, twigs, and leaflets mostly glabrous . . . . **black locust** (*Robinia pseudoacacia*) p. 183
    10. Fruit, twigs, and leaflets bristly-hairy . . . . **New Mexican locust** (*Robinia neomexicana*) p. 182
 6. Fruit not a legume; leaflet margins entire, serrate, or otherwise toothed.
  11. Leaves with three leaflets, strong odor when crushed; fruit a 1/2" to 1" diameter, 2 seeded samara that resembles an elm samara or hops, held in drooping clusters . . . . **common hoptree**❖ (*Ptelea angustifolia*) p. 185
  11. Leaves with many leaflets, with or without a strong odor when crushed; fruit not as above.

5. Leaflets usually 1" long or less, margins finely serrate; fruit a 12" to 18" long, brown legume, about 1" wide, with many small, hard seeds; usually thornless, though stout, branched thorns are present on native trees; very common . . . . **honeylocust** (*Gleditsia triacanthos*) p. 175

12. Crushed leaves have a strong, musty, disagreeable odor, leaves 1' to 2-1/2' long; 11 to 41 leaflets, typically glandular-lobed near the base; twigs very stout, pith solid, wide, light brown; fruit a yellow to red-orange samara . . . . **tree-of-heaven** (*Ailanthus altissima*) p. 187

12. Crushed leaves without a musty, disagreeable odor; pith solid or chambered; fruit a nut, capsule, drupe, or small pome.

13. Leaflet margins entire; fruit a drupe or nut .

14. Leaflets lanceolate, 10 to 12 on each leaf; fruit a 1/4" diameter red or blue drupe; rare and generally only found in southern Utah . . . . **Chinese pistache** (*Pistacia chinensis*) p. 190

14. Leaflets elliptic to obovate, 5 to 9 on each leaf; fruit a large nut . . . . **English walnut** (*Juglans regia*) p. 92

13. Leaflet margins distinctly toothed; fruit a capsule, nut, or small pome.

15. Fruit a large nut; flowers inconspicuous.

16. Pith chambered, light brown; usually no terminal leaflet; nut round **black walnut** (*Juglans nigra*) p. 90

16. Pith solid; terminal leaflet present; nut elongated . . . . **pecan** (*Carya illinoensis*) p. 94

15. Fruit a capsule or small pome; flowers showy.

17. Leaflet margins with coarse, rounded, irregular teeth; fruit a 3-valved papery capsule; flowers bright yellow and very showy . . . . **goldenraintree** (*Koelreuteria paniculata*) p. 212

17. Leaflets margins with fine, regular teeth; fruit a small, orange-red pome (apple-like); flowers white (**mountain-ashes**).

18. Buds densely hairy in winter; small to medium-sized tree; introduced . . . . **European mountain-ash** (*Sorbus aucuparia*) p. 158

18. Buds glabrous or only slightly hairy; shrubby tree; native to cool, moist canyon sites and rarely planted . . . . **Greene mountain-ash**❖ (*Sorbus scopulina*) p. 159

GLOSSARY

Achene small, dry and hard one-seeded fruit.

Acorn nut-like fruit of an oak with a scaly or warty cap or cup.

Aggregate fruit a fruit formed by attachment of pistils from the same flower, as in *Magnolia*.

Alternate leaves leaves arranged on alternating sides of the twig.

Ament see catkin.

Angiosperm class of plants that has the seeds enclosed in an ovary; includes flowering plants.

Annual rings a layer of wood — including spring-wood and summer-wood — grown in a single season; best seen in the cross-section of the trunk.

Awl-like leaves short leaves that taper evenly to a point; found on junipers and redcedars.

Berry fleshy fruit with several seeds.

Bisexual flower a perfect flower; a flower with organs of both sexes present.

Branchlet a subdivision of a branch.

Broadleaf trees having broad, flat-bladed leaves rather than needles; also a common name for hardwoods.

Cambium layer of tissue one to several cells thick found between the phloem and the wood; divides to form new wood or xylem and phloem.

Capsule dry fruit that splits open, usually along several lines, to reveal many seeds inside.

Carpel the individual unit of a pistil; simple pistils have one carpel and multiple pistils have 2 or more carpels.

Catkin a spike-like inflorescence of bracts at the bases of unisexual flowers, often flexible and hanging down (for example, inflorescences of willows and cottonwoods).

Chambered pith pith divided into many empty horizontal chambers by cross partitions.

Common name   familiar name for a tree; can be very misleading because common names vary according to local custom, and there may be many common names for one species.

Compound leaves   leaves with more than one leaflet attached to a stalk called a rachis.

Conifer   trees and shrubs that usually bear their seeds in cones and are mostly evergreen; includes pines, firs spruces, yews and Douglas-fir.

Cordate   heart-shaped.

Cork cambium   see phellogen.

Cross-section   surface or section of tree shown when wood is cross-cut; shows the circular growth rings.

Cultivar   a cultivated variety of a plant; a species can have no cultivars or many cultivars that may vary widely.

Deciduous leaves   leaves that die and fall off trees after one growing season.

Dichotomous key   a key to tree identification based on a series of decisions, each involving a choice between two alternate identification characteristics.

Diffuse-porous   a type of hardwood in which vessels in the spring-wood are the same size as vessels in summer-wood (maples, birches, poplars, etc.).

Dioecious   having unisexual flowers with staminate (male) and pistillate (female) flowers borne on different trees.

Drupe   fleshy fruit usually with a single stone or pit.

Elliptic   resembling an ellipse and about one-half as wide as long.

Entire margin   leave margins that are smooth (not toothed).

Estipulate   without stipules.

Evergreen   trees and shrubs that retain their live, green leaves during the winter and for two or more growing seasons.

Family   group of closely related species and genera; scientific name ends in "aceae".

Follicle   a dry fruit that splits open along one line, and is the product of a single carpel or simple ovary, as in *Magnolia* or milkweed.

Forest ecology   study of the occurrence of forest plants and animals in relation to their environment.

Genus   a group of species that are similar; the plural of genus is genera.

Glabrous   smooth, with no hair or scales.

Gymnosperm   large class of plants having seeds without an ovary, usually on scales of a cone; includes conifers and the ginkgo.

Hardwoods   usually refers to trees that have broad-leaves and wood made up of vessels; similar to angiosperms.

Heartwood   wood (often dark) made up of non-living cells found in the middle of a tree's stem.

Imperfect flower   a unisexual flower with either functional stamens or pistils but not both.

Inflorescence   the flowering portion of a plant; specialized stems bearing flowers.

Lanceolate   lance-shaped; about 4 times as long as wide and widest below the middle.

Lateral buds   buds found along the length of the twig (not at the tip); they occur where the previous year's leaves were attached.

Leaflets   small blades of a compound leaf attached to a stalk (rachis); without buds where they attach.

Legume   fruit that is a dry, elongated pod that splits in two, with seeds attached along one edge inside.

Lobed margin   leaf margin with gaps that extend more or less to the center of the leaf.

Lustrous   glossy, shiny.

Monoecious   having unisexual flowers with staminate (male) and pistillate (female) flowers borne on the same tree, though often on different branches.

Multiple fruit   fruit made up of a cluster of ripened ovaries or pistils that came from many separate flowers attached to a common receptacle.

Naturalized   nonnative trees that have escaped cultivation and are growing in the wild.

Needle-like leaves   very thin, sharp, pointed, pin-like leaves; found on pines, firs and some other softwoods.

Node   the point on a stem at which leaves and buds are attached.

Nut   fruit that is hard throughout and typically partly or fully enclosed in a leafy or leathery structure.

Obovate   inversely ovate; broader above the middle.

Opposite leaves   pairs of leaves arranged directly across from each other on the twig.

Orbicular   circular in outline.

Oval   broadly elliptic, with the width greater than one-half the length.

Ovary   the ovule- and seed-bearing part of a pistil.

Ovate   having the lengthwise outline of an egg, widest below the middle.

Ovule the egg-containing part of an ovary; becomes the seed after fertilization.

Palmately compound compound leaves in which several leaflets radiate from the end of a stalk (rachis); like the fingers around the palm of a hand.

Parenchyma unspecialized living cells present in many plants parts.

Perfect flower a bisexual flower with functional stamens and pistils.

Persistent leaves leaves that remain on the tree during winter.

Petiole a slender stalk that supports a simple leaf.

Phellogen generative tissue, also called cork cambium, outside the phloem that produces corky cells for stem protection.

Phloem inner bark of a tree that carries food and sugars from the leaves to other parts of the tree.

Photosynthesis process through which the leaves, with energy from sunlight, make food from water and carbon dioxide.

Pinna the leaflet of a compound leaf (plural is pinnae).

Pinnately compound compound leaves in which leaflets are attached laterally along the rachis or stalk; leaves may be once, twice, or three-times pinnately compound.

Pistil the ovary-bearing (female) organ of a flower; made-up of individual units called carpels.

Pistillate flower a unisexual (female) flower bearing only pistils.

Pith soft and spongy, or chambered tissue found in the middle of the stem.

Polygamo-dioecious having unisexual flowers with staminate (male) and pistillate (female) flowers borne on different trees, but also having some perfect flowers on each tree.

Polygamo-monoecious having unisexual flowers with staminate (male) and pistillate (female) flowers borne on the same tree, along with some perfect flowers on each tree.

Polygamous having some unisexual flowers and some bisexual flowers on a plant (can be polygamo-monoecious or polygamo-dioecious).

Pome fruit with a leathery skin, fleshy middle layer, and plastic-like inner layer containing several seeds (example — apple, pear, serviceberry).

Pseudo-terminal buds the uppermost lateral bud when located near the terminal position, but usually off to one side.

Pubescent covered with hairs.

Rachis the central stalk to which leaflets of a compound leaf are attached.

Radial-section surface or section of a tree shown when wood is cut down its length straight through the middle.

Rays ribbon-like groups of tracheids and parenchyma cells that move water, minerals, and organic substances in the xylem between the inner and outer rings and the phloem; best seen in radial sections of the trunk.

Rhombic with an outline resembling a rhombus (diamond-shaped).

Ring-porous type of hardwood in which the vessels in spring-wood are much larger than vessels in summer-wood (oaks, ashes, elms etc.).

Samara dry, usually one-celled, fruit with one or two flat wings attached to a seed (as on elms and maples).

Sapwood living wood, often light colored, found between the bark or cambium and the heartwood, the latter usually darker colored.

Scale-like leaves small, short, fish-scale-like leaves which cover the entire twig; found on juniper and redcedar.

Scientific names Latin-based names used world-wide to standardize names of trees and other plants and animals.

Semi-ring-porous type of hardwood in which the vessels in the spring-wood are somewhat larger than vessels in summer-wood; intermediate between diffuse-porous and ring-porous (black cherry, black walnut, etc.).

Serrate with teeth.

Shade intolerant trees that cannot tolerate low levels of sunlight for growth and survival, and typically thrive under high light (open) conditions.

Shade tolerant trees that can tolerate low levels of sunlight for growth and survival.

Shrub low-growing woody plant with many stems rather than one trunk.

Simple leaves leaves with one blade attached to a petiole, or stalk.

Sinus a recess between two lobes.

Softwoods usually refers to trees that are conifers or cone-bearing; conifers generally have softer wood than angiosperms or hardwoods, but there are many exceptions.

Solid pith pith that is not divided into chambers.

Species trees with similar characteristics and that are closely related to each other; species is used in both the singular and plural sense (specie is not proper).

Spring-wood wood on the inside of an annual ring, formed during the spring; cells are often thinner-walled.

Stamen   the pollen-bearing (male) organ of a flower.

Staminate flower   a unisexual (male) flower bearing only stamens.

Stipules   small, leafy appendages attached in pairs at the base of a petiole; often missing later in the growing season.

Strobile   also strobilus and plural strobili; a cone-like reproductive structure consisting of seed-bearing scales.

Sub-opposite   leaves that are closely, but not exactly, opposite one another on the stem.

Summer-wood   wood on the outside of an annual ring, formed during the summer; this wood is sometimes dark and cells are often thicker-walled.

Tangential-section   surface or section of a tree shown by cutting a tree lengthwise, but not through the middle.

Terminal buds   bud appearing at the apex, or end, of a twig; usually larger than lateral buds.

Toothed/serrated margin   leaf margin with coarse, fine, sharp or blunt teeth.

Tracheids   small-diameter cells in the wood of trees that carry water from the roots to the leaves and throughout the plant body; water carrying tubes in conifer xylem are all tracheids.

Tree   a woody plant with one to a few main stems and many branches; usually over 10 feet tall.

Twig   a shoot of a woody plant representing the growth of the current season.

Two-ranked   arranged in one plane along two sides of a stem; usually refers to leaf or twig arrangement.

Unisexual flower   an imperfect flower; a flower with organs of only one sex present.

Vessels   large-diameter tubes in the wood of hardwood, or angiosperm, trees that carry water from the roots to the trees.

Xylem   the wood of a tree, made up of strong fibers, tracheids and vessels.

INDEX OF COMMON
AND LATIN NAMES

The following index includes common and Latin names for all species mentioned in this book, with Latin names in italics. In many cases several common names for one species are included, and names are listed several different ways. For example, *Sorbus americana* also is listed as American mountain-ash; ash, American mountain-; and mountain-ash, American. Listing of a species under a common name is done for convenience and ease of locating the species in the book, and does not necessarily imply that it is closely related to other species under that common name. A mountain-ash (genus *Sorbus*) is not related to a true ash (genus *Fraxinus*), but is included under the common name ash and mountain-ash in this index. Family names are also included in this index.

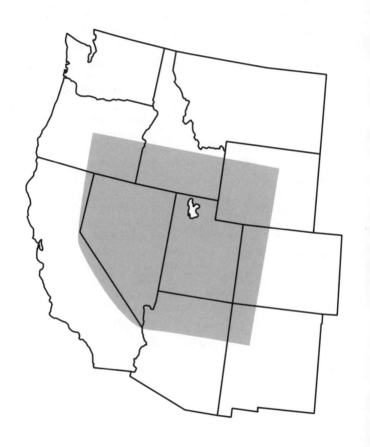